Stalls & Spins

TAB
PRACTICAL
FLYING SERIES

Other Books in the TAB PRACTICAL FLYING SERIES

Stalls & Spins

Paul Craig

TAB Books
Division of McGraw-Hill, Inc.
Blue Ridge Summit, PA 17294-0850

FIRST EDITION
SECOND PRINTING

Library of Congress Cataloging-in-Publication Data
Craig, Paul A.
  Stalls & Spins / by Paul A. Craig.
    p. cm.
   Includes index.
   ISBN 0-8306-4019-3 (h) ISBN 0-8306-4020-7 (p)
   1. Stalling (Aerodynamics) 2. Spin (Aerodynamics) I. Title.
TL574.S74C72 1993
629.132'3—dc20   92-29914
                                     CIP

Acquistions Editor: Jeff Worsinger
Book Editor: Norval G. Kennedy
Director of Production: Katherine G. Brown
Book Design: Jaclyn J. Boone
Cover Photograph: Thompson Photography, Baltimore, MD

Contents

PART 2: WHAT YOUR INSTRUCTOR NEVER TOLD YOU

Acknowledgments

MUCH CARE, LEARNING, PATIENCE, GUIDANCE, UNDERSTANDING AND time went into this work. First a special thanks to my family who tolerate me and my schedule. Thank you Dorothy and Gabrielle for your journalistic talents.

Much gratitude goes to John Benton, Don Culp, Larry Lambert, and Johnny Henley for support and lots of advice.

A special thank you to Raymond D. Whipple at the NASA Langley Research Center spin tunnel for help on this project and for his help with my college students on several trips to Hampton, Virginia.

Thank you Bill Kershner, for your help, practical advice, and your sense of humor.

Thank you to the staff of the Air Safety Foundation.

Thanks to David E. Arnold of Nashville, Tennessee, a life-long friend and talented artist.

Special thanks to Jamie Smith and the Jimmy Smith Printing Company of Greenville, North Carolina.

I always have deep gratitude and pride in those who pump life into Craig Communications of Nashville, Tennessee. Thanks again!

Finally a heartfelt thank you to a dedicated and knowledgeable group of truly professional flight instructors. This group knows and appreciates their aviation heritage, they work to help each other, and they do the job for all the right reasons. Several of these helped me with spin testing and spin photography. Thanks to David Masters, Bob Frederick, Linda Jusino, Fred Nauer, Jason Bagwell, Paul Curlee, Rob Ballard, David McDonald, Wendell Terry, Jamie Creel, and Tim Beglau. Lesson plans were prepared by my spring 1992 flight instructor group: Latty Bost, Doug Schultz, and Lisa Barrow. Thanks Maurice C. Green for always being there when I needed you and to all my aviation students at Lenoir Community College.

Introduction

August 9, 1896, Rhineower, Germany

It is early afternoon on a clear and unseasonably cool day. A man in his late 40s stands near a railing of a tower built from scrap lumber. He is wearing a flannel shirt, a tight fitting cap, and knickerbocker pants that have been heavily padded in the knees. The man straps on an unusual winged contraption and stares into the wind.

The man is Otto Lilienthal.

In the decades to come, he will be considered a visionary from the infancy of heavier-than-air flight science. Dreamers after him will read his findings and using his work they will build to ultimate success. Lilienthal had written: "No one can realize how substantial the air is, until he feels its supporting power beneath him. It inspires confidence at once!"

But on this day in 1896, he was just one man working toward a goal that few could see or understand. Aeronautics was not considered science then. Men who jumped off

Smithsonian Institution Photo Number 2B-16752

buildings with bed-sheets were not considered scientists, they were lunatics. Lilienthal fought public opinion as well as the wind and made more than 2,000 successful glider flights; he did use science and he did know more about the tricks of the air and his gliders than anyone else; he was committed to searching out the truth about flight; he said that no sacrifice would be too great. And he knew the dangers. He wrote in 1893 that the wind "was a treacherous fellow."

Lilienthal's gliders were fixed-wing. He had long since determined that any research into "flapping" machines was a dead end. In man-made flying machines, aerodynamics and propulsion would have to be separate interests. Lilienthal's gliders had no movable surfaces to control the craft. The glider was only controlled when the pilot shifted his weight from side to side and forward and aft.

On this day in August, Lilienthal dangles his hips and legs beneath the glider and swings his weight where it is needed. Stable, controlled flight can only be achieved, "by a constant and arbitrary correction of the position of the center of gravity," he reported.

Finally, the man at the top of the tower is ready. A small crowd gathered to see a man soar on nothing but air. Lilienthal took a leap into the onrushing wind and streaked upward. His legs were whirling in every direction it seemed; he hoped that each movement would steady the craft. He moved forward some 50 feet in the air now. The glider banked left then right, always gaining distance and altitude. Then the glider made a fast nose-up stroke. Lilienthal urgently threw his body forward, but this time with no reaction from the craft. One wing dipped, the entire glider followed. The air had suddenly forsaken him. He fell long and hard. The spectators converged on the now tangled heap of wire, splinters, and fabric. Lilienthal was uncovered and laid out on the ground. He reached up to one of his helpers: "Remember, sacrifices must be made!" Otto Lilienthal died the next day from his injuries.

Today we have a name for what happened to Otto Lilienthal: a stall/spin accident. But stalls and spins are really no accident, they can be predicted and avoided. Unfortunately, most modern pilots still have one thing in common with Lilienthal: We do not fully understand stalls and stalls certainly have the potential to kill us.

Wilbur Wright, after using the work of Lilienthal to move his own experiments along, said Lilienthal, "was the greatest of the precursors." That makes Lilienthal our pioneer as well.

Lilienthal also left us this advice: "One can get a proper insight into the practice of flying only by actual flying experience." Lilienthal knew that flight takes more than engineering and science, it takes skill. Flying is not a spectator sport. Practice of actual flight experiments such as S-turns, crosswind landings, chandelles, and all types of stalls, makes us better pilots. The great sacrifices have already been made for us, all we must do now is follow good advice. Like Lilienthal, fully understanding stalls and spins is a goal all pilots must work toward.

PART 1

The stall/spin myth

1
Why pilots
don't like stalls

I WAS WATCHING A LOCAL TELEVISION NEWSCAST ONE EVENING AND HEARD these words come over the airwaves: "According to officials at the scene, the small plane simply stalled and crashed, killing the pilot and his two passengers."

I am always very critical of the news media when it comes to reporting aviation topics. First, the average reporter knows nothing about airplanes but when on camera professes to be an expert; second, the news reporting works on a deadline. The problem is that determining the cause of an accident might take years, while the roving reporter on the scene needs a quick answer so he or she can form a headline or phrase to lead off the nightly newscast. The TV quote was a classical example of a misunderstanding driven by the need for speed.

Most, but certainly not all, general aviation accidents are investigated by the National Transportation Safety Board. Sometimes when the board has no one to send, the Federal Aviation Administration will send a representative to the scene of an accident. Either way, the first persons on the scene at general aviation accidents are the local airport officials and the local police and rescue services because the NTSB or FAA investigators have not arrived. When the reporter said "according to local officials at the scene," she meant a fireman who had been interviewed. Firemen are talented people and life savers, but they are probably unqualified to render on-the-spot probable-cause statements about airplane accidents; however, the news media will grab anybody who will say anything about an accident, even though by doing so the news media might reshape the story and prevent the discovery of the real truth.

Then came the phrase that should make any good pilot shudder: "the small airplane simply stalled and crashed." The report placed the terms "stalled and crashed" together as if to say that one causes the other. Anybody hearing that statement would logically assume that whenever an airplane stalls, it crashes as a result. This of course is not true, but if flight students believe what they hear, they will have a built-in fear of stalls before flight training even begins. For the same reason, many airline passengers are terrified of something called a "stall" because their perceptions tell them that a stall directly leads to death. This is how the stall/spin myth thrives.

DEFINITION

But the stall/spin myth is much deeper than this. What does the word *stall* actually mean? A large college dictionary lists 22 separate definitions for the word stall. The definitions range from the act of procrastination to a place to put a horse. Definitions 8 and 9 are the most interesting. Number 8 states: "The instance or the condition of causing an engine, or vehicle powered by an engine, to stop by supplying it with a poor fuel mixture or by overloading it." Anyone that drives a car has found themselves in a position where the car would not start or stopped running, usually in the middle of a busy intersection. Most of us would describe this situation as having the "car stalled." This is a term familiar to all drivers. Referring to an automobile as being "stalled," typically means the engine has quit.

When we humans hear things, we automatically make associations or use insights that help us understand what has been heard. If the word "stall" is familiar to us as meaning an engine when it stops running, it is understandable to think that when an airplane "stalls," that also means the engine has stopped running. But this is a great misunderstanding. An airplane stall has absolutely nothing to do with the airplane's engine. A sailplane can stall. When most beginning flight students are told that they are to learn stalls in the airplane, past experience causes the student to conjure up a scene where the flight instructor deliberately turns off the engine while in flight. The words "stall and crash" immediately come rushing back and the student starts developing an inherent dislike of anything called stalls. With beginning students, I try to avoid this situation by renaming stalls as "loss of lift" maneuvers.

Definition number 9 of a stall reads, "The instance or condition causing an airplane to fly at an angle of attack greater than the angle of maximum lift, causing loss of control and a downward spin." Look at the first part of the definition. This is a good description of an airplane exceeding its critical angle of attack. No mention is given to an engine. In fact, this critical angle of attack can be exceeded while the engine is running at full power, at idle, or without an engine at all. The term stall when referring to airplane aerodynamics has nothing to do with the operating condition of the engine. That last part is detestable: "causing loss of control and a downward spin." Perhaps the writer of this definition assumes that a stall, once entered, is unrecoverable and a crash will happen next; the writer apparently watches too much television news.

The fact remains that the word stall has several meanings. Unfortunately the most popular definition misleads pilots and passengers. I have been asked many times by nonpilots what I would do in the event my engine were to "stall" while in flight. I know instantly that this question is coming directly from the stall myth. They expect me to answer by saying something cute like "I get ready for my life to flash by in front of me." They are surprised to hear "I fully intend to fly the airplane to the ground and land." This blows their concept away because the phrase "fly the airplane" implies that I have control of the airplane. Their vision of what happens after an engine quits (stalls) is a directly vertical drop with wild gyrations of the airplane, stopped only by impact with the ground. I usually reply to their astonished looks: "Gliders fly every-day, under control, without any engine at all. Right?" Then I'm asked in amazement, "Don't you wear parachutes? What if the engine quits?" Personally, I will never jump out of an airplane. I explain that we train many hours for the possibility of an off-air-port emergency landing, and it is not a great deal different than a normal landing, you just find a spot, fly the airplane, and land, engine or no engine.

A BETTER UNDERSTANDING

One of the first goals of any flight instructor when teaching a student to fly an air-plane is to reach a point where they understand what a stall really is, how a stall is prac-ticed, and most importantly, why we practice stalls in the first place. More about the what, how, and whys later. Flight instructors must first realize that the stall misunder-standing does exist to some degree in every person. With the knowledge that a prob-lem of understanding is inherent in any flight training, the instructor must work overtime to overcome this problem of perception. Students who have not been prop-erly guided through the stall misunderstanding might develop real problems later on, perhaps during a critical flight maneuver, because they lack a solid foundation when it comes to airspeed control.

Think about your flight instructor(s). Did the instructor accurately explain this dif-ference in word meanings? Like any profession, there will be instructors that do a great job and others who do not. Unfortunately, certain instructors make stalls worse for stu-dents to learn than it has to be.

Any technical profession comes with a language or a jargon all its own, and avia-tion is certainly no exception. Flight instructors are taught not to use much "aviation-talk" with beginning students because, after all, they are beginners and they do not know the language yet. Let's listen to a typical instructor preflight briefing regarding stalls. Remember, the student brings preconceived ideas about this maneuver called "stalls" that are incorrect, yet these notions are all he has to go by until a smart flight instructor straightens things out or makes them worse:

"Well John, I was looking over the flight syllabus and you and I are up to lesson three today, and we have a good day for it. Lesson three is all about stalls. (FIG. 1-1)

"Stalls are just one of those things that pilots have to learn how to do, so let me tell you what will happen. We will climb up real high, so we have plenty of room to work.

Fig. 1-1

We will do a clearing turn to make sure we don't hit anybody up there, and we will raise the nose until it stalls. (FIG. 1-2)

"Now, we will know that we are stalling because the airplane will start to buffet and shake. (FIG. 1-3)

"After that, the nose will break (FIG. 1-4) and, we must be ready on the rudder, because one wing might fall off. (FIG. 1-5)

Now, go ahead and start the preflight and I'll be right out." (FIG. 1-6)

The terms that the instructor used in this discussion were normal terms within the flight training game. But from the new student's perspective, the instructor has inadvertently made stalls appear dangerous, if not deadly. The student desperately wants to be part of this training game and does not want to look bad, so he or she says nothing and starts the preflight inspection with all the wrong ideas about what is going to happen and why.

Fig. 1-2

A worse situation might exist where the instructor deliberately scares a student with stalls. Anytime this happens, it is completely unprofessional. If your flight instructor does it or has done it, get a new instructor. I have known instructors who would execute a stall with no warning or explanation. The instructor would rationalize this behavior by saying "it is sink or swim time," meaning that the student was forced to overcome his fears alone and if he could not do it, he would never be a good pilot and it was better to weed them out early. Again, if any instructor takes this approach to any aspect of training, get another instructor. All the built-in fears about stalls will be compounded when the instructor does not do the job properly and the student will shy away from all practice of slow airspeed maneuvers. Because landing the airplane is also a slow airspeed maneuver, a fear of stalls could delay or prevent a student from soloing. The student would develop mental road-blocks all through the initial training and beyond. There is never a reason why a student should be kept in the dark about what is going to happen inside the airplane.

Fig. 1-3

BARRIERS

Students have barriers to understanding stalls. The situation might simply be their perception of the word, or horror stories from other students, or been compounded by an unprofessional instructor, but no matter how the misunderstanding arrived, it must be dealt with and solved.

I learned to fly in the infamous Grumman American Trainer. I really loved that little airplane with its sleek lines, and its bubble top that could slide back to make it an open cockpit. I stalled, soloed, and eventually passed a checkride in that airplane. At the time, I never knew that NASA was also flying that same model. The difference was that NASA's modified Grumman Trainer had a parachute packed into the tail (FIG. 1-7). The NASA test pilots would deliberately stall and spin the airplane in an attempt to discover why, when the Trainer got into a spin, it would not come out. The test pi-

Fig. 1-4

lots would attempt a spin recovery, but when all attempts failed, they would pull a cable and release the tail parachute. The open chute would stabilize the airplane to re-
sume normal flight.

Because of this, all the Grumman Trainers had a sign on the instrument panel:
Spins Prohibited. As a young and naive flight student, I did not know what a spin was.
I actually thought then that the sign meant that you should not make sharp turns using
excessive brakes while taxiing on the ground. That would have been a spin. First-hand
experience at how the aviation jargon can cause student misunderstandings.

A misunderstanding of stalls will lead to an unhealthy fear of stalls. This fear will
prevent the student from practicing stalls. Students can develop a real stigma about
stalls. Some pilots never stall except on the flight reviews. If stalls, or any other maneuver, are not practiced, the pilot will not be as sharp and safe as they should be. Ultimately, the stall myth that leads to the misunderstanding of stalls is a safety issue.

Fig. 1-5

LAWS OF LEARNING

Why do students and many certificated pilots shy away from stalls and stall practice? The reasons might come from deep within ourselves. Flight instructors must learn the "Laws of Learning" before they become instructors. The laws were written by Dr. Edward L. Thorndike of Columbia University in the early 1900s, suggesting some simple principles that govern how people learn or are unable to learn new concepts.

The Laws of Learning are readiness, effect, exercise, intensity, primacy, and recency. The laws provide insight regarding why learning and practicing stalls is so hard for us to do.

Readiness

The Law of Readiness states that when someone is ready to learn, they will learn faster and better. Being ready to learn means that the student is eager and anxious to

Fig. 1-6

get started. The student is hungry for the knowledge. This law almost needs no definition. In your own case, you can certainly think of topics you would enjoy learning more about, and other topics that you could care less about. Personally, I would have no problem sitting for three hours at a seminar on how the Wright brothers first flew. The three hours would seem like no time at all. But, if I had to sit through a 30-minute lecture on the historical significance of Romeo meeting Juliet, I would not be able to stand it.

It is all a matter of what we individually prefer. What we want to learn, we will learn. If a flight student brings a negative perception of stalls to the airport, that student will not be eager to go out and do stalls. If the instructor forces the student to do them anyway, the student will be uncomfortable and this deters learning. Any human's number one concern is their own safety. If the student thinks that learning and practicing stalls is dangerous and that their safety is in jeopardy, the student will not be "ready" to learn, consequently they would not learn well. An unfortunate revolving door be-

Fig. 1-7. *The modified Grumman trainer used in the NASA spin research project.*

gins. The pilot does not practice stalls because he does not like stalls. But he cannot overcome the problem without stall practice. Some pilots fly for years carrying the knowledge that they do not fully understand stalls and stall characteristics. Their stall knowledge is less than it should be because they really did not want to learn about stalls in the first place.

Effect

The Law of Effect states that learning is strengthened when accompanied by a pleasant feeling or weakened when accompanied by an unpleasant feeling. If stalls are presented in a way that knocks down the walls of misunderstanding and simultaneously builds up the reason why stalls are so important to good pilots, the student will learn better. If stalls are presented in a way that increases anxiety, the student will not learn as well.

Exercise

The Law of Exercise states that repetitious actions help people remember the action. The specific skills that are necessary to fly an airplane safely are not yours forever; many Federal Aviation Regulations deal with this fact. Takeoffs and landings, night flying, and instrument flying all have minimum practice requirements, called *skill-level proficiency.* The whole idea behind flight reviews and instrument competency checks is to assure proficiency. Not using a skill means losing a skill. The more you exercise, the greater the proficiency. The more you exercise the better you learn and remember; therefore, practicing stalls is the best way to greater understanding and safety. But if a pilot just does not like stalls, he or she will not practice and no proficiency is gained.

Intensity

The Law of Intensity states that learning is greatly enhanced when it is presented in an interesting way. The "science of teaching" is knowing the subject matter to be taught; the "art of teaching" is being able to hold the attention of the student. If a lesson is presented in a dramatic, exciting way, it will be more easily understood. The worst possible situation is being forced to learn something you do not care about from a boring teacher. Reading this book about stalls and spins might go a long way toward understanding them, but you will get more learning done by actually stalling an airplane than reading about stalling. All the best diagrams, videotapes, books, and photographs can only take you so far. To really learn how an airplane feels, sounds, and looks in a stall, you must experience it for yourself.

Primacy

The Law of Primacy states that what is learned first will have a bigger impact on the learner than what is to follow. This places a burden on the flight instructor to teach a topic correctly the first time; "unlearning" an idea is tough. You must make every effort to learn the proper method initially. If the topic is stalls, the student should understand basic aerodynamics first and there should be no question what stalls are, how they are performed, and why they are important to do from the very beginning.

Recency

The Law of Recency states that if you learned something yesterday you are more likely to understand and use the topic today than if it had been presented six months ago; recent learning implies the use of short-term memory. This is why students can successfully cram for a test. They might pass the test, but will they subsequently recall what they learned? If you practice stalls on a regular basis, recent experience will properly serve you; your proficiency and understanding will be much greater.

The myths about stalls need not remain a mystery. We can analyze why we don't like stalls and therefore why we are not as good at them as we know we should be. Knowledge overcomes mystery. The more you know about what stalls are, how they are performed, and why they are so important, the safer pilot you will become.

2
Spin training

ON APRIL 15, 1991, THE FEDERAL AVIATION ADMINISTRATION CHANGED the laws that govern how pilots are to be trained in regard to stalls and spins. Federal Aviation Regulation (FAR) 61.97(h) calls for recreational pilots to have knowledge of "stall awareness, spin entry, spins, and spin recovery techniques." FAR 61.105(a)(6) for private pilots and FAR 61.125(a)(4) for commercial pilots also have the same stall/spin awareness requirement. All of the laws come under the heading of "aeronautical knowledge." The laws do not require a recreational, private, or commercial pilot to actually learn how to spin and recover from spins in an airplane. This requirement only calls for the pilot applicants to have knowledge of the topic. The only regulation that does require in-airplane spin training is FAR 61.187(a)(6), which pertains to instructor training. Before a person can take the flight instructor practical test, he or she must have had another flight instructor complete a course of spin training with them. This training includes spin entries both to the left and to the right, and spin recoveries. The instructor who teaches the course must have been a flight instructor for more than 24 months and given at least 200 hours of instruction.

These changes stopped short of requiring spins to be taught to everyone. But, the fact that spin awareness has been written back into the regulations reflects a compromise in a fight that has been raging now for more than 50 years. To spin or not to spin has been a topic that has been debated everywhere from small airport hangars on Saturday afternoon to the halls of the United States Capitol.

LOGICAL ARGUMENT "FOR"

The argument for spin training is logical. If a pilot ever unintentionally finds himself in a spin, he would have a better chance of recovery if he had actually been trained to recover. The job of a flight instructor, among other things, is to take the student to the "edge" of their experience and let them look over the side. With safety ensured by the instructor, the student can go where it is not safe for them to go alone. In the beginning, this "edge" is at the airplane preflight. It would not be safe to fly an airplane that was inspected by someone who did not know what they were doing. The instructor teaches a student how to preflight and the edge of their experience expands. In the air, the instructor shows the student various maneuvers that will ultimately allow the student to fly alone, but before the training takes place, it would be dangerous for the student to solo.

The solo skill is still just over the edge of their ability. As training continues, the student will push back the edge, but one cliff does not have to be crossed: the spin. Currently, we train students for all sorts of possibilities. Having an engine quit in flight is a very rare occurrence, but that does not stop us from teaching forced landing procedure. Someday the student might experience an engine-out emergency and when that day comes the pilot would have a greater chance of a safe outcome if he had practiced the procedure time and time again. It would seem logical that the same way of thinking should apply to spins as well. Training for emergencies does not guarantee a safe result but it does increase the chances. Spins are emergencies that, like engine-outs, are rare but can happen. The more possibilities that a pilot is ready to handle, the safer that pilot will be.

PRACTICAL ARGUMENT "AGAINST"

The argument against spin training is practical. Spinning can be hard on the airplane, especially its gyroscopic instruments. If all students were required to receive spin training, schools would probably have to set aside one airplane as the designated spin airplane to protect all the other airplanes from spinning. This would increase the overhead cost of running the school. Insurance coverage might be higher for spin training, which would further cut into meager flight school profits. Many students who were afraid to spin would simply choose not to fly and the school would lose more business. It boils down to a classical safety versus dollars conflict. But, how unsafe is the lack of spin training?

National Transportation Safety Board statistics show very few accidents that were attributed to spins alone. Most spin accidents occur because of some other factor that distracts the pilot and prevents him from maintaining flying speed. The spin therefore is just a symptom of a larger problem. If the larger problem can be solved, there would be no spin and therefore the actual spin threat is low. Training everyone to spin would increase the danger manyfold and more accidents would take place in the name of safety than would ordinarily take place without the training. Mandatory spin training to overcome a minimal problem would be overkill, literally.

Passionate proponents are on both sides, and the issue might never be solved by regulation or lobbyists. A spin training history lesson will show how and why the recent regulatory changes were determined.

GENEALOGY OF SPIN TRAINING REGULATION

Prior to 1949, spins were required for private pilot applicants, there was no such thing as a recreational pilot then. After talking with several pilots who flew and taught before 1949 I began to understand how different things were then. The checkrides were very informal with very few do's and don'ts: no practical test standards. The examiner might not have even flown with the applicant, but rather observed from the ground. A short application was filled out, and the test began. Private pilot applicants had to do a 720° steep power turn using at least 60° of bank, stalls, a one-turn spin, and make three precision landings. The landings had to be three-point in the tail-draggers and touchdown had to be within 100 feet of a predetermined line on the runway or pasture, as the case might be. Commercial pilots had to do a two-turn spin and recover within 20° of their original heading. At the examiner's discretion, all or part of the test could be administered from the ground. The examiner would simply give a list of maneuvers to the applicant and the prospective pilot would take off, fly over the airport within sight of the examiner, and put on a checkride airshow. There was no minimum requirement for teaching spins before the applicant took the flight test. Today, we have very strict rules on what a person must do before he or she is eligible for a checkride (chapter 25); back then you did not even need an instructor endorsement.

"We did spins all the time with students and with no stigma attached," said Don Culp, FAA designated examiner, formerly a flight instructor in the 1940s. "Spins were just like any other maneuver, they were a normal part of teaching people how to fly." There were very few "ratings": no multiengine rating, instead, pilots were rated by horsepower. If a checkride was passed in an airplane that had a 200-horsepower engine, a certificate was issued that allowed the pilot to fly airplanes with 200 horsepower plus 50 percent. If a pilot was rated for 500 horsepower and wanted to fly an airplane that had two 200-horsepower engines, that was legal because the two engines together were not more than the total horsepower rating. "Things have certainly changed since those days," Culp said in a disappointed tone.

The biggest change then came about in 1949 when the Civil Aeronautics Agency (CAA), forerunner of the FAA, deleted spins from pilot certification requirements. On June 15, 1949, Civil Aviation Regulations (CAR) Amendment 20-3 went into effect. The document stated:

"This amendment eliminates spins from the pilot certification requirements and, in lieu thereof, provides for dual instruction in the prevention of and recovery from power-on stalls and power-off stalls entered from all normally anticipated flight attitudes. It is believed that the deletion of the spin requirements and the placing of greater emphasis upon prevention of and recovery from stalls will result in greater air safety in two ways: (a) it will emphasize recognition of and recovery from stalls which, on the basis of available accident statistics, has been proved to be the most dangerous maneuver to pilots; and (b) elimination of the required spin maneuver will act as an incentive for manufacturers to build, and operators of schools to use, spin-resistant or spin-proof aircraft."

What was the atmosphere that lead to this decision? I am sure that the writers of this landmark aviation legislation were sincere in their belief that the elimination of required spins from flight training would make aviation safer. In the four years preceding the amendment, 48 percent of all fatal accidents had been attributed to spins. This was not 48 percent of all accidents, 48 percent of accidents with a death. Of the 48 percent, many were "combination" accidents where other factors were involved, such as fuel exhaustion leading to pilot panic, which distracted the pilot from flying. The pilot, while worried about the engine, allowed the airplane to stall and then to spin.

But something more than statistics led to the no-spin decision: politics. After World War II, aviation business leaders were eager to turn gains in war time technology into profits. Airplane manufacturers wanted the American public to perceive the airplane as the invention that would replace the automobile. If learning to fly was quick, easy, and inexpensive, they could sell more airplanes. A movement began to make the acquisition of a private pilot certificate as easy as getting a driver's license. Steep-turn bank angle requirements were relaxed to 45°. The eight-on-pylon maneuver was eliminated. There was discussion to eliminate "full" stalls and teach "imminent" stalls instead. In this movement, teaching spins was high on the hit list. If people were afraid of spins they might not learn to fly and the industry would lose a potential customer. The result was a full-scale effort on the part of manufacturers, business groups, and pilot groups, to lobby congress for pilot training changes. In 1949, Amendment 20-3 deleted the spin requirement and it has never been overturned.

NTSB RESEARCH

Twenty years after the spin was deleted, the National Transportation Safety Board (NTSB) conducted a study and did statistical research on pilot training requirements and stall/spin accidents in 1967, 1968, and 1969. The study was the first impartial attempt to judge the results of the 1949 amendment. The special study was adopted on September 13, 1972, and concluded that 27 percent of all fatal general aviation accidents could be linked to a spin. This was a significant reduction from 48 percent in 1949, but the NTSB also understood that aviation participation had grown and a higher total number of accidents had occurred; 27 percent of a higher total number might not have meant fewer spin accidents. The safety board concluded that in order to change the trend, "impetus of renewed, revitalized, and reoriented accident prevention efforts responsive to the needs of the general aviation system as a whole, can serve to mitigate this trend significantly."

The NTSB study turned up new information about the detailed causes of a stall/spin accident. It was determined that 60.5 percent of all stall/spin accidents took place during "noncommercial" flights. Noncommercial generally refers to pleasure or business related flights usually conducted by pilots with less time and fewer ratings than commercial pilots. The conclusion to be drawn is that less experienced pilots have a greater chance of being in a stall/spin accident. Another 19 percent of the accidents took place during "instructional" flying. This is a disturbing statistic because the people doing the instruction are required to have spin training. Many people point to this as evidence that spin training does not necessarily eliminate spin accidents, so why expose everyone to the risk?

Thirty-six percent of the stall/spin accidents occurred during landing. Twenty-four percent of the accidents took place during takeoff. Together, 60 percent of the stall/spin accidents took place in and around an airport traffic pattern. Specific causes related to "traffic pattern circling," "final approach," and "go-around" were cited.

Forty percent of these accidents took place during the "in-flight" phase. Although several of these could be linked to pilot negligence due to "low-level acrobatics," "buzzing," and "low passes," a relationship was established between the pilot's attention to flying the airplane and stall/spin accidents. A list of "pilot-involved" factors was discovered that distracted the pilot's attention and this in turn lead to a stall/spin accident:

- Fuel exhaustion due to inadequate preflight preparation
- Fuel starvation due to mispositioning of fuel selector
- Lack of familiarity with the airplane
- Continuing VFR flight into adverse weather conditions
- Improperly loaded airplane weight or center of gravity
- Carburetor icing
- Improper use or failure to use anti/deicing equipment
- Engine malfunction or failure
- Alcoholic impairment of efficiency and judgment

The study also uncovered additional noteworthy revelations:

- 16.7 percent of the accident-involved airplanes were piloted by student pilots
- 42.8 percent of the stall/spin accidents involved private pilots who had not been required to have spin recovery training
- 96 percent of the stall/spin accidents took place during VFR weather conditions
- 90 percent of the accidents took place during daylight hours
- 97 percent of the stall/spin accidents were determined to be caused by "pilot-error"

The NTSB concluded the report with a list of recommendations. The final recommendation of the 1972 study charged the FAA to "evaluate the feasibility of requiring at least minimal spin training of all pilot applicants."

When the NTSB recommends that a change be made, they have no regulatory means to require the change. After the 1972 special study was adopted, no significant change was made by the FAA regarding stalls and spins.

FAA MOVEMENT

In January of 1980, the wheels at the FAA began to slowly turn. The FAA was still very opposed to spin training, but took a new direction: pilot distraction. On the strength of their own study, Report number FAA-RD-77-26 entitled: "The General Aviation Pilot Stall Awareness Study," the FAA directed pilot examiners to deliberately distract pilot applicants during flight tests. The report cited the previous NTSB special study together with their own data to conclude that, "most stall/spin accidents occurred when the pilot's attention was diverted from the primary task of flying the aircraft." As a result of the report, the FAA published "Advisory Circular 61-92: Use of Distractions During Pilot Certification Flight Tests (Appendix A)."

This sheds some light on examiners that are seemingly aggravating during a checkride. It is bad enough that you are nervous, but the examiner is directed to deliberately ask questions during critical flight operations. The advisory circular states that "intentional practice of stalls and spins seldom resulted in an accident. The real danger was inadvertent stalls induced by distractions during routine flight situations. . . . Distractions may be included in the evaluation of performance to determine that the applicant possess the skills required to cope with distractions while maintaining the degree of aircraft control required for safe flight."

Examples of distractions were listed in the advisory circular, but not limited to:

- Simulate radio communications
- Read outside air temperature gauge
- Remove objects from the glove compartment
- Identify terrain features or objects on the ground
- Reverse course after a series of S turns
- Identify fields suitable for forced landing

The examiner could ask a pilot applicant to perform a turn-around-a-point and while the task is being performed, ask to see a navigation plotter that is in the back seat. The pilot is then required to do two things at once and still maintain safe airspeed, altitude, and ground track. I had an instrument student on a checkride who was asked by the examiner while on a partial panel ILS approach, "Do you have a dog?" The student never looked the examiner's way, but said, "I had a Labrador retriever as a child and we are now at decision height." The most extreme case of distractions I ever heard was an example told by aviation writer Ernest K. Gann. He described an airline test that was required for promotion to captain. As he began an instrument approach, the company examiner struck a match and held it in front of the pilot's face as he flew. As the match would burn down, the examiner would light another match. This continued throughout the entire approach and after landing. The point was that if the pilot could fly safely with a match in his face, he might be more able to fly safely when real flames were in his face someday.

The 1980 advisory circular did not make spin training mandatory but it did signal a readiness to address the problem. The FAA clearly took the position that stalls and spins do not lead to many accidents but that stalls and spins are the off-spring of other problems. Rather than requiring spin training, they placed a greater emphasis on diversion training. By curing the illness, the FAA hoped to prevent the symptoms.

CONGRESSIONAL "SPIN"

The United States House of Representatives held a hearing in June 1980 that specifically dealt with spin training. The Subcommittee on Investigations and Oversight heard testimony from pilots and representatives of aircraft manufacturers, NASA, FAA, AOPA, and the military regarding mandatory spin recovery training. Jim Lloyd of California opened the hearings by asking the question: "Would spin training as a requirement for a private pilot license result in a net saving of lives?" He observed that after 30 years (referring to the 1949 amendment) we are raising the question of whether or not we should do what we did 30 years ago without question. If we returned to required spin training would, "this be beneficial to the aviation community? Would there be a saving of lives? Would we instill greater confidence (in pilots)? Would we come up with a better product, namely the private pilot as an aviator in today's aviation world?"

FAA, GAMA, and AOPA opposed mandatory spin training for student pilots. AOPA's Air Safety Foundation favored spin training but did not testify.

Bernard A. Geier testified for the FAA and maintained that the FAA's "Stall Awareness and Avoidance Program" was adequate to reduce stall/spin accidents without actual spin recovery training. The idea of distraction training while operating at slow speeds was Geier's main point. He said that the FAA was conducting flight instructor and student clinics on stall/spin avoidance and would hold more in the future.

Elwood Driver testified for the National Transportation Safety Board and cited the stall/spin accident report that was adopted by the NTSB in 1972, wasting no time in calling everyone's attention to the fact that the NTSB had recommended "minimal spin training for all pilot applicants" in 1972, but the FAA had not acted on the recommendation. "The FAA's actions were good as far as they went, but they were insufficient," he reported. Then Driver drew the battleline that ignores the actual accident statistics:

"We keep pulling out that link which says keep the guy from getting into trouble (by spinning), but what are you going to do when he does get into trouble? He has got to know what to do (to recover from a spin). It does not occur very often but it is awfully catastrophic to the one guy that it does occur to."

This is the "it is worth it if we can save one life" theory. When you attack the problem on the basis of one individual, you attempt to eliminate all risk and even though accident rates might be low, it is not low enough until no accidents occur. Unfortunately in the real world, the price of transportation is risk.

Requiring a Cessna 150 to have a collision avoidance system (TCAS) would certainly make the flying safer, but who would pay for it? It boils down to an issue of "how much does safety cost?" and if we cannot afford safety, then how much risk will be deemed acceptable. The FAA looks at risk levels versus cost of implementing a plan. Simply stated, how many people can get killed before the number exceeds "acceptable limits" and money must be spent.

Roger Boggs, a retired FAA accident investigator, laid the blame for stall/spin accidents at the doorstep of his former employer: "Ignorance is prominent in pilot error. Most ignorance is voluntary. I know of only one area of ignorance which was decreed by regulation and which the government has sponsored ever since: spin training." He concluded by pointing out that, "the FAA has stringent rules and enforcement against violators for all types of emergency and safety situations except the most deadly of them all, spins, which isn't even on the list."

Scott Crossfield, the first man to fly faster than Mach 2, testified and disputed the antispin arguments one by one:

- Spins damage aircraft and instruments: "A very dubious premise at best."
- Students are afraid of spins: "Fear as a reason to protect students from spins is absurd."
- Instructors are afraid of spins: "Just as absurd."
- Inadequate training areas: "Just a rock to hide behind."
- Discouragement of aspiring pilots: "Pure fiction in light of the heavy extracurricular demand for spin training by the neophyte groups."

Crossfield's last conclusion was that all "respectable" aviators are convinced that spin training would result in a net savings of lives. Only those who would be inconvenienced continue to voice disagreement.

OPINIONS

In the committee's final list of conclusions and recommendations, great support was shown for overturning the FAA's 1949 no-spin amendment. The votes came in from each group:

FAA, no
AOPA, no
GAMA, no
NTSB, yes
EAA, yes
FAA-retired, yes
System safety, yes
Lockheed, yes
U.S. Army, pass
U.S. Air Force, yes
U.S. Navy, yes
Science & Technology, yes
NASA, undecided

The report concluded, "The only disagreement appears to stem from other than safety considerations from trade groups and the FAA. It can be concluded without equivocation that the experienced aviator overwhelmingly demands that aspiring pilots be trained to protect themselves and be able to recover from post-stall gyrations, incipient spins, and spins."

Recommendations: "The subcommittee recommends that some form of spin recovery training become a requirement for a private pilot license. (Specific recommendations):

"1. An unbiased phase I study and analysis be conducted to determine a proper and realistic syllabus for such training.

"2. An additional phase II study be conducted designed to develop an implementation plan to accomplish restoration of spin training to flight training. Such a plan must have the basic protection for the grandfather rights of current aircraft certification, current instructor and private pilot certification, and the entire logistic and economic structure of the flight training industry.

"3. Firm (implementation) dates and milestones acceptable to the committee be established and considered mandatory."

Never underestimate the ability of the FAA to look the other way even in the face of a U.S. congressional hearing. Obviously, the FAA did not accept any of these recommendations to return spins to required training.

PRACTICAL TEST STANDARDS

In the mid-1980s, measures were taken by the FAA to improve the pilot standards put teeth to the notion that pilots were just not as good as they should be. Several changes took place following the collision of a commercial airliner and a single-engine airplane in the Los Angeles Terminal Control Area. The flight test guides that had been used to determine whether or not a pilot would pass a checkride were replaced by the practical test standards. The "guides" were aptly named. The examiner used the book's guidelines, but administered the test any way he wanted. Under the "standards," the examiner is required to have the applicants perform exact tasks. In this way, the tests are to be uniform, no matter which examiner you might take a test from. Every examiner is different and even with the practical test standards in use, checkrides still vary widely.

Next, the designated examiners were not allowed to renew the right to administer flight instructor practical tests. This turned the job over to the already tight-scheduled inspectors at the flight standards district offices. The only conclusion that can be drawn from this change is that the FAA believed that substandard flight instructors were getting passed into the system. Once turned loose, these supposedly inadequate instructors produced inadequate students and the entire system was less safe. By reeling in the flight instructor testing responsibility, the FAA could ensure that only highly qualified flight instructors were in the training marketplace.

The FAA produced the "Back to Basics" series in 1987 to improve awareness of lapsing standards. Accident prevention specialists across the country delivered lectures and video tape presentations of several topics of interest to general aviation pilots. One presentation was "Stall/Spin Avoidance." The FAA had moved a little farther along the scale from 1949 when the stall/spin topic was taboo, past the point where the stall/spin topic was only considered as a result of a distraction, and arrived at actual recognition of the fact that pilots today just do not know much about stalls and spins.

The FAA published Advisory Circular 61-67B: Stall and Spin Awareness Training (Appendix B), in 1991. AC 61-92 on distractions has been canceled. The 1991 advisory circular was intended as a guide for pilots and instructors to meet the Federal Aviation Regulation changes that make stall awareness, spin entry, spins, and spin recovery techniques a mandatory ground school topic.

CAREFUL APPROACH TO TRAINING

This whole chapter has dealt with mandatory spin training or the lack of it. Of course, spin training goes on everyday whether it be required or not. Today, without a rule that forces a pilot to have spin training, the spin experience is optional to all except instructor applicants. The decision is personal. If you do decide to seek actual spin training be very careful. Due to the pilot hiring boom of the last decade, instruction has become a transition profession. There are very few career instructors anymore. Instructors that are around have trained in a nonspin environment. The spin training that is required for the flight instructor test has no specific guidelines and can vary widely from very good to very bad. As a result, just because a person holds a flight instructor certificate does not guarantee that that person is a qualified spin instructor. The FAA understands this and changed the flight instructor checkride in 1991; if a flight instructor applicant fails the checkride due to a lack of stall/spin knowledge, he or she must bring to the reexamination an airplane that is spinnable and take the FAA inspector spinning. In theory, this will increase the spin proficiency of flight instructors. In practice, the effort might fall short of this goal because FAA inspectors are not thrilled about doing spins in various unfamiliar airplanes. An inspector can avoid spins by not failing an applicant on spin topics.

Before you spin an airplane accompanied by an instructor, ask about their spin experience and their familiarity with the specific airplane in which spin training is completed. Do not attempt to spin without proper instruction. Do not attempt to spin solo without proper instruction.

As the new FAA initiative on stall/spin awareness begins to take hold, there should be a greater number of instructors who have advanced spin training and can teach you safe spin recognition and recovery. Spin training can be safe and yield safer pilots. Until the regulations change again, if you want voluntary spin training you should read about stalls and spins, ask questions and seek out quality instruction.

PART 2

What your instructor never told you

3
What is spinnable?

PILOTS ARE VERY FAMILIAR WITH PARTS 61 AND 91 OF THE REGULATIONS, which are the rules of flight and certification. But, what about the rules for airplane certification? Part 23 (Appendix C) is the chapter of the regulations that manufacturers must adhere to when planning to build and sell an airplane. Like other Federal Aviation Regulations the language is very legalistic and thorough, but select areas still cannot be completely regulated. What happens to airplanes in stalls and spins is one area.

Light airplanes must receive an airworthiness certificate issued following the rules of FAR Part 23.221 entitled, "Airworthiness Standards: Normal, Utility, and Acrobatic Airplanes." Before the airplane is certificated, it must pass some tests just like a pilot. The tests include the airplane's operating limitations, engine, handling characteristics, equipment, structures, and flight performance. Stall demonstrations are part of the certification process.

Any airplane must show certain stall characteristics that will later provide the pilot with at least the ability to recognize and recover from a stall. First, the airplane's control surfaces must remain effective up to the event of the actual stall. The design must allow the ailerons to correct for roll and the rudder to correct for yaw until the full stall occurs. The effectiveness of these controls will gradually diminish as the airplane gets slower, but right up until the end, there must be some effect. If a pilot lost control of the airplane prior to the actual stall due to the airplane's design, the pilot would be powerless to recover from an imminent stall. This condition would be unsafe and the aircraft would not be certificated.

ROLL PREVENTION

Another criteria of certification is that the airplane must be able to prevent an unwanted roll of greater than 15° or an unwanted yaw of 15° during stall recovery. This means that as soon as the stall has been broken, the control surfaces must come back to life. This allows the pilot to make the proper control movements to get out and stay out of trouble.

A pilot must be alerted with adequate stall warning. The airplane should not just stall without sending a message first. The message might only be a buffet or vibration as the airflow on the wings starts to churn. The warning might be a device: stall warning light, alarm, or horn may be used. The warning must begin between 5 and 10 knots above the stall speed. The warning must continue throughout the stall and only stop during the recovery when the airplane is flying again.

If the airplane's recovery from a full stall requires more than 100 feet in the FAA flight tests, this information must be given in the airplane's flight manual. Also, if the nose of the airplane pitches more than 30° down during the demonstrated full stall that information must also be included in the manual and be available to pilots who will stall the airplane.

CATEGORY

The actual category of certificate that is issued depends upon additional tests. The stress or the loading that an airplane can handle is determined. G-load stress is measured in two directions: positive and negative. The natural force of gravity pushes you down in the seat where you are sitting. A positive G-force would simply add to that force. In airplanes, we really cannot speak of "up" or "down" because as airplanes turn, other forces affect the airplane and pilot in directions other than toward the center of the earth. For now, a positive G is a force that pushes you farther down in the seat during a steep power turn. A negative G-force works the other way. It pulls you out of your seat, like going up and over the hump on a roller-coaster. Airplanes are designed to handle forces from both directions. The degree of their strength helps to determine which category they are assigned. Part 23 uses TABLE 3-1.

Table 3-1. Categorical stress limits

Category	Positive G load limit	Negative G load limit
Normal	+2.5 to +3.8	40% of positive or −1.52
Utility	+4.4	40% of positive or −1.76
Acrobatic	+6.0	50% of positive or −3.0

In addition to the certification category, the airplane might be prohibited from certain maneuvers. Normal category airplanes are not authorized to do acrobatic maneuvers and spins. The definition of an acrobatic maneuver: an intentional maneuver involving an abrupt change in an aircraft's attitude, and abnormal attitude, or abnormal acceleration not necessary for normal flight. This is not to say that a normal category airplane cannot be forced to do an acrobatic maneuver or spin, it can. But if one of these maneuvers is performed, the airplane might experience structural damage or come apart.

For an airplane to receive a normal certificate it has to be spin tested through one turn or a three-second spin, whichever takes longer. Normal control movements are used in recovery. At one time, the normal category required a six-turn spin test with "free-control" recovery. That requirement was relaxed to the present day standard in the early 1960s. When the rule was changed, the FAA published Advisory Circular 23-1, "Type Certification Spin Test Procedures." The one-turn spin test was discussed in the circular: "These (one-turn) tests are considered to be an investigation of the airplane's characteristics in a delayed stall (recovery) rather than true spin test." The FAA does not require normal category airplanes to be tested in a developed or stabilized spin. If you are flying a normal category airplane and enter a spin and do not recover within one turn, you become your own test pilot. Past one turn, the airplane's characteristics are unknown. The airplane might recover normally, or it might be impossible to recover, you just do not know. Stall recovery in normal category airplanes must be sharp. Stall and spin awareness must be sharper.

ACROBATICS

Limited acrobatics are authorized in utility category airplanes. To determine the authorized and unauthorized maneuvers, look inside an airplane's flight manual. Information about authorized maneuvers that are shown in the type certification must include a recommended maneuver entry speed. If a maneuver is not listed, it is not authorized. Some maneuvers can be listed as prohibited in the manuals. Again, the airplane in question can perform the maneuvers that are not authorized but there is no assurance that the airplane will come out of the maneuver in one piece. Utility category aircraft testing is really a mystery. The regulations say that utility airplanes must be tested to "either the normal or acrobatic category limits." This means that testing of utility category airplanes has a range of possibilities. The pilot must check with the manufacturer to determine how the airplane was actually tested.

Acrobatic category aircraft are tested in spins of up to six turns or three seconds, whichever takes longer. The recovery must be made using normal control movements and recovery must be achieved within one and one-half turns after the recovery is initiated.

Manufacturers attempt to design airplanes that are spin-proof or at least spin-resistant. But the current regulations do not require the development of such airplanes. Airplanes today do stall and they do spin if the pilot allows it. Do not think you are immune from stalls or spins just because you decide not to deliberately perform these maneuvers. The next chapter examines situations that happen on every flight. Manufacturers have not developed a pilot-proof airplane.

4
Stall/spin threats

AN FAA PILOT EXAMINER ONCE ASKED A PRIVATE PILOT APPLICANT ON his checkride to perform a departure stall. The only problem was that the student had just taken off and the airplane was still within the confines of the traffic pattern and below 1,000 feet AGL. The examiner hoped that the student would override this request when the student realized that they were too low to do the maneuver safely. The poor applicant faced a choice between doing what the "all-knowing and all-powerful" examiner told him to do or to use good judgment. Unfortunately the applicant decided that if an examiner said it was okay to do a stall at low altitude, then it must really be all right. The applicant began the maneuver and the examiner ended the test.

This story has a hidden message about how stalls are practiced versus how stalls can kill. Nobody should ever deliberately stall an airplane below a safe altitude for recovery, but that is exactly where fatal stalls occur. Everyday students and flight instructors take off and fly to the "practice area." This practice area, with its freedom from traffic and safety of altitude, is where most pilots learn the airplane's tricks. Stalls are routinely practiced in a unrealistic environment where there is plenty of altitude and warning. Stalls that kill usually occur without altitude and with little early warning. I am not advocating the practice of stalls at low altitude, I am only pointing out a misunderstanding about stall threats.

While practicing intentional stalls, you should be at least 1,500 feet above the ground as a bare minimum; never purposely stall an airplane without enough altitude for a spin recovery.

Most pilots think of stalls as a practice area maneuver only; stalls are a threat to any maneuver. Pilots should learn about stalls and practice stalls with more urgency because real stall threats do not happen in the practice area. Stalls and certainly stall recoveries are maneuvers that are required outside the training environment in real flying. This chapter probes stall situations that will be a part of your next flight.

TAKEOFF

In practice, every takeoff is a little different than the one before. So many factors work together to make a takeoff interesting. Aircraft weight, density altitude, runway length, runway surface, runway slope, weather conditions, and pilot technique (or lack of technique) change to make every takeoff a challenge. Unfortunately, the potential for a stall or stall/spin accident also changes with these variable conditions. Flight training moves through a series of takeoff variations that in time lose their real meaning. We repeat short-field and soft-field takeoffs without really understanding what is important about the maneuvers. We memorize a set of speeds and we mechanically go through the motions in training, on checkrides, and throughout our flying career. But these maneuvers and others are actually practiced to prevent stalls on takeoff. Your flight instructor probably never mentioned that. Let's look at the maneuvers again, but this time with some real practical applications.

Normal takeoff is an everyday occurrence, but people still get into trouble because they do a poor job of airspeed control. The airplane starts developing lift when it starts to move forward on the takeoff roll. Of course, far too little lift is being produced to take off, so we allow the airplane to accelerate to a speed where enough lift is produced to offset the weight of the airplane. As the pilot reaches a speed that produces enough lift, he should slightly rotate or pull back on the control wheel. This deflects the elevator into a position that will bring the tail down and the nose up. When the nose rises, the wing's angle of attack increases and this produces even more lift, now in excess of the airplane's weight, and it flies.

Very elementary, but failure to reach or maintain flying speed is still a category needed in National Transportation Safety Board takeoff accident statistics. After leaving the runway, the airplane should be allowed to accelerate to a speed required for a safe climbout. A real understanding of "what controls what" is required to do this job. Placing the airplane's nose too high will result in reduced climb performance and reduced airspeed. Placing the nose too low will not allow clearance of obstructions and will also reduce climb performance. Strict attention and familiarity with the airplane is essential. Speed control during takeoff becomes more complicated when other factors are involved.

Short field

If the runway is short and obstructions are present at the takeoff end, a short-field technique might be required (FIG. 4-1). A short-field takeoff is a private pilot maneuver because it is required by the FAA's practical test standards. Student pilots

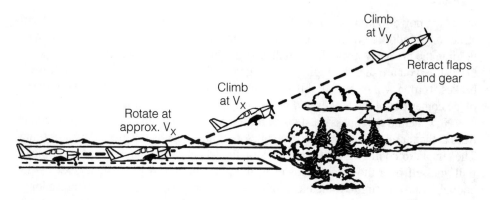

Fig. 4-1. *Short-field takeoff technique.*

practice short-field takeoffs all the time, but seldom do they consider the maneuver a stall threat. In a real takeoff, where trees or power lines are in the takeoff path, there will be a great temptation to get the airplane off early and climb out steep to clear the obstructions; however, if airspeed is not controlled properly, the airplane cannot do what it is asked.

The takeoff should not be attempted without taking advantage of all available runway. In training, we usually simulate this by taxiing as close to the end of the runway as possible, then turning to line up with the runway centerline. A pilot would do more if this were a real takeoff where real danger existed from colliding with obstructions. The pilot could stop the engine and pull the plane backward so that the main wheels are at the edge of the available runway. The load could be reduced; any extra weight could be removed, including unused seats. Or take off with only enough fuel to land at an airport with a longer runway to refuel. We do not go to these drastic extremes just to practice, but pilots should think about what might face them someday and that the proper short-field technique is not just a checkride maneuver but the difference between a safe departure and a disaster.

Traditionally, pilots on short-field attempts hold the brakes as the power is increased to the takeoff setting. Doing this does not shorten the ground run on takeoff. There is no "sling-shot" effect. Having full power when the brakes are released as opposed to a gradual increase of power while the plane is rolling will reduce ground run, but holding brakes themselves does not do anything. The reason we hold the brakes is to give us time to inspect the operation of the engine. The pilot makes sure that full power is being developed prior to committing to the takeoff. If the engine were not developing full power, you would rather not discover it upon lifting off the runway. At that point, it would be too late to turn back, and chances are good you would not clear the obstruction.

Verify that the engine is functioning properly by checking the oil temperature and pressure gauges, as well as the tachometer. Listen for smooth engine operation. Any hesitation in the engine, like a fouled spark plug or improperly timed magnetos, could lower the power output to a level that will not allow the airplane to pass over the obstruction. In addition to your ear, you can detect a rough engine with your feet. While holding the brakes, you can feel small changes in vibration through the rudder pedals. Only after you are sure the engine is giving you all it has to give should you release the brakes. Torque will be high at this moment, so be ready to apply right rudder if the airplane comes out of the brakes and veers away from the centerline.

Now mental toughness must come in. It is very hard to just sit there and watch the trees at the far end of the runway getting closer and closer as the ground run continues. The temptation will be great to pull back on the wheel early in an attempt to physically pull yourself over those trees; however, the pilot must wait until the airspeed is fast enough to sustain flight. If the elevator is deflected too early, greater drag and a longer takeoff run will result. Keep the elevator neutral until rotation speed. The pilot must know his airplane here; all the practice slow flight, minumum controllable airspeed, and stalls must pay off now. The pilot should have a good understanding of what pitch angle will provide a best angle-of-climb speed (V_x). As the airspeed increases, an indicated airspeed will be reached that is just below the best angle-of-climb speed. Upon reaching that speed, the pilot pulls back on the wheel and places the nose of the airplane precisely at the pitch angle of best angle.

During the rotation, the airplane will continue to accelerate. Airspeed stops increasing upon attaining the speed that gives the pilot the greatest gain in altitude over a short distance. And this climb rate easily clears the obstruction. After the danger of obstructions is past, the pilot can lower the nose slightly and accelerate to the best rate-of-climb speed (V_y). This sounds good but it is very hard to do in practice. Most pilots really have a hard time raising the nose to a point in space that will exactly yield the best angle. What we really do is chase the airspeed indicator. While on the takeoff roll, our attention is divided: outside, keep the plane straight and watch the upcoming trees; inside, watch the airspeed. For this reason, rotation can be started too late and as we pull back on the wheel, the airplane accelerates past the best angle speed. Now the pilot is in the air and remembers that the airplane book says the proper speed for this maneuver is five knots fewer than the current speed.

If there is a flight instructor—especially a pilot examiner—in the right seat, there will be mental pressure to produce the book speed on the indicator. (At this point, the pilot is not thinking about the trees, only how to impress someone else.) The pilot raises the nose in an attempt to lose the extra five knots, but rather than aim the nose to the proper pitch, the pilot is watching the airspeed indicator. But the airspeed indicator is not an instantaneous instrument; it has a time lag between what is indicated and what is real. By the time the instrument indicates a five-knot loss of airspeed, the actual loss is 10 knots. Now the pilot is in real trouble: full power, low to the ground, and too slow. The airplane is on the brink of a power-on, takeoff stall. If the airplane does stall in this situation, a successful recovery without hitting the ground or the trees is unlikely. The pilot might have spent hours practicing stalls but did not recognize that a short-field takeoff can be a dangerous stall threat. He approached the stall without even knowing he was doing it; therefore, if a stall does happen, it will catch him completely by surprise. A surprised pilot cannot react immediately and properly. To help develop the ability to control airspeed with pitch position, not airspeed indications, refer to chapter 6 on minimum controllable airspeed.

Most people believe that the reason for learning short-field takeoff technique is to fly out of a short field. Wrong. If an airplane actually were caught in a short field where a safe climbout was in doubt, would the FBO manager send a student pilot out to fly the airplane home? Of course not. Even though the student pilot might have diligently been practicing short-field takeoffs in preparation for a checkride, the student is not ready for the real situation. Short-field takeoff technique is taught to student pilots to help them learn to fly safely in critical situations. Nobody would advocate the practice of flying just above stall speed, nose high, power full, at 50 feet above the ground. That would be too dangerous. But that is exactly what we are doing on a short-field takeoff. If a student pilot can take an airplane into a potentially fatal situation, yet control the airplane safely, then the FAA calls that "meeting the standards." As a pilot gains experience there might be real short-field takeoffs that need to be made, but by then the lessons of airspeed and stall prevention should have been learned. The real reason that short-field technique is initially taught is to prevent a stall accident.

Soft field

Another common practice maneuver with stall potential is the soft field takeoff. Many years ago I was flying with my father and as we rolled out on final approach to a grass runway he asked, "How is it different landing on grass?" I nervously replied, "I don't know. I've never done it before." I do not think that made him very comfortable, but he sat there quietly as I made my first real soft field landing. Like many pilots, I had never made a takeoff or landing from a grass or sod runway during my flight training. If you have not done takeoff and landings on "other than hard surface," you should try it. First, check your insurance policy and perhaps call the company to see if you are covered on grass, or check your FBO's rental policies regarding grass runways. If you can go to a well-kept grass airport, you should practice real soft-field takeoffs and landings.

No matter how smooth and flat the grass might look, the ride on the landing and takeoff will be surprisingly bumpy compared to concrete. The plane will vibrate and rattle as you contact and roll on the grass. It will be easy to see why soft-field techniques were invented. Imagine a "worst-case" field where holes or large rocks are hidden in tall grass. To take off in these conditions, a pilot would want to be on the ground as little as possible. The longer the ground run, the greater the chances of damage to the airplane. Of course you would walk the field looking for anything that you might hit, but the takeoff roll must be as short as possible even after you have removed rocks and branches. Consult the airplane's handbook for the proper use of flaps for a soft-field takeoff. The use of flaps is a trade-off. Flaps will produce extra lift and extra drag. If the main concern is a minimum ground run, then accepting the extra lift will reduce the time on the ground. In the air, the extra drag produced by the flaps can cut down climb performance. It is all a matter of what result is desired. If flaps are recommended for soft-field takeoff, the flaps are intended to help get the airplane in the air sooner, above the rocks, mud, and holes.

The takeoff run begins using takeoff power and back pressure on the control wheel. In a very short length of runway, the airflow over the elevator will have enough force to lift the nosewheel off the ground. If the nosewheel is in the air, there will be one less thing that could strike debris on the ground and to cause friction. As the airplane accelerates, the effectiveness of the elevator is increased so the pilot must push the control wheel forward slightly so the nose does not get too high. If the nosewheel is pulled off the ground and the same amount of pitch is held during acceleration, the tail will hit the ground. The idea is to allow the nosewheel to pass just above the terrain. This nose-high attitude also increases the wing's angle of attack. Slowly, the weight of the plane is being transferred from wheels to wings. Eventually, a speed will be reached where the main wheels roll off the surface. What happens next can be dangerous and is a stall threat.

An airplane is still to slow to climb when the airplane first comes off the ground. The lift of the wings is being aided by *ground effect*. As the airflow comes off the upper chamber of the wings, a downwash is established. Underneath the wings, the air is also deflected downward. In flight, this downwash is not a factor, but when the downwash strikes the ground, the air molecules have nowhere to go so they move up and "pressurize" the underside of the wing. This provides a cushion of air that is utilized in a properly executed soft-field takeoff. If the airplane can ride the air to a climb speed rather than roll on the ground to a climb speed, the ground run will be greatly reduced. Reducing the ground run of a soft-field effort is the whole idea.

But here is the problem: If the pilot believes that just because the airplane is in the air that it can climb, he might be tempted to start climbing out of ground effect too early. At this moment, the airplane is fast enough to produce ground effect and take advantage of it, but still too slow to make a normal climb. Any increase in altitude at this speed will cause a *mush* and probably a descent back to the ground (FIG. 4-2). Up until now, no obstructions have been discussed, but most soft fields will have something to climb over at the end. It would be easy for a pilot flying in ground effect and seeing a fence ahead to pull back on the wheel. As the plane rises out of ground effect it will lose the lift produced by ground effect and this brings the pilot to the brink of disaster. A stall/spin accident is about to happen.

Fig. 4-2. *Climbing out of ground effect without sufficient airspeed.*

36

The pilot again must have some confidence in what lift can do, given the proper airspeed, and show some mental toughness. The pilot, after leaving the ground in ground effect, must lower the nose and allow the airplane to accelerate. The wheels will be just above the ground and free from friction, and possible damage. The fence at the end is getting closer but the pilot waits until flying speed is achieved before raising the nose. The airplane should then climb at the best angle speed to clear any obstructions ahead, or the best rate speed if no obstructions are present.

In practice, the most common error is allowing the airplane to accelerate to a climb speed before leaving the ground. If the pilot then lowers the nose (because that is what they have been told to do) it is not very practical. There would be no reason to deliberately delay the climbout after a climb speed is reached. The pilot needs to bring the airplane off earlier to take advantage of ground effect.

On an actual rough runway, the terrain might toss the airplane into the air too soon. As the airplane accelerates, it gets light on its wheels. If the plane hits a bump, the wheels will come off the ground. If the pilot is in the air prematurely, but mistakenly thinks he can climb, a mush back to the ground is inevitable, and the actual ground run will be longer. In the worst case, the pilot could nurse the airplane higher with inadequate and failing airspeed until a stall is induced. This pilot would probably not even practice a full-power, flaps-down stall even with the safety of altitude, but is allowing the plane to perform the same maneuver close to the ground. Mastering speed control that is required to properly execute a soft-field takeoff is the same as mastering speed control for stall prevention. Ultimately stall prevention is the real purpose of the maneuver.

Crosswind takeoff

Crosswind takeoffs have hidden stall potential. If a crosswind is present, the pilot must take the proper corrective action to assure that a proper ground track is maintained and proper airspeed achieved. The crosswind takeoff is much like a normal takeoff except that the ailerons must be used in a way that will prevent early liftoff. If the wind comes from the right of the airplane's nose during the takeoff roll, the pilot must rotate the control wheel to the right. This brings the right aileron up and spoils lift on the right side. Meanwhile, the left aileron is down, which increases lift (FIG. 4-3). The wind coming from the right cannot get under the right wing and "skip" the plane along on the left main wheel. If the wind did get under the right wing and lift the plane into the air prematurely, the pilot would be in a precarious position—the wings would be banked away from the wind, the airplane's direction of travel would be toward the edge of the runway instead of down the runway, and the speed would be too slow to sustain flight. So, the pilot must recover from a turning, full-power, near-stall while low to the ground.

The way to avoid the problem is to hold the upwind wing on the ground with aileron pressure. At the beginning of the takeoff roll, the airflow over the aileron will be minimal and therefore the deflection of ailerons should be full. As the ground roll

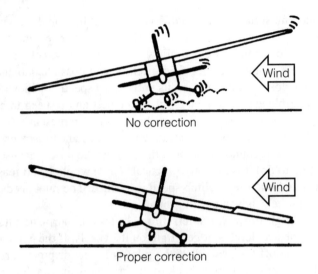

Fig. 4-3. *Crosswind correction.*

continues and the airflow increases, the ailerons become more and more useful. The pilot should reduce the amount of aileron deflection gradually until liftoff. In extreme conditions, at the speed of liftoff, the aileron deflection might not have reached neutral. This will cause the airplane to lift off one wheel at a time. First the nosewheel comes off the ground, then the downwind main wheel, then the upwind main wheel. This requires some finesse. The airplane will be in a bank as it comes off the ground. Too much aileron pressure could cause the upwind wingtip to touch the ground.

The liftoff speed should be faster than on a normal takeoff. Hold the airplane on the ground longer than usual. This will allow the airplane to "pop" off the ground and have enough flying speed to produce an immediate climb. If the airplane is stalled into the air at a speed that is too slow, the wind will toss the airplane downwind like a leaf. When the wheels do leave the ground, the friction of the wheels will go away and this allows the crosswind to carry the airplane sideways; you can prevent this with a *crab angle* established just after liftoff. With additional liftoff speed, the airplane can quickly gain altitude so that a further banking of the wings will not make the upwind wheel touch down. Once a crab angle is found that will prevent the airplane from drifting off the runway's extended centerline, level the wings and make a normal climbout. Care should be taken in gusty winds to maintain even more airspeed so that an inadvertent stall is not produced by changing airflow.

DENSITY ALTITUDE

If a takeoff is attempted with adverse density altitude conditions, a stall threat is very present. I teach flying in an area near sea level elevation. My students, while in training, will never take off from an airport that has an 8,000-foot density altitude.

Nevertheless, they must be prepared to deal safely with the situation. If the elevation is high, the temperature is high, and the humidity is high, the takeoff performance of the airplane will be low. To simulate a high density altitude takeoff, you should practice using partial takeoff power. Be very careful not to turn this into a real emergency; use the longest runway available; ideally, have an instructor on board.

Set the power on takeoff to simulate the reduced power the engine will have at high altitude. Try 2,000 to 2,200 rpms with a fixed-pitch propeller, or 20 inches of manifold pressure with a constant-speed propeller. The initial acceleration will be surprisingly slow as compared with your usual takeoff roll. As you use up runway and still have not reached flying speed, the tendency will be to raise the nose and coax the airplane into the air early. The end of the runway is coming up, so the pilot hauls back on the wheel in order to make it fly. But the airplane simply is not producing the lift required, so it stalls back to the runway. Under the worst density altitude conditions, no liftoff might be a possibility. The pilot cannot force the airplane to fly by applying elevator to the problem.

In real application, pilots face combination situations. A takeoff might need to be made on a hot and humid August afternoon from a wet grass runway at 4,500 feet MSL that is surrounded by 50-foot trees, with a 12-knot crosswind. If a safe takeoff is to be made with several adverse conditions present, the pilot will need good judgment and a good understanding of the airplane's limitations. Remember that takeoffs are always optional.

REAL LANDINGS

The FAA's 50-foot tree has been cut down. The new practical test standards no longer mention a 50-foot obstruction, but the performance of a short-field landing has not changed. The short-field landing technique is required for private and commercial pilot certification, but that does not prevent widespread misconceptions about the maneuver. The reason a short-field technique is taught is not to lure pilots into 1,500-foot landing strips. The real application is airspeed control.

Sometimes things can get out of hand. I was evaluating a student pilot (a would-be private pilot) on the downwind leg of the traffic pattern when I asked him to demonstrate a short-field landing. I also asked him to make a complete stop on the runway after landing and to do all this within the first 1,000 feet of the runway. First, I noticed that abeam the runway numbers he went through a normal prelanding check that included the reduction of power and dropping 10° of flaps. We started to descend and had lost at least 300 feet from the traffic pattern altitude when we turned on the base leg. He dropped the flaps to 20° in the turn and by the time we reached the base-to-final turn, we were only 300 feet above the ground. His approach speed was slow, just about what the book says to fly, approximately 1.3 times the stall speed in a landing configuration. The wind was not strong, fewer than 10 knots, but it was straight down the runway, which reduced our ground speed on final. This increased our rate of sink. The student added the full amount of flaps: 40°.

He then noticed that we were low and sinking fast, so he raised the nose slightly to keep us from reaching the ground too soon. This dropped our airspeed another few knots. Seeing that the airplane was still descending, now headed for the approach lights, he added power. Then more power. We cleared the threshold lights with the airspeed reading slower than the white arc, nearly full power, and nose high. With the runway made, now the student chopped the power and the nose dropped. Soon we were inches above the ground, he pulled on the control wheel once more but there was no float left in the airplane. We crunched down on the runway. The student applied heavy brakes even though we were so slow we really did not need any. We came to a complete stop. I was scared. I was also mad that I let that approach get that bad without doing something myself. I looked over at the student and he was grinning a big smile: "That was almost as good as the one I did the other day. I got it down in less than half the distance you gave me."

The student thought that the goal of the maneuver was to plant the airplane on the runway and stop it short at all costs. He had completely missed the purpose of the maneuver and almost killed us in the process. A short-field landing requires good judgment, knowledge of the airplane and wind conditions, and great airspeed control. According to the FAA practical test standards, short-field landings should be made with full flaps, but the key is to place the airplane in a position where full flaps are actually needed. To begin with, delay the descent on the approach and remain deliberately high. Bring the flaps in one setting at a time and control airspeed. Using judgment and familiarity with the airplane's glide characteristics, get to a position on final approach where you can lower the remaining flaps, ease the power back, control speed with pitch, and touchdown with minimum float. If you approach the runway without anticipating the need for full flaps, you will be too low to use them.

Many times, while attempting a short-field landing, pilots have noticed that they were too low, or located approximately where they would be on a normal approach. Then a conflict hits them. They know they really do not need any more flaps, but the standards say that they must use full flaps in order to complete the maneuver. So, they overrule good judgment, they put the flaps down to full, and then are forced to add power in order to make the runway. This is like stepping on the gas and the brake at the same time, which makes no sense. The short-field landing maneuver's success or failure is not measured by how far it takes you to stop, it is measured by the airmanship displayed during the approach.

The student I was riding with had done a minimum controllable airspeed demonstration for me. But I would have rather he not do it 20 feet above the approach lights. The entire final approach we flew was on the edge of a potentially fatal, low altitude, power-on stall. Ironically, the same student was very reluctant to do a power-on stall when we were at 4,000 feet. He freely admitted that he just did not like stalls, but he was perfectly happy with doing what amounted to a stall entry on final approach. He firmly believed that stalls only happened at high altitude and that he was in no danger of stall down low.

SLOW MEANS STALL

Anytime you get an airplane as slow as it can go in flight, a stall accident is possible. When properly making a soft-field landing, the airplane will touch down at its slowest possible flying speed. The airplane needs to touch down slowly to avoid damage from objects on the ground or just the fact that the field is not as smooth as it looks from above. The FAA's practical test standards do not dictate what flap setting should be used at touchdown, so use what is well matched with approach speed and angle. Flaps will add drag to help slow the airplane down and add lift, which will keep the plane in the air longer. The approach to this landing can be a normal angle unless real obstructions are in the way; however, the approach speed should be somewhat slower than normal. Consult the manufacturer's recommendations. During the flare to land, the idea is to prevent touchdown until the slowest possible flying speed is reached. As the pilot pulls the control wheel back to begin the flare, the airspeed will slow and the airplane will sink. Now add more back pressure and the speed will slow even more and the plane will sink even more. Hold the airplane off.

The wheels should start rolling on the runway while the wings still support the airplane's weight. Then gradually, the weight is transferred to the main wheels. Holding continued back pressure will keep the nosewheel in the air and out of mud or holes. Some airplanes can use a little power in the flare to help roll the wheels on the runway, but if too much power is used, the airplane will climb in the flare and will be too high when the speed bleeds completely off to make a soft touchdown. Applying power after the main wheels are rolling on the ground will keep airflow on the elevator and help keep the nosewheel in the air longer. Do not apply brakes. The brakes will slam the nosewheel to the ground and ruin the soft-field effect. It is possible to mistime the flare so that the lowest possible speed is reached while the airplane is still several feet in the air. Getting slower and slower without anything for the airplane to land on will produce yet another stall-and-fall threat.

The airspeed indicator is not a speedometer. It relies on the airflow for its information, so how good is it when the airflow is made up of a thin atmosphere? When attempting to land at airports with high density altitude conditions, the airspeed indicator can be misleading. The indicated airspeed on the instrument should still be used, but the actual speed of the airplane through the air will be faster than indicated because the same quantity of air molecules is necessary to produce a reaction on the airspeed indicator's diaphragm at high and low density altitudes. When the air is thin, the number of molecules available to move the diaphragm is reduced, so the airplane must go faster, therefore piling up more molecules to indicate the same speed.

If an airplane's approach speed is 75 knots indicated at sea level, the approach speed will also be 75 knots indicated at 5,000 feet. The difference is that at 5,000 feet, the indicated speed of 75 knots might be 85 knots true airspeed. This means that after landing, the brakes will have to dissipate greater speed, probably taking more runway than 75 indicated knots at sea level. Also, the stall will occur at the same indicated speeds as at sea level but the true airspeed will be greater.

5
Clearing turns

IT SEEMS THAT MOST PILOTS MAKE CLEARING TURNS JUST FOR SHOW. IT IS very typical for a flight instructor to advise a student on his way to a checkride to remember to make clearing turns. But, of course, people are creatures of habit, so the student forgets to do clearing turns on the checkride because he never did them in the first place. Many students who are about to perform a maneuver have asked me, "Do you want me to do clearing turns?" I always respond by saying, "What do you want to do?" Then they always do them because they do not want to look unsafe. Just the fact that they asked tells me that they feel clearing turns are a nuisance that instructors invented to increase the Hobbs time on the airplane. Also, students feel that some maneuvers require clearing turns while other maneuvers do not. Most people believe that a clearing turn might be a good idea before doing a stall, but never think about it before a steep turn. Then, if they do a clearing turn, they do not actually look for traffic. They make the turns with a stiff neck, get them over with, pacify the examiner, and then get on with the flying. They never really believe that clearing turns are a part of a safe maneuver.

I have observed students do clearing turns in many ways. It can be anything from a quick raising of a wing to a complete 360° turn. The fact is that there is no single way to clear the area. You should be practical. We should do clearing turns so that we avoid midair collisions. Typically, a clearing turn is a single 180° turn or two 90° turns in opposite directions (FIG. 5-1). This allows you to look in places that are blind spots created by the airplane. Above the wings for high-wing airplanes and below the wings for low-wing airplanes are the biggest blind spots. In order to see around the wings, you must move the wings by turning (FIG. 5-2).

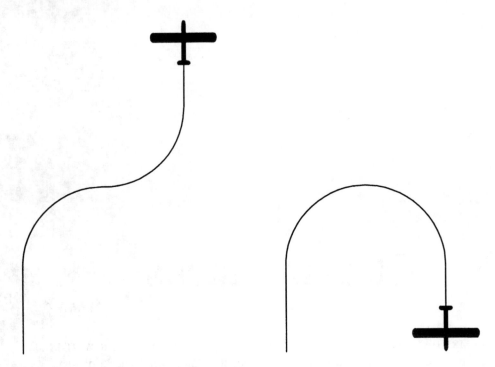

Fig. 5-1. *A clearing turn may be two 90° turns or one 180° turn.*

While in the turn, look for traffic in areas that would present the greatest danger. If you transition from a cruise to a minimum controllable airspeed, you are essentially slamming on the brakes. In a small single-engine trainer, this transition could take you from 90 knots to 45 knots in a short amount of time. Imagine you are driving your car on a highway behind another car. You and the driver ahead are traveling at approximately the same speed. Then, without warning, the driver ahead hits the brakes and cuts his speed in half. In order to avoid a collision, you will have to recognize that the car is slowing down, and slow down yourself. The lead car's brake lights help to recognize the change in speed, but airplanes have no brake lights. If one airplane is in trail behind another, and the lead airplane slows down rapidly, the trailing pilot might not recognize the change in time. By executing a clearing turn, you can look behind, but very few pilots do a thorough job of "checking their six."

OFFSETTING UNPREDICTABILITY

I believe our experience driving cars does effect how we think about collision avoidance. While driving down a highway, we expect the other drivers to stay in their lanes. And as long as we stay in our lane, then there will not be a crash. But no lanes are in the air. Another airplane can come at you from any and every direction and even in three dimensions. Car drivers do not worry about other vehicles hitting them from

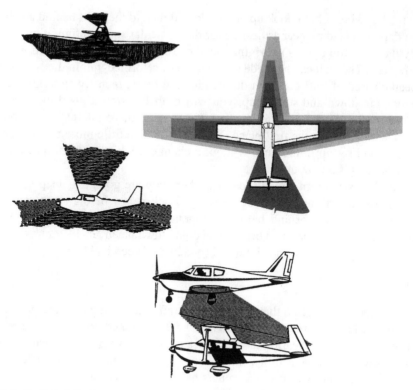

Fig. 5-2. *Built-in blind spots.*

above or below, but airplane drivers do. Even though every pilot knows there are no protected lanes in the sky, we still fly like we drive. We look and fly straight ahead, and we think that is enough to be safe. But we are wrong.

Clearing turns are not married to certain maneuvers; the turns should be used in various forms for every maneuver. During long climbs, the pitch of the nose and the heading of the airplane should be altered slightly to avoid constructing a "pilot-induced" blind spot. If you hold the same pitch and heading through a climb, you cannot see directly in front of the airplane. Make small adjustments that will allow you to see in the blind spot. This is a clearing turn. Even small heading changes deserve a look in the direction of the turn. Raise the wing and look to see if the space you plan to occupy is already vacant. In a small airplane, everybody on board can look for traffic. Do not have passengers act as if they have settled into coach-class on an airliner; no reading the newspaper; get everybody involved looking out the windows.

During flight training, a clearing turn can take up time and break up the flow of the lesson, but be practical. When setting up to do a stall, slow down while in the clearing turn. Start a gradual turn to the left. While the right wing is high, look above and behind, then on the left, look behind and below. Start to slow the airplane down with proper pitch and power changes. Now make a right turn back to the original heading.

While the left wing is high, look up and back, and then to the right behind and below. Set the flaps and landing gear as desired for the particular stall configuration.

By the time you reach the original heading, the airplane is in a position to perform the stall. The stall can be made and recovery performed within the area that has just been cleared of traffic. If you do the clearing turns, then fly straight and level while slowing down and setting up, you will probably stall a good distance from where the area was confirmed to be clear. If you do that, you defeat the purpose of doing a clearing turn in the first place. Yes, it will take a little more piloting skill to slow down and set up in the turn, without a change in altitude, but improved pilot skill is what this is all about.

Never do a steep turn without looking where you are going. A steep turn is like cutting across several lanes without signaling. Look below before steep spirals and spins. Look above and behind before Chandelles and Lazy Eights. Look for crop dusters, towers, power lines, and birds when doing low maneuvers like: turns around a point, S turns, pylon eights, and simulated (or actual) forced landings.

SAFE PILOTING

Pilots should understand that watching for traffic and doing clearing turns is just safe piloting. Clearing turns are not a ritual that are performed prior to a specific set of maneuvers. Do not do a clearing turn just because an examiner, or instructor tells you to do it. Show some responsibility, some authority of pilot-in-command. Clear traffic so you will not be hit by traffic. Examiners have an old trick to determine whether a flight test applicant really looks for traffic or just does clearing turns by rote.

They will set you up by saying, "Hold a heading of 270° and show me minimum controllable airspeed." The dutiful applicant, not wanting to do anything that would upset the examiner, follows the directions to the letter. He holds the heading, reduces the power, drops the flaps, and essentially slams on the brakes without looking if anybody was tailgating. The examiner now has you where you do not want to be. As tough as it might sound, the applicant should have overridden the examiner by saying, "OK, I'll give you MCA on a heading of 270 after I check for traffic." Do the turns, slow down during the turns, then keep the maneuver quick and to the point. This will show good judgment and good decision making, and you will impress the examiner. You will also reduce the chance of getting run over.

6
Airspeed transitions and minimum controllable airspeed

ONE OF THE MOST FUNDAMENTAL CONCEPTS TO BE CONQUERED WHEN learning to fly is to understand "what controls what" in the airplane. Flight instructors often use straight and level airspeed transitions and minimum controllable airspeed maneuvers to teach the control of airspeed. Unfortunately, very few students make a solid connection between flying around at slow airspeeds and controlling the airplane on approach to landings, but that is the true value of the maneuver.

First, we must understand "what actually does control what" with regard to airspeed. To make matters worse, the control of airspeed depends on how much airspeed you have. A range of speeds will produce a "power-is-speed" situation. At this speed, the more power you apply, the faster the airplane will travel. Also at these speeds "elevator (pitch)-is-altitude." In other words, if you pull back on the wheel, objects on the ground will get smaller, and if you push forward on the wheel, objects will get larger. These arrangements of power/speed and elevator/altitude go well with our everyday understanding of how an airplane should be controlled.

When we drive a car and want to go faster, we step on the gas pedal—power is speed. This is an easy transfer for the mind to handle. Also, it makes sense that when we point the nose at the sky, by pulling back on the wheel, the airplane goes toward the sky. Our cars usually do go where we point them. All this makes perfectly good sense and we are comfortable with it. Because these relationships do make sense they are called "normal command." So, normal command of an airplane means that speed can be changed by adding or reducing power to the engine; we go up when we aim the airplane up and we go down when we point the airplane down. Simple, no problem.

REVERSE COMMAND RANGE

Unfortunately, these relationships for speed and altitude do not always stay the same. A range of speeds where the relationships turn around is called "reverse command." In this range, adding power does not necessarily increase airspeed. In fact, the airplane can be in a position where even full power cannot increase the speed of the airplane, and the speed can even be decreasing. In this reverse command speed range, the relationships become: "elevator-is-speed" and "power-is-altitude." The dividing line, where normal command stops and reverse command takes over exists at an airplane's maximum endurance speed. Maximum endurance deals with time. Perhaps you are wondering which level-flight speed requires the least amount of power? The least amount of power, and therefore the least amount of fuel, would mean the airplane could stay aloft the longest amount of time.

Figure 6-1 illustrates the power required to maintain level flight and the speed ranges that determine "what will control what." The speeds that are to the slow side of the maximum endurance speed are the very speeds that every pilot must master in order

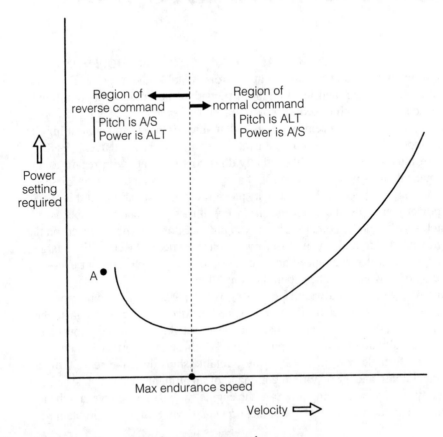

Fig. 6-1. *Regions of normal and reverse command.*

to avoid stalls and make good landings. In small airplanes, used primarily for flight training, practically entire flight lessons are performed without ever getting fast enough to reach normal command. Teaching level-flight airspeed transitions and minimum controllable airspeed maneuvers will teach how the airplane responds in the reverse command speed range. If the student makes the proper transition from practice maneuver to actual flying, they will act properly when it really counts in the reverse command region.

Think about your last approach to a landing into a brisk headwind. The wind slows down the approach and gives you the impression that you are "swimming upstream." You notice that at the current rate of descent that you will never reach the runway. What did you do to solve the problem? You must know "what controls what" with regard to airspeed and altitude and be ready to apply the correct rules when taking action. If you employed the normal command reaction, you would pull back on the wheel because normal reaction would increase your altitude by pointing the nose up. You would also maintain or even reduce power so that the airspeed would not get too fast for the landing attempt. But would this set of control inputs actually solve the problem? No, because normal inputs don't solve problems when reverse inputs are required. To solve this problem the pilot should add power, not to increase airspeed but to reduce the rate of altitude loss. This lengthens the time the airplane will remain in the air and this allows the airplane to glide a farther distance to the runway.

At the same time, the pilot might have to lower the nose so the airplane does not get too slow on the approach. The solution required the pilot to understand that at approach speed, power is altitude and elevator is airspeed. The minimum controllable airspeed (MCA) maneuver proves this fact and allows the student to practice in the reverse command region with the safety of altitude. During the properly executed MCA maneuver, the airplane teeters on an unsteady fence. At the slowest possible airspeed, only the addition of power can stop a descent. If the pilot gets mixed up and attempts to raise the nose in an attempt to gain altitude, a stall will immediately result. If this happens down low on a landing approach, the result might also be fatal.

Many pilots have painted themselves into a corner "behind the power curve." (Figure 6-1 position A) Most airplanes (and every small propeller driven airplane) have a speed that is so slow that the engine cannot save them with power. A pilot on final approach seeing that he is too low could attempt to stay away from the ground by pulling the nose up away from the ground. But this time the airplane does not go where it is pointed, it keeps going down even though the nose is up. The airspeed will get slower and slower. The pilot now adds power to stop the loss of airspeed, but the speed gets still slower. The additional power slows the rate of altitude loss but the plane is still sinking. The airplane will either stall as the pilot continues to slow down by continued elevator back-pressure or will collide with the ground with full power but no control over the rate of descent. A rocket engine might have been powerful enough to lift the airplane out of this situation, but small single-engine training aircraft are not equipped with rocket engines.

Understanding and reacting properly at speed within the reverse range is not natural and requires practice. Without this vital understanding, so many areas of flight can become hazardous. An airplane in flight cannot hover like a helicopter or hang like a hot air balloon, it must always maintain a safe airspeed.

AIRSPEED TRANSITION TRAINING

To start overcoming the built-in misunderstanding about the reverse command speed range, try an exercise that will prove the relationships of airspeed and altitude. Perhaps an instructor should go along with you. Clear the area and watch for traffic; when clear, hold a constant heading and let the airplane find a cruise airspeed. Then, while holding a constant heading and altitude, slow the airplane down by 20 knots. First, reduce power. The power reduction will not directly slow the airplane down, but the reduction will prevent the airplane from climbing when elevator is applied. Second, gradually move the control wheel back. This will raise the nose and slow the airspeed. If the airplane climbs, reduce more power. If the airplane sinks, reapply some power.

Eventually, the proper amount of pitch and power will be found that will hold the reduced airspeed steady while maintaining altitude. Now, change the speed; stay above stall, but reduce airspeed by 10 more knots or increase by 10 knots. By transitioning from one airspeed to another, the pilot is required to fine-tune the pitch/power relationship. Each speed will require a different combination of power amounts and pitch amounts. Try maintaining speed, heading, and altitude during configuration changes. Hold a predetermined speed and lower the flaps or extend the landing gear.

AIRSPEED INDICATIONS

The airspeed indicator during these transitions will lie to you at first. Because the instrument's indication lags, you really cannot trust it to give you pitch information during the transition. For instance, if you wanted to fly 70 knots and your current speed was 85 you would know that the way to slow down would be to raise the nose. As the nose came up, the airspeed indicator would not do anything at first. If you continued to raise the nose until the indicator came to life and reached 70 before you stopped pulling back, you would have exceeded the proper nose pitch. Even after you have stopped pulling back, the airspeed indicator will continue to show a speed reduction. Because you are now too slow, you push forward on the wheel to get the speed back, but by the time the indicator says 70, you have again overshot the pitch and are going too fast.

The solution to this problem is to ignore the airspeed indicator during its lag time. Start by raising the nose to the position that you estimate will give a speed of 70 knots and hold the pitch constant. Now, watch the airspeed indicator stumble across the speed markings until it stops and remains stationary. It might not stop at 70 knots. It might stop short at 75 knots, which will require the pilot to fine-tune the pitch with just a little back pressure to achieve 70. This method allows you to feel how pitch changes speed, rather than the "hit-and-miss" method. After you get well acquainted with the airplane, positioning the pitch will be your primary means of airspeed control, and the airspeed indicator will be used for verification.

There are countless applications in real-world flying where speed changes must be made smoothly and without sacrificing altitude or heading. Many pilots have trouble changing speeds, or do so at the expense of other duties. This prevents a pilot from staying ahead of the airplane and leads to more problems. An instrument pilot must slow to approach speed from cruise speed; the speed transition must take place simultaneously with radio communications, chart reading, approach planning, and basic attitude instrument flying. If the speed change diverts the pilot's attention from these other vital duties, the approach proficiency will suffer. Instrument approach tasks have a tendency to snowball. A minor distraction gets the pilot behind in approach preparation, but the pilot can never catch up due to the fact that the demands of the approach never stop coming.

If a pilot has trouble slowing the plane down while maintaining altitude on the outbound portion of the procedure turn, he will not be able to tune in the CTAF frequency. When it is time to change radio frequencies, the proper frequency will not be readily available and the pilot must take time to work the radio dials. While this is going on, the final approach fix is passed, but the pilot forgets to note the time over the fix because his attention is on the radio. Now, without the inbound time, the approach is all but blown, because now the missed approach point cannot be determined. The pilot got behind and was snowed under.

The same thing happens to student pilots in the traffic pattern. The transition from cruise to approach speed usually starts on the downwind leg. If the student has trouble finding the proper pitch, power, and flaps that will provide a good downwind speed, he might drift away from the pattern in a crosswind. The inside speed distraction could prevent the pilot from looking outside for other airplanes entering the pattern. But if the pilot changes speeds efficiently, the mind can move ahead to other important decisions that keep the pilot ahead of the airplane.

MCA IN-DEPTH

Performing the minimum controllable airspeed maneuver might be different from one airplane to the next but the basics will be the same. Clear the area of traffic and start a speed transition from cruise to slow flight. The name of the maneuver implies the slowest possible flying speed, so gradually lower the flaps one notch at a time to the full flap position when inside the white arc. Lower the landing gear on retractables. Slow the airplane down with a combination of reducing power and increasing pitch. Many students gain or lose altitude as they approach the maneuver. This is because they do not control the pitch/power relationship well. Do not hurry into the maneuver, make the speed reduction gradual so that if the airplane starts to climb or descend, you can recognize it early and make the proper power adjustment. You should not gain or lose more than 50 feet at anytime from cruise speed to MCA and back to cruise.

As the speed continues to drop, the power will have to be increased to maintain altitude. This exactly mirrors the rising power curve when slower than maximum endurance speed. This tells the pilot that he is on the "back side." You might need to add carburetor heat in the beginning of the maneuver when the throttle is reduced, but as the power comes back up, to maintain altitude, move the carburetor heat back to cold. The carburetor heat usually affects the engine by approximately 100 rpm. The extra 100 rpm can make the difference between a descent and level flight when you finally arrive at MCA.

The minimum control speed should be just on the brink of stall. The airspeed indicator should be steady at a position that is slower than the stall speed with flaps up. This means the needle points to a speed that is slower than the slow end of the green arc (V_{S1}). The needle would, at the same time, be just faster than the slow end of the white arc (V_{SO}) (FIG. 6-2). If level flight is maintained at this speed, it is only because the flaps are down. The flaps produce the extra lift that is required to fly at this speed and any retraction of the flaps now would result in an immediate stall. The pilot must make very small pitch adjustments here. If the wheel is pulled back any farther, then a slower speed will result. At MCA, you are already at the slowest possible speed, so any speed reduction will produce a stalled condition. The wheel cannot come back without stall, and the wheel cannot go forward or the airplane will speed up and will not be flying at MCA any longer.

Fig. 6-2. *Minimum controllable airspeed indication.*

The airplane is on the fence. If the airplane begins to lose altitude now, the pilot has only one choice: power. Pulling back on the wheel will not cause the airplane to climb, the airplane would lose altitude as it stalled. Only power can hold the altitude. The ability of an airplane to hold altitude or climb is based upon how much "excess" power is available from the engine. Figure 6-3 shows the relationship between the power that would be required to maintain level flight at a particular airspeed and the power that is actually available from the engine. The greatest rate-of-climb is found where there is the greatest gap between what is needed to climb and what can be provided by the engine. On the slow end of the chart, where MCA takes place, the gap narrows.

The power available from the engine, of course, varies widely based on altitude, and temperature. On hot days at high altitude the power available curve will move

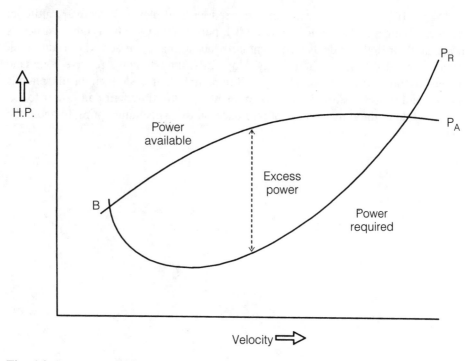

Fig. 6-3. *Power available versus power required.*

down the chart making the gap even more narrow. While flying at MCA in small trainer airplanes, the pilot can easily reach a point where the power that the engine can provide equals the power that is needed to fly straight and level at MCA. If the day is hot, and the plane full of fuel, even full power might not hold level flight at MCA. When this happens, a "deficit" of power (position B) is realized, or in other words, this slow speed just requires more power than the engine can give.

PITCH/POWER PROOF

When flying MCA, the pilot can feel the near-stall performance of the airplane. It feels sluggish and slow. Movement of the flight controls does not produce a quick response. The airplane is lazy. But the biggest advantage of flying this slow speed is to prove the pitch/power relationship. Here at MCA, a change in pitch will change the airspeed to either too slow, which causes a stall, or too fast, which takes you away from MCA. While at this speed, pitch has no ability to cause the airplane to climb, only power can do that job.

The desired end result is greater safety when flying at slow speeds close to the ground. Airspeed transitions and MCA practice are the same as approach to landing practice.

Do not fly minimum controllable airspeed without plenty of recovery altitude; however, flying slowly at a low altitude is a part of every flight. Flight instructors know that their flight students will eventually face a final approach where additional altitude is needed to make the runway. Hopefully, that student's reverse command airspeed training will kick in and they will remember that at slow airspeeds, pitch is airspeed and power is altitude. In that moment of truth, they will add power to extend the glide to the runway and not pull back on the wheel attempting to avoid the ground below.

7
Takeoff stalls

M Y FIRST FLIGHT LESSON WAS AN "INTRODUCTORY" FLIGHT THAT A school offered to get potential students hooked on flying. It worked. I have been flying ever since. That lesson cost $5 in 1973. I remember that I did more actual flying than I thought that I would and the flight was not just a ride, but a real lesson. The one thing that stood out in my mind the most was the fact that the instructor let me take off. I am sure that he really did most of the work with rudders, and trim, but I believed I had taken off on my first try. I also remember that before landing, the instructor took over. He did not let me attempt to land on my first try. This made me believe that landing must be tougher than takeoff, and it probably is, but people still get into takeoff trouble.

The National Transportation Safety Board completed a study of general aviation takeoff accidents and concluded that 19 percent of all accidents occur during the takeoff phase of flight. What is more important is the high percentage of these accidents that are fatal. Ten of every 100 takeoff accidents will kill at least one airplane occupant. The landing phase of flight has a higher total accident rate, but only 4.4 out of every 100 landing accidents involves a fatality.

Once again the "pilot error" is listed as the overwhelming cause of takeoff accidents. In 87 percent of all takeoff accidents and 90 percent of all fatal takeoff accidents, the blame is placed on the pilot. Many situations in flight can overwhelm a pilot's workload. When a pilot is overworked or is "behind the airplane" a flawed decision can easily occur, but this should not be the case on takeoff. Remember that takeoffs are always optional. You can never be forced into the air. A pilot should have the luxury of time to plan a takeoff and consider all its factors.

Fig. 7-1

THINK IT THROUGH

Unfortunately, of the "pilot error" takeoff accidents in the study, 30 percent were caused by the pilot's improper preflight preparation or improper takeoff planning. A pilot should be aware of any factor that might affect a takeoff: crosswinds, rough terrain during the ground run, obstructions to climb over, weight of the airplane, and density altitude. Before pushing the throttle up, make the takeoff in your mind. On multiengine takeoffs, the need for planning is even more critical. Do not wait until you are accelerating down the runway to go over all your options.

Do not let anyone or anything rush you into the air without proper preparation. How many times have you been halfway through your pretakeoff checklist when you heard an impatient pilot behind you racing the engines? Corporate airplanes and airliners behind schedule will often pressure you to get out of the way. You probably have looked out the rear of your small airplane only to see a window full of Boeing 737 nose gear. Even the air traffic controllers might attempt to rush you occasionally. The controller will say, "How much more run-up time will you need Cessna 1234N?" ATC is really saying "get out of the way." Be as considerate as possible, but do not replace safety for expedience. If the taxiway has an expanded area provided for run-ups, that does not block the main taxiway, use it, but never allow yourself to be pressured into the air before you are ready.

MAINTAIN FLYING SPEED

Of the pilot-error takeoff accidents, another 29 percent were blamed on the pilot's failure to obtain or maintain safe flying speed. This takes us back to stall awareness. A pilot who allows the airplane to get too slow and stall low to the ground, as would be the case on a takeoff, has very little opportunity to recover without hitting the ground. And the study has shown that striking the ground after a low altitude stall has a very poor survival rate. So, stall prevention on takeoff is the same as fatal accident prevention.

Stalls that simulate a takeoff condition should be practiced with plenty of altitude for recovery. Using high altitude, of course, does not present the real picture that would be seen if indeed a stall were encountered low to the ground after takeoff, but it just is not safe to make this demonstration too real. Because it is too dangerous to practice down low, this places a great responsibility on the pilot to recognize and prevent a stall from fully developing when on an actual takeoff. Before practicing takeoff stalls, imagine the urgency that would be present if this were taking place 50 feet above the ground. These stalls are often called power-on or departure stalls. No matter what you call them, you should put the airplane in a condition that is most like takeoff and climb-out.

Configuration of the airplane during takeoff stall practice depends upon the airplane. Power-on stalls should be practiced with the airplane looking just as it does at liftoff. This might mean that flaps are partially lowered and the landing gear is down. On small trainers, the gear is always down and usually no flaps are needed for takeoff. If the gear is retractable, then power-on stalls should also be practiced with gear up to simulate a stall after or during gear transition.

When you are in level cruising flight, the plane will be traveling faster than it was at lift-off, so, to practice a takeoff stall, you must first slow down to takeoff speed, perhaps during clearing turns. If you add full power and start raising the nose with a cruise airspeed, the airplane will have a greatly exaggerated nose pitch when the stall finally occurs. The higher the nose angle going into the stall, the greater the pitch down angle will be when the stall happens. Also, it will take longer for the stall to take place simply because the airplane has more speed to lose. This prolongs the approach to stall and can lead to other problems like uncoordinated flight.

PRACTICE AND REALITY

Understand that development of a practice takeoff stall is different than the development of an actual takeoff stall; in practice, the plane is already flying and speed must be decreased to reach liftoff speed; in reality, the plane would have just accelerated along the runway and just begun to fly with increasing speed. Because of this difference, it is easy for a pilot to be surprised by the real thing. We practice to make things more familiar and therefore more manageable, but real situations where stalls might occur are too dangerous for practice. The result is a stall accident can happen to someone who does practice stalls. Be practical. Do what is safe in practice, but understand reality.

Slow the airplane down, first by reducing power, then raising the nose gradually and maintaining altitude. When the liftoff speed is reached, set the power for takeoff; in small airplanes, this means push the throttle as far as it will go; on other airplanes, you might need extra attention to the manifold pressure gauge so that the proper setting is achieved if it is less than full power. Once power is applied, start raising the nose and let the airplane climb-out. Then increase the pitch of the nose to an excessive attitude beyond the normal pitch angle for climb. Some airplanes require that the increase in power and pitch be simultaneous.

As the nose is raised with the power high, torque and P-factor will affect the airplane. To maintain the desired heading, and to keep the ball in the center (coordinated flight), ever-increasing amounts of right rudder should be applied. Also, as the speed diminishes from liftoff to stall speed, the airflow over the elevator will be reduced. This will cause the elevator to be less effective. Increasing amounts of elevator back pressure on the control wheel will be required to maintain the pitch angle as the airplane gets slower. The control wheel might be all the way back before the stall occurs.

SENSORY INVOLVEMENT

Stalls are practiced so the pilot becomes familiar with the symptoms of a stall. Hopefully, if the pilot ever again hears, sees, or feels these symptoms, a recovery will be made immediately and the airplane will never actually stall. Stall recognition is our highest priority. Get your senses involved in stall detection.

First, as the speed diminishes, the sound of the wind around the airplane will change. The airflow will be slower and the angles that the air strikes the airplane will be changing. The engine will sound differently, as well. As the climb continues, the engine will labor and slow down. Listen for these changes because these are the first clues. Next, the control wheel will have less and less effect on the airplane. At a fast speed, air flows over the aileron, elevator, and rudder with great force and any deflection causes an immediate response to the pilot's request. But near stall speed, the airflow is slow and the responsiveness is reduced. If, at cruise airspeed, a pilot rotated the control wheel one inch to the left, the airplane would start a turn to the left as the deflection occurred. But, at near-stall speed, the same one-inch deflection might not cause the airplane to move at all. The same loss of response takes place with the rudder and elevators. The pilot must recognize the difference in how the controls feel and respond at all speeds. As the air over the wings changes from a smooth to a turbulent flow, the airplane will begin to buffet or shake. The power-on stall buffet is usually more predominant than a power-off stall buffet. The buffet can be felt in the controls, but also in the seat of the pants.

Finally, you can watch for the stall. With practice, a pilot can recognize the pitch angle that will produce a stall. With understanding of the straight-ahead pitch angle that will cause a stall, the pilot can simply never allow that pitch angle to be achieved during liftoff and climbout. If the angle is ever reached, the pilot can know that a stall is just about to happen and take recovery action. Of course, all this recognition by sound, feel, and sight takes place all at once. The brain must handle all these incoming signals, interpret the signals, and act based upon the interpretation; the action required is recovery.

EXECUTING A PROPER RECOVERY

As the full stall takes place, the nose will pitch down, even though the pilot is holding the control wheel all the way back. The airplane might start a roll either left or right. If the rudder is used properly to keep the airplane in coordinated flight during the entry to the stall, there will be less roll tendency. Remember, if this were a real situation, the ground would be directly beneath the wheels. When the nose pitched down, we would see a windshield full of twisting earth, not sky. Our reaction must be immediate and correct.

First, get the airplane flying again. A stall is the loss of lift. Lift is the only force that will prevent the airplane from striking the ground, so, whatever it takes to replace the lifting force must take place now. The actual aerodynamics are explained in Part III, but for now, realize that the nose must be placed at an angle less than the critical angle. When the nose pitches down in the stall, the job of lowering the nose to below the critical angle is done for you. The pilot should place the nose either on the horizon or just below the horizon and achieve flying speed. Lose as little altitude as possible because by now the treetops would be at eye level. The engine power was set during the entry to the power-on stall; if the power setting is at maximum, no additional power is available; if the power setting to enter the stall is less than maximum, advance the throttle and use maximum power to get out. A constant-speed prop should be set to the high rpm position during the stall entry so that maximum power can be applied without damaging the prop or powerplant.

If the airplane begins to roll, level the wings using the rudder. In a full-wing stall, the ailerons will be inside the turbulent stalled airflow, which means that the ailerons will not help stop the roll; however, the rudder is more effective because it is not inside the stalled wing airflow. At this moment in the life of a stall, the rudder will do you more good than the ailerons; if the left wing dips during the stall recovery, apply right rudder. Soon thereafter, as the speed increases and the stall is broken, the ailerons will become effective once again and can be used to level the wings. But be careful, the use of ailerons can actually aggravate the stalls; if the left wing dips in the recovery and the pilot turns the control wheel to the right to compensate, the left wing could increase its stalled condition. When the pilot turns the wheel right, the aileron on the left side moves down. This changes the chord line of that part of the wing, which changes angle of attack to a higher value. This value might further exceed the critical angle and bring on more stall. A touch of pilot finesse is required to know when the aileron should be used, all based upon angle of attack and the speed yielded. Once the wings are level and the speed is increasing, start climbing.

Follow through

Many pilots end the maneuver by just flying straight and level during acceleration. That works fine at altitude, but in reality, trees and power lines would be passing the windows. The maneuver is not complete until you have avoided obstructions, so climb at best angle for at least 100 feet and then accelerate to best rate.

Before every stall, select a simulated ground altitude. When practicing a stall at 5,000 feet MSL (assume at least 1,500 feet AGL) fly as if the ground were at 4,700 feet. Perform the stall and recover without hitting the simulated ground. When in the recovery, if you scrape 4,700 feet, you must begin an immediate obstruction-clearance climb back to at least 5,000 feet. Hopefully, you can control the altitude loss so that the airplane never gets as low as 4,700 feet before a positive climb is possible.

TURNS

Power-on stalls should also be practiced while the airplane is in a turn. The entry to a turning stall is the same as with wings level. Slow the airplane down to the liftoff speed, bank the wings either left or right approximately 20°, and then raise the nose past the critical angle of attack. This maneuver simulates a departure turn out of the traffic pattern. Takeoff or climbout power is again used in the maneuver. As the stall is approached during a left turn, the bank will want to steepen because of the turning tendencies of torque and P-factor. Right turns will tend to be shallow because of these turning effects. The turning effects will feel like they are getting more powerful as the speed decreases. Because the power setting is constant, the torque and P-factor actually have the same force, but because the control surfaces now have less airflow, they cannot counteract the turning force. The effect the pilot sees is an increase in the turning tendencies and this will affect coordination throughout the maneuver.

Compounding the problem is that the outside wing is moving faster and producing more lift in the process. As the airplane slows down, the radius of the turn becomes smaller. The wings travel on a different arc around the turn; the wing tip on the inside of the turn has a shorter arc than the wing tip on the outside of the turn; a shorter arc means a slower speed and that means less lift. The outside wing is traveling faster, producing more lift; the extra lift on the outside wing causes an over-banking tendency; this over-banking tendency is very apparent during steep turns with full power; the tendency is reduced when the bank is only 20°, but it is one more force that complicates the turning stall.

To overcome all these forces, the ailerons and rudder will need to be constantly adjusted. Getting the bank too steep will have an affect on the pitch. The steeper the bank, the harder it will be to maintain a high pitch-angle that is necessary to stall. When approaching the turning stall, a constant angle of bank and angle of pitch should be maintained, but because the control forces are decaying with reduced airflow, these constant angles can only be held by changing control wheel position. This is tough to understand. As the plane slows down, the only way to hold constant pitch and bank is to move the control wheel. Control effectiveness depends upon two things: airflow and amount of control surface (aileron, elevator, rudder) deflection. If the same force is to be maintained and one factor is reduced, the other factor must be increased. In this case, the factor reduced is airflow, so to maintain a constant force, the control surfaces must increase deflection, compensating for the loss of control effectiveness. The result is that the control wheel is moving, but the airplane's attitude is not moving, which leads to some awkward control situations. In order to maintain proper pitch, bank, and coordination, you might have to actually cross control: hold aileron one way and hold rudder the opposite way. This situation is especially possible in a power-on stall while turning to the right. Right rudder is needed to overcome torque and P-factor and at the same time left aileron is needed to prevent the bank from becoming too steep.

When a full stall takes place, as the nose pitches down, the airplane might also roll. Which way it rolls depends upon the design of the airplane and whether the airplane is slipping or skidding when the stall occurs. The preferred roll would be toward the raised wing. Upon stalling, the nose will pitch down and that is good; if the roll counteracts the banking wing, and the wings level themselves, then that would be great. All the pilot has to do is allow the airplane to accelerate and maintain flying speed. But it's not always that easy; anytime the airplane rolls, it's due to uneven lift, even in normal turns; therefore, if the airplane rolls in a stall recovery, something has caused a greater loss of lift on one wing.

RUDDER REVIEW

If the power-on stall is entered with coordinated controls (ball in the center), the raised wing should stall first, producing a roll motion toward the raised wing. As the airplane slows down approaching the stall, the wings lose lift and the airplane will start to slide sideways in the turn. This changes the effective relative wind to the airplane. In a right turn, as the airplane starts to slip, the ball will move to the inside of the turn. Figure 7-2 illustrates that the relative wind is striking the airplane from more of an angle on the right side. The wind strikes all of the right wing with no problem, but the airplane's fuselage gets in the way of a portion of airflow that would have hit the left wing. This area of the wing then becomes lost to the production of lift making the total lift from the left wing reduced; if the right wing's lift remains the same, this reduction in left-wing lift causes the left wing to drop, which causes the roll "over the top." As the speed increases in the recovery, and as the pilot uses rudder to return to coordinated flight, the wings should start producing equal lift again, which allows the pilot to maintain wings level as the rest of the recovery is made.

It is possible for the roll to go the other way; if the airplane is allowed to skid into the stall, the lower wing could stall first. In this case, the lowered wing is partially

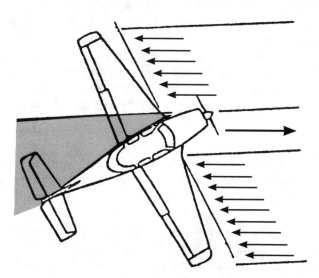

Fig. 7-2. *Airflow is "blanked out" by the fuselage.*

blocked off from the relative wind and will lose more lift than the raised wing; if the low wing stalls first, an "under the bottom" roll will result, and you will find yourself on your back. This is easy to say, but do not panic, allow the roll to continue until the sky is up and the ground is down again and then make a normal recovery. This recovery will take more altitude and if close to the ground, you might have none to spare.

Many pilots fly around as if they are driving a truck—they do not use the rudders much, if at all. Stalls teach many things and among them is the proper use of the foot pedals. A stall can be greatly aggravated by the improper use or neglected use of the rudders.

In the power-on stall recovery, get the airplane flying again, stop any roll tendency, and lose minimum altitude. Flying speed depends upon the angle of attack, so lower the nose. The manufacturer has designed the airplane to pitch down when stalled, so half the battle is won. There is probably no need to push the wheel forward all the way or abruptly. As the nose falls through the horizon, the pilot merely catches the nose at a good recovery attitude, which is at or just below the horizon; no need to push the nose way over so that the pilot is looking down at the ground, which would lose too much altitude and bring an examiner out of his seat. Neither represent good form. The initial recovery from a roll is use of opposite rudder; if the left wing were to fall, apply right rudder. As the airspeed increases, the ailerons become more and more effective and can be used to stabilize the roll at the wings-level position. Power and pitch then are used during the practice stall and recovery to keep the airplane away from the ground and obstructions. All this should happen in an instant.

IMMINENT STALL

Sometimes instructors and examiners will ask a pilot to perform an imminent stall or a full stall. Confusion exists between the two types and how they should be performed. An imminent stall is a flight condition approaching a stall but the aircraft is not completely stalled. During normal flight operations, an imminent stall should be the only stall encountered because hopefully the pilot will recognize the stall symptoms prior to a full stall and execute a proper recovery. An imminent stall can be demonstrated with any power setting and any configuration of flaps and landing gear.

Warnings

What determines the imminent stall? The answer usually is "the first indication of a stall." But which indication should be used?—a mechanical stall warning or aerodynamic stall warning. Many mechanical devices have been designed and installed in airplanes to give the pilot some "heads-up" about an imminent stall. As part of a National Transportation Safety Board study, various mechanical stall warning devices were tested to determine how well they did their job alerting the pilot about the upcoming stall and hopefully prompting the pilot to take recovery action prior to the full stall.

The study concluded that warning lights installed on the instrument panel of an airplane were "almost totally ineffective." Most of the accidents that made up the study took place in VFR conditions during daylight hours. It is very hard to tell if the stall warning light is on or off when bright sunlight comes inside the cabin. When the light does come on, the study said that there was not enough difference to alert the pilot adequately. The stall warning device could go off, but the pilot still be unaware of the potential danger.

The use of a horn warning was better, but not great because the horn's sound can be discarded by a pilot's brain that is already preoccupied with another emergency. In the study, many pilots stated that prior to their accident, they did not remember hearing the horn, even though the respective horns were tested and were functioning properly. The best stall warning device was determined to be a "tactile" warning device, or a system that alerts the pilot's sense of touch. Airliners use the "stickshaker." The stickshaker actually vibrates when the stall is imminent. The NTSB study found that the stickshaker was 99 percent effective with respect to alerting the pilot to an imminent stall. Unfortunately, small airplanes do not have stickshakers or any other tactile device. The cost of the stickshaker system requires a general aviation pilot to rely on less effective systems.

An aural interrupted horn, the horn goes on and off repeatedly, was found to be 84 percent effective. Unfortunately, an airplane might have several systems that have warning horns that sound alike; it is easy to get a stall warning horn confused with a landing gear warning horn. This is just another reason to be thoroughly familiar with any airplane you fly. A continuous stall warning horn was effective 64 percent of the time in the NTSB study; this horn is supposed to come on and stay on until the airspeed increases. The problem is that when flying on the fringe of a stall, the horn will cycle on and off as the airplane changes speeds, which is particularly true during flight at minimum controllable airspeed. When this happens, the continuous horn sounds like an interrupted horn, and this might cause further confusion with other warning systems that might have an interrupted signal.

Warning systems

The systems are triggered by some device that is outside in the airflow and can sense a change in angle of attack. The simplest and most common device is merely an inlet in the leading edge of the wing (FIG. 7-3). Inside the leading edge opening is a line that leads to a reed that is similar to the reed of a woodwind musical instrument. While flying with angles of attack that are lower than the critical angle of attack, the airflow is allowed to pass into the inlet, but air going in does not cause the reed to "sound off." When the angle of attack becomes critical and a stall is imminent, the inlet is positioned so that the airflow passes over the opening. Airflow across the opening consequently produces a low pressure inside the inlet that draws air out through the reed making the sound. This is why it is necessary to "suck" on the leading edge of the wing at the inlet in order to test the stall warning system; this really looks weird, not to mention the fact that you can get bugs in your teeth. (Try forming a "gasket" with your thumb and forefinger, place them around the hole on the leading edge, then put your

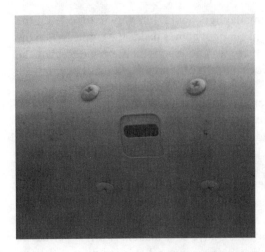

Fig. 7-3. *Inlet-type stall warning device.*

lips on the "gasket." Rather than inhaling, which might pull a bee or wasp down your throat, close off your throat with the back of your tongue and merely open your mouth to pull air out of the inlet to activate the reed.)

Another device uses a flap. Not to be confused with a wing flap, stall warning flaps are small and attached on the leading edge of the wing (FIG. 7-4). At a low angle of attack, the airflow holds the flap in the down position. When the angle increases, eventually the airflow will hit the underside of the flap and push the flap up. When the flap is up, the warning is electrically sounded. Some airplanes have more than one flap, each used during a different configuration of wing flaps.

The best device is an angle of attack (AOA) indicator. The wing will always stall at a particular angle of attack regardless of airspeed, power setting, weight, or G force. A device that would deliver the exact angle of attack to the pilot would provide the pilot with the best information. The AOA indicator uses a probe that is usu-

Fig. 7-4. *Tab-type stall warning device.*

ally attached to the fuselage (FIG. 7-5). The probe determines the angle of the airflow relative to the airplane and this information is displayed on an instrument in the cockpit. The pilot then places the pitch of the airplane at the desired angle of attack for the flight operation. In the case of a stall recovery, the proper angle to climb, yet remain flying, can be seen on the indicator. Once again, cost prohibits widespread use of AOA indicators on small airplanes.

Fig. 7-5. *Angle of attack probe and indicator.*

When to recover

So, when demonstrating (practicing) an imminent stall, do you raise the nose until the first indication from a mechanical warning device and then recover? No. Imminent stall recovery should be initiated from the first indication of aerodynamic warnings. Mechanical devices are designed to go off before the actual stall. When the warning first goes off, the airplane is not stalling, it is supposed to be approximately 5 to 10 knots faster than the stall, but these devices might not be that accurate. Select airplanes will warn you of a stall only after you are in the midst of a stall. And there is more to it than the accuracy of the device; stall recognition is a pilot skill. If you can only recognize a stall by a horn or light, your safety is in jeopardy. If your warning device fails, you must be able to recognize a stall without the device.

If you approach a stall and recover when a horn is heard, then the aircraft did not stall and you did not accomplish anything except to test the horn. If you do this with an examiner, you will leave doubt in his mind: "Is this applicant's ability to keep out of a stall only as good as the warning device?" The examiner will not know for sure. When performing imminent stalls, continue past the mechanical warning to the aerodynamic warnings before initiating the recovery. Go to the brink of aerodynamic stall, then recover, proving that you have the piloting skill necessary to recognize imminent stalls.

In any stall recovery, the aerodynamic warnings must be perceived by the human body. Use hearing to determine changes in airflow and engine sound. Sense the change in direction. The airplane will "mush" prior to stall. Understanding that a motion has changed is *kinesthesia*. With practice, a pilot can "feel" the imminent stall by direction and lack of control pressures.

FULL STALL

A full stall is approached and recovered from the same way as an imminent stall. The difference is that the pilot continues to hold the pro-stall control pressures past the imminent stall and until the nose pitches down by itself. Before demonstrating a stall, plan ahead. Determine to what point you will take the stall before recovery. When performing stalls on FAA checkrides, make sure it is clear before you begin whether or not an imminent or full stall is required. If only an imminent stall is requested, but you did not get the message and do a full stall instead, the examiner will think that you do not know the difference. Or worse, he might believe you know the difference, but did not or could not control the airplane as he wished.

Let's hope that all takeoff and departure stalls that you might encounter in a real, low altitude situation, are only imminent. That way, a full stall will never develop close to the ground where the results might be fatal.

8
Landing stalls

YOU ARE ON FINAL APPROACH TO A LONG RUNWAY. THE WIND IS CALM AND of no factor. The airplane's speed and approach path is just right. Everything is looking great, then without warning the airplane starts a violent left roll and the nose pitches up. Is it wind shear? Is it wake turbulence? This is a situation that could happen to a pilot who was otherwise doing all the right things, but finds himself approaching or actually in a low altitude, power-off stall. The airplane is virtually out of control and accelerating to the ground. Fast and correct action is required right now.

Like all other stalls, the real occurrence of an unexpected stall down low is nothing like an expected stall practiced at high altitude. Pilots must learn to anticipate stall situations so that if a stall happens by surprise, the recognition and recovery time is reduced.

Landings are one of the highest cause-factors that lead to a stall or stall/spin accident. Thirty-six percent of stall/spin accidents in an NTSB report took place during the landing phase of flight. Landing, of course, takes place at the end of a flight. Pilots will therefore have greater fatigue at landing than at the beginning of the flight. Mentally, the pilot might have already finished the job of getting the airplane to the proper airport and relaxed too much.

Many years ago, a military demonstration flying team put on its usual show of great flying skills, coordination, and timing. When the demonstration ended, the jets got in sequence to land, the pressure was off. The last airplane touched down prior to the concrete at the threshold of the runway. The landing gear was damaged and the airplane skidded off the side of the runway toward a temporary grandstand that had been set up for local officials to watch the show. The jet came to a halt just in front of the grandstand. No one was hurt, but it was sure embarrassing. The pilot, arguably one of the best in the world, probably took the landing too lightly. Mentally, that airplane was already tied down. This is just one of the factors that makes landing accidents too common.

PROPER CONFIGURATION

When practicing approach to landing stalls, the airplane should be placed in a configuration as if on final approach. This way, there is little or no difference between practice and the real thing except altitude. Climb to an altitude for practice that will allow at least 1,500 feet separation between airplane and ground during the recovery, and of course clear the area. Slow the airplane down to a speed that would be normal for the final approach to the runway. Reduce the power and gradually raise the nose to reduce the speed. As the speed decreases, add flaps and perform a normal prelanding checklist. For practice in complex airplanes with retractable landing gear and constant-speed propellers, go through a complete GUMPS checklist. Put the landing gear down and make sure the prop control is in the high rpm position. Trim the airplane just as you would in the traffic pattern. Most small airplanes land with no power; therefore, turn the carburetor heat on and reduce the throttle to idle. If the airplane has an approach power setting other than idle, place the throttle in the correct position.

When the airplane is in the landing configuration and the speed is at approach speed, smoothly raise the nose to an angle beyond the critical angle of attack. All stall recognition techniques discussed in chapter 7 still apply. Detect the stall by using sight, touch, and hearing. The airplane will vibrate and buffet in the imminent stall. The airplane's nose uncontrollably pitches down, even though the elevator is full up (control wheel full back), when the full stall is reached.

In practice, it is a good idea to make power-off stall recoveries with and without power. Making the airplane start flying again after a stall is only a function of angle of attack. As long as the nose is lowered below the critical angle, the airflow will again be smooth over the wings and lift will again be produced. This can all be done without power. Power only reduces the altitude that will be lost in the recovery. The amount of altitude lost should not be a factor during high altitude stall practice. A power-off recovery simply demonstrates that a stall is a lack of airflow and the airflow can be replaced with pitch.

Do not let power-off recoveries dull your senses regarding the urgency of a low-altitude stall; if a stall occurs down low, the first priority is to make the airplane produce lift again, but the power must be applied to arrest the descent and initiate a climb away from danger. Separate the situations that are being practiced. Power-off recovery technique proves the aerodynamics of a wing. Power-on recovery technique is a real-life method of avoiding an accident.

REALISTIC PRACTICE

To add a little realism to an approach stall, try this method. Select a long and straight road, fence row, or railroad track. This straight landmark will be the runway.

You could even use a real runway if you were high enough. Fly a traffic pattern to the runway, but do it approximately 2,000 feet higher than you normally would when making an actual landing. Clear the area, then enter on the downwind leg and begin a prelanding checklist as you should always do prior to a real landing. Slow the airplane down, pull on carburetor heat, add flaps, everything normal. When you are abeam the simulated landing spot, reduce the power and start a glide. Turn base to the runway, continue gliding, and add another notch of flaps. Control the airspeed at the normal approach speed. Lead the roll into the final approach so that you are directly on the simulated runway's centerline.

Turns from downwind to base and from base to final can be clearing turns, as well. You should be looking for traffic just as you would in the traffic pattern. Now on final approach, add full flaps, and reduce the power to idle. Select an altitude that represents the ground elevation. Maintain approach speed until approximately 50 to 75 feet above the altitude you chose to represent the ground. Now raise the nose to begin a flare, but deliberately overdo it. Allow the critical angle of attack to be exceeded and cause the airplane to stall. When the full stall is reached and the nose pitches through the horizon, initiate the recovery.

The goal now is to recover and climb out without going through the altitude designated as ground elevation. Catch the nose with the elevator and place the nose at or just below the horizon. Add full power and push carburetor heat to cold. Take out some but not all the flaps. (Consult your airplane's manual for the recommended procedure.) Full flaps usually cause too much drag to allow a rapid reversal of an airplane's direction from going down to going up. But flaps also provide lift, which is greatly needed right now. Start a climb as soon as possible and get away from the simulated danger.

PRIORITY: ESTABLISH THAT CLIMB

Anytime the airplane is losing altitude, the landing gear should remain extended. The idea is that you would want the gear to help absorb the shock of impact, but as soon as the airplane can be coaxed into a climb, the gear should be retracted. Do not wait until the vertical speed indicator shows a number on the plus side of zero. Retract the landing gear at the first indication of needle reversal. In the stall, the VSI will show a descent, for instance, 500 feet per minute and increasing. As the airplane transitions from a descent to a climb, the VSI needle will pause during the transition. If the needle stops increasing at 700 feet per minute down and then moves back to 600 feet down, then 500 and continues in that direction, you know you are gaining altitude.

The VSI has a built-in lag in its indication. When the VSI first shows a climb, the airplane has already been climbing for three to six seconds. Bringing the gear up as soon as possible reduces drag and that might make the difference in a successful recovery. As altitude and speed increase, the remaining flaps can be retracted; however, bring the flaps up one notch at a time to gradually compensate for the loss of lift.

The airplane in the stall might have a tendency to roll left or right, but this roll will not be as pronounced in a power-off stall as in a power-on stall. Entry to the stall should be coordinated and the recovery should use rudder opposite the direction of the roll just as discussed in chapter 7.

In the recovery, a secondary stall can result if the pullup is too abrupt. If the ground were just under the wheels at the time of the stall, the pilot could stall again in his anxious attempt to prevent striking the ground. This makes the recovery with a simulated ground elevation even more valuable because the pilot would have been well practiced at recovery and immediate climb without causing a secondary stall.

POWER OFF IN A TURN

Power-off stalls should also be executed from turns. The best demonstration is the turn from base to final approach in the traffic pattern. Using the same simulated traffic pattern discussed in this chapter, induce the stall in the turn. Control the bank angle of the turn during the entry to the stall. Use approximately 20° bank and hold the bank constant until the airplane stalls. As always, keep the airplane in coordination. If the airplane begins to slip, the raised outer wing will stall first and will dip abruptly. Bring the nose up to the stalling angle of attack gradually but allow the airplane to stall before passing 90° of heading change. This will best simulate the 90° heading change during the base-to-final turn. Enter the power-off stall from left and right turns. The recovery from a power-off turning stall is the same as before: nose down to a flying angle, wings level with coordinated use of rudder and aileron, and full power to reduce altitude loss.

CROSS-CONTROL

The most dangerous approach to landing stall situation is the cross-control stall. It also can take place during the low-altitude turn from base to final. In this case, the pattern is planned poorly and the airplane overshoots the runway centerline in the turn.

I used to think that good landings simply happened according to what the pilot did on the runway. I quickly learned that a good landing is planned long before the airplane arrives on the ground. You spend many flight lessons working on the basics of airspeed control, altitude control, and wind-drift control. All these skills must come together to produce a successful landing. The simplest ground reference maneuver has to be the parallel course. This maneuver teaches pilots that the airplane does not always fly in the direction the nose is pointed. A man in a canoe paddling across a current of water must aim the bow of the boat upstream to cut straight across a river. The airplane is also in a moving current. The current of air has the same effect on airplanes as water does on canoes.

One of the basic skills of flying is to manipulate the airplane across the ground while compensating for wind drift. The ultimate ground reference maneuver is the traffic pattern. One circuit around the pattern involves all flying skills: speed control, use of flaps, power changes, altitude control, wind drift correction, radio procedures, collision avoidance, and lots of good judgment. All the best airspeed control needed for properly landing an airplane will do no good if you cannot get the airplane to the runway in the first place.

The worst case deals with a crosswind through the traffic pattern. If is is a direct crosswind, then the airplane will either have a direct headwind or direct tailwind on the base leg. It would be best to land on the runway that offers a headwind on base, but you might not have a choice. If a tailwind is unavoidable on base, think ahead. Start the turn early so that you can line up with the centerline and begin experimenting with slip or crab angles needed to land. If you begin the turn onto final at the normal position, the tailwind will push you through the centerline (FIG. 8-1) and leave you with some poor choices.

Fig. 8-1. *A tailwind on base leg can cause a final approach overshoot. This situation can lead to a cross-control stall. Go around.*

Faced with an overshoot, the best solution might be to just go around the pattern again and understand and predict the wind better the second time around. But the centerline can be regained by tightening the radius of the turn. Just like the downwind portion of a turn-around-a-point maneuver, the wings must have a greater bank to maintain proper radius when the airplane has a greater groundspeed. But, turning steeply while low in the traffic pattern is not a good idea either. So the pilot is tempted to maintain constant bank yet increase the rate of turn by using the inside rudder.

If the pilot is in a left traffic pattern, and overshoots the centerline, the left rudder will yaw the airplane toward the runway. With left rudder applied, the airplane will pivot and the right wing, which is raised, will increase its speed. The increased speed will increase lift on the right wing and the airplane will overbank. Now the pilot must use right aileron to overcome the overbanking tendency. All these deflected control surfaces will add drag to the total airplane and the pilot will have to raise the nose to maintain the proper airspeed and possibly add power to overcome a rapid rate of descent.

Stop here. The pilot has right aileron, left rudder, nose high, power increasing, and altitude going away. The name cross-control stall is derived from this situation where ailerons are going one way and rudders another way. This is not a pretty picture. The pilot is on the edge of a skidding stall. When the critical angle of attack is exceeded, the wings will stall unevenly. The wing on the outside of the turn is moving faster and is producing more lift than the slower wing on the inside of the turn.

When the pilot adds aileron pressure to prevent the overbank tendency, the inside wing's aileron will move down. This adds drag to the lowered wing and yanks it back, inducing a roll "under the bottom." The roll that takes place will be rapid and possibly uncontrollable until the bank has passed 90°. The airplane would continue to roll, if the pilot does not take action, until it is on its back. Short final, upside down, failing airspeed, and no room to recover, that is the result of a cross-control stall.

Cross-control practice

When practicing cross-control stalls, get plenty of altitude. The landing gear should be down. Check your airplane's manual to determine if "flaps up" is recommended for this maneuver because many airplanes' stress loading would be exceeded with flaps down in a cross-control stall; this thought might scare you even more regarding an actual cross-control stall in the traffic pattern because when executing a normal approach to landing, most likely the flaps are lowered. If the manufacturer recommends against the use of flaps in the situation, it can only mean that in addition to the problems of a low-level cross-control stall recovery, you would have to deal with the flaps ripping off.

Begin the demonstration by slowing to approach speed and start a turn, perhaps a concurrent clearing turn, to simulate the base-to-final turn. This turn is assumed to overshoot the runway. Apply rudder pressure in the direction of the turn, but maintain aileron pressure necessary to hold the bank angle. Increase back elevator pressure so the nose does not drop, subsequently increasing all control forces until the airplane stalls.

If you catch the stall in its imminent stage, the recovery can be made by releasing control pressure on the aileron and rudder. This returns the airplane to coordinated flight. Break the stall with elevator and recover with power; however, if the stall cannot be arrested early, an abnormal attitude will quickly develop; if the airplane rolls inverted during the stall demonstration, release the control pressures but allow the roll to continue until the airplane is back to straight and level, then break the stall and apply power. When the plane is rolling to inverted and back to right-side-up again, there will be a great altitude loss. Do not add power too soon. If power is added while the nose is still pointed at the ground even more altitude will be lost; when executed with plenty of altitude, this should be no problem provided you have no traffic below. In the traffic pattern, there simply will be no room to recover before impact with the ground.

Pay more attention to ground reference maneuvers. They are related to stalls in the traffic pattern because poor wind drift compensation can cause a dangerous final approach leg. The best way out of a crossed-control stall is a go-around.

9
Accelerated stalls

MOST STALL ENTRIES HAVE A COMMON LOOK: NOSE ABOVE THE HORIZON attitude and slow airspeed indication. But all pilots have heard that a stall can happen at any attitude, at any airspeed. So, what factors must exist for the airplane to stall in a "nonstall-like" situation? The fundamentals of what affects the stall speed must first be understood.

The airplane's wings have a particular angle of attack that will cause the airflow to spill over the upper wing surface. When the airflow is not smooth, lift is destroyed. But lift is in opposition to weight, so the amount of weight in the airplane will dictate how much lift is required for flight.

As the airplane's total weight goes up, the stall speed also goes up, but the critical angle of attack stays the same. The amount of lift produced depends on several factors; one of these is the speed of the smooth airflow over the wing. The faster the air flows, the greater the lift. A pilot can vary the speed of the upper chamber airflow in flight by changing the airplane's pitch angle. As long as the stalling angle, or critical angle, is not exceeded, the airflow over the wing will get faster as the nose comes up. The higher the pitch angle, the greater the lift produced.

HEAVIER WEIGHT MEANS HIGHER PITCH

In a situation where the airplane is heavy, a higher pitch angle will be required from the start to offset the extra weight. There is greater weight to be carried, so more lift is needed. The airplane can supply the extra lift, but to do so, the nose must be raised. That is great, except the exact angle of stall does not change. If a pilot deliberately flies with the nose high, he is that much closer to the stall angle with less margin for error between cruising flight and stalled flight. If the pilot raises the nose a little more, a stall will be reached at a higher than normal airspeed.

ARC ANGLES

The airspeed indicator has stall speeds indicated on the dial (FIG. 9-1). The green arc of the airspeed indicator is the normal operating range. The fast end of the green arc is the beginning of the caution range and is designated V_{NO} for maximum structural cruise speed. Anytime the air is turbulent, flight speeds should be kept in the green arc to protect the airframe from damage. Turbulence is similar to speed bumps in a parking lot; to prevent damage to your car, you must slow down to drive over speed bumps; likewise, you must slow the airplane to pass through the bumps in the air. The slow end of the green arc is the stall speed in a clean configuration. Clean specifically means flaps up and this speed is designated V_{S1}. The white arc of the airspeed indicator is the flap operating range; the fast end of the arc is the fastest speed

Fig. 9-1. *Airspeed indicator color code arcs.*

that the airplane should be allowed to fly with the flaps extended. The slow end of the white arc is the stall speed in a landing configuration, gear and flaps down, and is designated V_{SO}.

Some airplanes have a "blue arc" that indicates a range of speeds faster than the white arc where flaps may be extended but not full flaps. For instance, it might not cause any damage to lower only 10° of flaps between the speeds of 90 and 110 knots. But to lower 20° or 30° of flaps the speed must be lower than 90 knots. In this example, the "blue arc" would be from 90 to 110 knots; however, do not expect to see the "blue arc" on the airspeed indicator because it is usually on the flap-position indicator. This blue arc should also not be confused with the "blue radial line" found on multiengine airspeed indicators. That blue line marks the best rate of climb speed with only one engine.

By looking at the airspeed indicator, two stall speeds are displayed: flaps up and flaps down. This ought to be simple, just keep the speed above those two speed positions and a stall will never occur, right? Wrong. The airspeed indicator lies. The speeds on the indicator can only be trusted when the airplane is flying straight and level at less than gross weight. At any other time, the speed at which the airplane stalls is not shown. The key to understanding this is weight; anytime the weight goes up, the wings must produce more lift to carry it, typically accomplished by increased angles of attack. When the angle needed is greater than the critical angle, a stall will result no matter what the airspeed indicator reads.

The extra weight that is causing the higher stall speed does not have to be too many passengers, luggage, and golf clubs. A smart pilot will determine the total weight of the airplane and keep the weight within limits, but the pilot will have little control over another element that influences weight.

LOAD FACTOR

The airplane's wings must provide lift to counteract all "down" forces. Weight or gravity is the "down" force that we understand, but while flying, forces of motion can team-up with gravity to compound the lift problem. The first airplane in FIG. 9-2 is flying straight and level. The lift exactly opposes weight and the airspeed indicator is telling the truth. The second airplane is in a steep-bank turn and other forces come into play. First, the lift vector that is keeping it in the air has been leaned over due to the fact that the lift produced by the wings is at right angles to the wings when looked at from this position. The lift vector is divided into two parts: horizontal and vertical. The horizontal component to the force is actually causing the airplane to turn. Because the total lift vector is not aiming straight "up" there is less total effective lift. This is why in a steep turn more power and more elevator back pressure is required to maintain a constant altitude. The pilot must get back some lift by lengthening the total lift vector.

In opposition to the horizontal component of lift is centrifugal force. Centrifugal force is like "artificial gravity." You have seen this phenomenon before many times; a carnival ride has approximately 20 people stand with their backs to the wall of a large

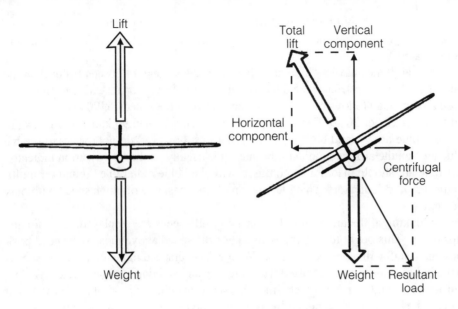

Fig. 9-2

barrel that starts to spin pressing everyone against the wall. At a particular speed, the barrel's floor drops out leaving the rider's suspended in what looks like midair. Gravity did not change its direction, centrifugal force is doing the job.

Do not forget the space station in the movie "2001: A Space Odyssey." The station was set into rotation so the people on the outside of the wheel could walk around as if on earth. From the diagram you can see that centrifugal force and gravity join forces to produce a resultant load. The airplane, and the human body, cannot distinguish between the effect of gravity and the effects of motion. From the wing's point of view, it is simply being asked to carry a greater load. A greater load requires more lift and, therefore, a greater angle of attack. The greater the angle of attack, the closer to stall.

Load factor and stall speed relationship

Due to load factor, the stall speed will be higher. Load factor exists during all turns and turbulence, but the increase in load factor with bank angle is not a straight line. Figure 9-3 illustrates the dramatic increase in load factor as a coordinated turn exceeds 50° of bank angle. At 60° angle of bank, the wings must provide twice as much lift to maintain a constant altitude. The mass of the airplane has not changed, so the pull of gravity on the airplane has not increased. Centrifugal force in this tight turn is the difference. Recall the issue of stress loading during airplane type certification; if a normal category airplane with a +3.8 G-load limit was placed into a coordinated, constant altitude turn of 75°, the plane could bend, break, or worse. Fortunately, the airplane would probably stall before reaching that point. *See* chapter 17 for more about airframe stress factors.

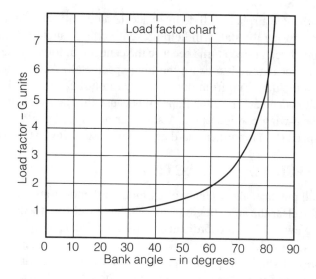

Fig. 9-3

Pilots must be smarter than airspeed indicators. When load factor is present, the pilot must understand that the airplane will stall even though the airspeed indicator is in the green arc. An inventor should come up with a device that senses load factor and couple that with a "sliding" green arc on the airspeed indicator. When turning, as the G-force increased, the slow end of the sliding green arc on the instrument would increase. The pilot would know the current stall speed for that maneuver and keep the airplane faster. It would work, but pilots should not have to rely on such an invention.

When a stall happens at a speed faster than marked on the airspeed indicator, it is referred to as a high-speed or accelerated stall. Two situations will require the wings to support more lift than in normal straight and level flight. The first situation is overloading the airplane, so that it has too much to carry in the first place. The second situation is when forces produced by motion compound the existing airplane weight. Either situation can produce an accelerated stall.

Before attempting to practice accelerated stalls, refer to the airplane's manual. Because an accelerated stall happens at a greater speed, the stall will be more rapid and more severe, which might exceed the limitations of the airplane. Determine if accelerated stalls are authorized for your airplane.

It is important to practice and understand accelerated stalls because they can happen without warning. For instance, a pilot flying an airplane at maximum gross weight makes a quick turnout after takeoff to allow a faster airplane to depart behind him. The bank angle used in the turn is steep, but the pilot does not anticipate any problem because even though he is at a climb speed, it is well within the green arc and above indicated stall speed. Just then, the airplane stalls. The pilot is caught off guard, not expecting a stall at that speed.

Knowing what the airplane will do in an accelerated stall and just how fast the indicator will read during the stall will help prevent getting caught off guard. Accelerated stalls are practiced in steep turns because the centrifugal force of the turn provides the extra load factor required to cause the high-speed stall. Accelerated stalls could also happen in a rapid pull-up from dives, or even in turbulent air. When entering an accelerated stall maneuver, bring the flaps up because the flaps cannot stand as much stress as the clean-wing configuration. Also, enter at a speed slower than the design maneuvering speed (V_A) to further guard against over stressing the airplane.

ACCELERATED STALL PRACTICE

Like all stall practice, allow plenty of altitude for demonstration and recovery and watch for traffic, clear the area. Begin in straight and level flight with a normal cruise power setting. Now roll into a coordinated, constant altitude, steep turn. The airplane will begin to lose altitude if elevator back pressure is not increased. So far, this procedure is the same as flying a steep-turn maneuver. As the turn is established, add excessive back pressure and bring the nose up in a smooth motion. Here the stall speed will be rising under the load factor and the airplane's speed will be falling due to the nose-up attitude. The two speeds will eventually meet and a stall will occur. The nose pitch and wing roll will be more sudden than in other stalls. Unless the airplane is skidding, the roll will be "over the top" and this will help bring the wings level; if the stall is entered with uncoordinated skid, the airplane will roll under. The pilot must take swift and correct action to prevent development of an extended accelerated stall; the speed is fast, the wings stalled, the airplane in a roll—this will soon be a spin entry. Near the ground, there would be very little time or space to recover.

In the recovery, break the stall with forward elevator pressure, and level the wings with coordinated opposite rudder and aileron. Add full power to stop the altitude loss and climb to a higher, safer altitude.

The accelerated stall demonstration proves that angle of attack is the factor that produces stall, not indicated airspeed. A stall actually can happen at any speed. Until the "sliding green arc" airspeed indicator is invented, the pilot must recognize a situation where a high-speed stall is imminent and prevent the stall from happening.

10
Go-around

MANY FACTORS MUST COME TOGETHER FOR A LANDING TO BE SAFE AND successful. Sometimes all the factors do not show up at once and best judgment requires a rejected landing attempt. A faulty approach might lead to a go-around. It is better to add power, and go around the pattern again than to paint yourself into a corner. If the choice is a go-around or a "behind-the-power-curve" situation, take the safer option. If the choice is a go-around or an overshoot across final approach, definitely go around. The problem is that a go-around will make you late and look like you blew the approach. Most pilots try to salvage a landing at all costs, but this might not be healthy.

THINK AHEAD

When teaching instrument flight, the student and I always discuss the idea of a missed approach. At the end of an instrument approach, you must plan to execute a missed approach, not land. This way, if you do get to the missed approach point and cannot land, you are already mentally prepared to execute the missed approach procedure; however, if you have it in your head that you will definitely land, it becomes harder to do the right thing down low. If a pilot gets to the missed approach point and does not see the runway, but mentally is not thinking about the possibility of a miss, he will be tempted to fly a little farther and a little lower, hoping to find the runway. This can be fatal. The same idea extends to a VFR approach. The actual landing is only an option. The pilot should plan the go-around and be ready and willing to execute it on every approach.

It is not unheard of to have the runway blocked while approaching to land. Animals, vehicles, and other airplanes could enter the runway causing a quick reaction to go around. During periods of airport construction, vehicles driven by people that are unfamiliar with airport operations could get in the way. Or another airplane could pull out onto the runway to begin a takeoff roll allowing you no safe room to land. At tower-controlled airports, it is very important to use and understand the proper phraseology with the controllers.

A pilot waiting in the runup area for takeoff contacted ATC: "Tower, this is two-one-four-six Romeo." The tower controller replied "Four-six Romeo, go ahead." With that instruction, the pilot put the microphone in its place, added power, and taxied onto the runway for takeoff. At this moment, another small airplane was on short final. The controller instructed the airplane on final to go around. The pilot on the ground thought that the phrase "go ahead" meant "go ahead and takeoff" when it meant "go ahead with your next radio request."

RUNWAY INCURSION

Another situation took place with a pilot who did not know the true definition of the words "go around." Two student pilots were in the traffic pattern doing touch-and-go landings. On one circuit, the first pilot's airplane blew a tire and came to a skidding halt on the runway centerline. The second pilot was turning base to final at the time. The tower controller, seeing the conflict, radioed to the airplane on final, "Zero-one Lima, go around, disabled aircraft on runway." The pilot simply replied "Roger," and continued the approach to the runway. The controller saw that the pilot did not start the go-around climb, so, once again he said, "Zero-one Lima, go around, disabled aircraft on runway." The pilot said, "Roger," and kept coming. The controller, now frantic said, "Zero-one Lima do you see the aircraft ahead on the runway?" The pilot reported, "Roger, I have him in sight." "Zero-one Lima, go around, disabled aircraft ahead." The student pilot continued in. He touched down before reaching the other airplane, slowed to taxi speed and "went around the disabled airplane on runway." He then returned to the runway centerline and took off again. The student had done exactly as he was told. The problem was that the pilot's definition of "go around" was different than the controller's definition.

Runway incursion is no joke. Getting two airplanes on the same runway has resulted in several accidents and the loss of many lives. At controlled airports, listen and be alert. Practice the proper radio terms and brush up on their definitions, which are found in the FAA's *Pilot/Controller Glossary*, typically part of an *Airman's Information Manual*. At uncontrolled airports, you are your own controller. Before taking the runway for takeoff, make a 360° turn on the taxiway. Look at the entire traffic pattern and determine who else is out there. No matter what airport you take off from, controlled or uncontrolled, look at the final approach leg to be sure that another airplane is not coming. Looking for traffic like this sounds very "low-tech" in today's world of air traffic control, radar, and collision avoidance systems, but it is great insurance that costs only a few seconds.

If an airplane does take the runway while you are on final approach, you must assume that the pilot ahead will continue the takeoff roll without ever seeing you. In this case, you should not fly over the runway, initiate a go-around procedure, and start a turn as well. Get away from the other aircraft by diverting at a right angle. Refrain from making condemnations on the radio and use your energy and full attention to fly the airplane. If a ground vehicle blocks the runway while you are on final, the go-around should be flown over the runway because the runway is free of obstructions, the traffic pattern will not be disrupted, and there will be no turns down low.

EMERGENCY PROCEDURE

The go-around procedure should be treated as an emergency. It can be critical because the airplane must transition in such a short time. One second, the airplane is slow, dirty, and low; the next second, the airplane needs to be fast, clean, and climbing. Because this transition cannot take place instantaneously, the quicker the pilot can make a decision to go around, the better. The farther into the approach the airplane gets, the more critical a go-around will be. The worst situation would be a go-around required from the landing flare where no altitude can be lost.

Each airplane will have a specific procedure for a go-around that should be committed to memory and followed, but all procedures have several things in common. At the moment that the decision is made to reject a landing and go around, add take-off power. The pilot must provide the best opportunity to stop the descent and transition to a climb. At the slow approach speed, power equals a gain in altitude. The next step is to reduce the airplane's total drag so that the power will have its greatest advantage. Usually, the flaps should be retracted before landing gear retraction because full flaps might produce more drag than the landing gear. The flaps should be brought up one notch at a time. If an airplane in the landing flare has an airspeed that is slower than the green arc, yet still faster than the slow end of the white arc, the flaps are keeping the airplane in the air. At this airspeed, a complete retraction of the flaps will produce an immediate stall and altitude loss.

Simultaneously, the airplane must climb and be cleaned up. Bring the flaps up to an intermediate position and leave them there. As soon as the pilot gets the first indication of a climb, the landing gear should be retracted. While the airplane is still in transition from a descent to a climb, there is still the possibility that the airplane will contact the ground. For that reason, leave the gear handle alone until you are sure the airplane is traveling away from the ground. Recall that the first indication of a climb is any upward motion of the vertical speed indicator. Let the speed increase to provide a safe climb out; use the best rate of climb (V_Y) unless obstructions are ahead; use the best angle of climb speed (V_X) to clear obstructions. Do not let the airplane over accelerate, but rather turn that speed potential into altitude. Gradually retract the flaps in stages, each time controlling airspeed and climb. Directional control is essential as well. When the power is added for the go-around, the forces of P-factor, torque, and slipstream will all combine to turn the airplane. Right rudder must be applied and held.

MAINTAIN AND GAIN

The go-around procedure and the approach to landing stall recovery procedure are the same thing. In both cases, the pilot's goals are the same: maintain flying speed, gain altitude.

There are other times when a go-around should be executed. One of the most important times is after a faulty landing touchdown; if the flare is excessive, the airplane will float and gain altitude. The airspeed soon dissipates and this leaves the airplane without flying speed but still 10 feet in the air. The airplane is going to "drop in." The pilot should realize that this could damage the airplane and its occupants; a go-around should begin before touching the ground. Other times the airplane will contact the runway and bounce. The bounce might be the result of too great an airspeed when the airplane originally touched down. The wings are still producing lift and the airplane simply flies back into the air. The problem is that after any bounce, the airplane's attitude might not be correct for landing. The airspeed will die off even faster after the ground has been contacted the first time. As the airplane comes down the second time, the nosewheel might contact the ground first. The airplane will then "porpoise," or worse, the nose gear could collapse. The nose gear is not designed to take the same shock as the main gear; if the nose gear strut breaks, the propeller will strike the ground and now there are major problems. Do not allow any of this to happen; if the airplane bounces, before it comes back down, promptly and safely execute a go-around.

CLIMBOUT STALL

Another danger associated with the go-around is a stall in the climbout. It is normal to use "up-elevator" trim to establish a stable glide speed during the approach. If the trim is left in the up position when takeoff power was applied, the nose of the airplane will pitch up rapidly. As the nose pitches up, the wings will reach a critical angle of attack and stall. In addition to repositioning the flaps and landing gear, the pilot should be ready to adjust the elevator trim while in the go-around procedure. The go-around can be dangerous because so much has to happen quickly and it all might catch the pilot by surprise. The go-around procedure should be rehearsed as part of the prelanding check. The possibility of a go-around should never leave the pilot's mind until taxiing off the runway.

Pilots should practice an elevator trim tab stall in simulation of a rejected landing go-around. Set up the maneuver by simulating a traffic pattern at a safe stall altitude. Start a downwind leg by reducing power, extending the first notch of flaps, and extending the landing gear. Using the turns to look for traffic, make a base leg and extend another notch of flaps. Turn on final approach and reduce the throttle to idle. Now trim the nose up to maintain a "hands-off" glide speed. Everything is now just as it would be prior to touchdown. Begin a flare and then begin the go-around procedure. Add takeoff power. The elevator trim will pop the nose up and P-factor and torque will turn the airplane left. For the demonstration, do not stop these forces with control movement, allow them to continue into the imminent stall. As soon as the imminent stall is felt, take recovery action.

More than the normal force on the control wheel will be necessary to break the stall. The trim tab is working against you, so to relieve the heavy pressure, adjust the trim tab to a nose-down position. Do not attempt to break the stall with the trim tab alone. The control wheel must come forward even though it will be harder to push than usual. After the stall has been broken, adjust the trim to an easier position. From this point, all normal stall recovery and go-around techniques should be used to safely climb away from the situation.

The altitude needed to recover from a full elevator trim tab stall will probably just not be available if the go-around is initiated in the final stages of the landing approach. If a go-around must be made from a low altitude, anticipate the nose-up pitch that the trim tab will cause and hold the wheel in proper position. This will not take super human strength, but the pilot must be ready for it.

11
Unusual
attitude recovery

ALL STUDENT PILOTS PRACTICE FLIGHT MANEUVERS UNDER THE HOOD, but most student pilots do not know the real value of the hood. It is not used to train student pilots how to fly in clouds and it has only limited value when training potential IFR pilots how to fly in the clouds. There are two good reasons why VFR pilots are taught to fly with the training hood. First, it does instill some trust in the instruments and it helps develop a mental picture of the airplane's attitude. The second reason is to train the pilot's eyes to scan. If the pilot can gather information quickly off the instrument panel, then the pilot is able do a better job of tending to other matters—the biggest responsibility beyond flying the airplane is to look for other traffic. When a pilot's scan is slow, his eyes stay in the cockpit too long and neglect watching for other aircraft. The hood forces pilot's eyes to move quickly to control the airplane. So, practicing under the hood enhances the ability for the pilot to "see" without the hood.

NOTEWORTHY AWARENESS

The buzzword of the '90s has been "situational awareness." This concept describes the ability of the pilot to make good decisions based on total knowledge of a particular situation. The most basic situational awareness to the pilot is the situation of the airplane he or she is flying; if the airplane is in an attitude or moving in a direction that the pilot is unaware of, the pilot becomes just an occupant. It is essential for a pilot to regain aircraft situational awareness if the awareness is ever lost. Unusual attitude recovery is practiced to train pilots to recognize an aircraft situation and provide a cure for that situation. This maneuver can be performed with or without the IFR training hood. With the hood, the pilot must paint the picture of the aircraft situation only with the flight instruments. This adds one more step in the mental process involved in returning to situational awareness.

In a real flight situation, the airplane can be tossed into an unusual attitude in a number of ways. The severity of the unusual attitude depends upon how quickly the pilot recognizes a problem and solves the problem. The pilot can become momentarily distracted by something as simple as dropping a pencil; the pilot does not want the pencil to get caught in the rudder pedals, so he tries to find it. While looking down and groping for the pencil, the airplane changes attitude due to turbulence; when the pilot looks up again, the airplane is not where the pilot left it. The pilot must regain awareness of the airplane's position, determine if any action is necessary, and take action if any is needed. If the pilot overreacts, or reacts in the wrong way, the airplane's attitude problem could go from bad to worse.

TREND DETECTION, PROPER REACTION

When using flight instruments alone, trends must be detected; if airspeed is increasing, altitude decreasing, and VSI showing a descent, the indicator needles on each instrument must be reversed. The pilot, with control movements, must make each needle's directional trend stop and turn around. The same is true if the airspeed is decreasing, altitude increasing, and VSI showing a climb. The trends cannot be allowed to continue.

If the pilot detects the nose is low in an unusual attitude recovery, care should be taken not to overspeed the airplane. If it is assumed that turbulent air can cause a real unusual attitude situation for a pilot, we must assume that the yellow arc of the airspeed indicator is off limits in a recovery. The yellow arc is the caution range and these speeds are too stressful to the airplane in bumpy air. During a nose-low recovery, it might be necessary to reduce engine power to keep the airspeed in the green arc of the normal operating range. Once the nose of the airplane has been brought back to the horizon, power can be restored to maintain level flight or begin a climb. The wings might become banked in a nose-low unusual attitude as well. The wings should be brought back to the level position using ailerons before the nose is raised. Pulling the nose up with the wings banked will tighten the turn and induce a greater load factor. Level the wings as the power is reduced, followed by raising the nose to the horizon. This should all be one smooth motion.

If the pilot detects a nose-high attitude, the danger of an inadvertent stall is real; if the pilot recognizes and reacts quickly, the stall should be avoided. The pilot who is surprised by the nose-high attitude will not be completely sure how close to stall the airplane has progressed. At the first recognition that the airplane's pitch is higher than normal, lower the nose with forward elevator; if a stall is imminent, this should break the stall entry; if the wings are also banked, delay leveling the wings until after the stall is broken and the nose is back at a normal position. When leveling the wings, coordinated rudder and aileron should be used. As forward elevator is used to lower the nose, add full power. The exact condition of the airplane might still not be completely understood by the pilot. It is better to establish a power setting that will arrest any altitude loss and start a climb. If an imminent or full stall was entered, use the complete stall recovery procedure.

If the nose is low and wings are banked in an unusual attitude recovery, level the wings first, reduce power, then raise the nose to the horizon. If the nose is high and the wings are banked, lower the nose first, add power, then level the wings.

Your next unusual attitude recovery might not be a prescribed training maneuver, but the result of some real distraction. But no matter how big the distraction, nothing is more important than flying the airplane. The distraction might be as minor as dropping a pencil or as major as an engine fire. In any case, the pilot must meet any urgent demands of the distraction while simultaneously piloting the airplane. If the airplane is left unattended, a stall or stall/spin accident is inevitable. The unusual attitude recovery becomes another stall and spin preventer.

12
Commercial
certificate maneuvers

MANEUVERS PRESCRIBED FOR THE COMMERCIAL PILOT CERTIFICATE ARE misunderstood because they simply are not practical. An air traffic controller will never request, "Three-seven Bravo, give me a lazy eight out there for spacing." The maneuvers determine a pilot's degree of aircraft control. On a commercial pilot checkride, the examiner looks to see if the applicant uses good planning, judgment, coordination, airplane familiarization, and attention to outside references. In every case, the pilot should anticipate all corrective actions needed and employ them early so that no problems are ever detected. The commercial maneuvers are speed control maneuvers, but with a greater demand for accuracy.

CHANDELLE

A chandelle is a 180° climbing turn where airspeed is sacrificed for altitude. It is not a stalling maneuver, but the pilot should "flirt" with the stall at the top of the maneuver. It requires that the pilot get the greatest performance from the airplane. The amount of altitude gained during the maneuver depends upon the airplane, and the density altitude, but the pilot must gain as much altitude as possible with the given conditions. Because the end of the maneuver will be slow and near stall speed, an altitude should be selected that will allow for a safe stall recovery if a stall does occur. Always look for other aircraft.

The chandelle can be divided into two parts (FIG. 12-1). The total maneuver is a 180° turn. For the first 90° of the turn, the bank will be held constant and the pitch in-

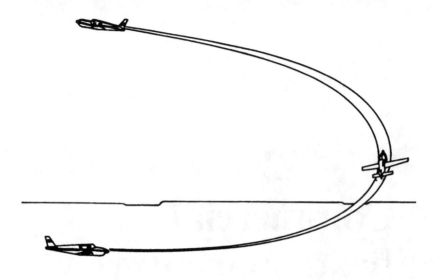

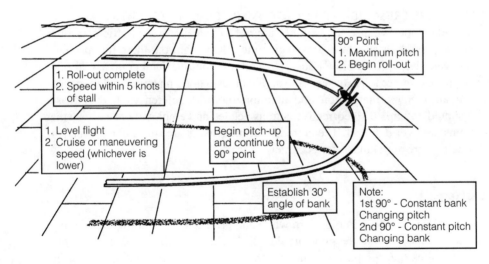

Fig. 12-1. *The chandelle.*

creased; in the second 90° of turn, this is reversed (the pitch is held constant and the bank is relaxed until the wings are level at the top of the maneuver).

Proper entry

Enter the maneuver no faster than the design maneuvering speed (V_A) or what the manufacturer suggests. This speed is important; if you begin the maneuver above V_A, any abrupt control movement could cause damage to the airplane; if you begin the maneuver slower than V_A, then maximum performance cannot be achieved. In some airplanes, a dive must begin the maneuver to obtain the V_A speed. The power setting at entry should be a cruise setting. Locate a reference point, preferably on the horizon, and put one wingtip on the point. (That reference point, or a similar reference point selected for a subsequent precision maneuver, helps determine successful completion of the maneuver.) Flaps and landing gear should be up. Constant-speed propellers should be set at high rpm. Clear the area and accelerate to V_A and then begin a 30° banked turn toward the point. When the bank has been established, begin a smooth pull up and add power. Airplanes with a fixed-pitch propeller should use full power; airplanes with a constant-speed propeller should set the power for a normal climb setting.

If the nose is allowed to rise before the bank reaches 30°, airspeed will be lost too early, and the maneuver will have trouble at the top. The sequence is "bank, then yank," but yank is not a good term because the application of all control inputs must be smooth and coordinated. While holding the 30° bank, the pitch should be ever increasing. The proper angle of pitch must be determined with practice. The pilot must aim the nose to a point above the horizon that will ultimately produce a reduction in speed equivalent to stall speed at the top of the maneuver. If the nose is raised too high, the speed will run out before the maneuver is completed. If the nose is too low, the speed will never get slow enough to meet the requirements of the maneuver. The nose should start to rise as soon as the bank reaches 30° and continue to rise until the 90° point of the maneuver.

At the 90° point, you must accept whatever pitch has been obtained. The wings are still banked at 30°; if the bank and pitch were held constant now, an accelerated stall would take place; to prevent this from happening, the bank is slowly relaxed. (The second 90° of the maneuver takes much longer than the first 90° because the bank gradually moves from 30° to wings level.) At the 90° point, the airspeed should be 25 to 30 knots faster than stalling speed. If the pitch were too high during the first 90°, the speed left over for the second 90° would not be sufficient. The pilot will have to do one of two things: continue holding the pitch where it is and ultimately stall or lower the nose some, which means maximum performance is lost. As far as airspeed is concerned, the pilot is a spectator in the last 90° of turn. This is where good planning will have paid off. The needle on the airspeed indicator should begin the maneuver at V_A and move to V_{S1} plus 5 without stopping, slowing down, or speeding up.

As the bank moves from 30° to wings level, the load factor of the turn slowly goes away. As the load factor diminishes, the stall speed gets slower. Because of the turn's load factor, you are much closer to stall speed the last 90° of the maneuver than is indicated on the airspeed dial. A common error is holding the bank in too long or bringing it out too fast. If you hold 30° too long, you will not allow the airspeed time to decrease to stall speed. The reference point will arrive at the opposite wing tip too early with 10 to 15 knots of airspeed to spare. If the 30° is brought out too fast, the reference point will never arrive at the opposite wing tip and a turn of 180° will not be completed.

Proper exit

As the airplane slows down, especially during the last 90°, the control surfaces will become less effective. Ever increasing elevator back pressure will be required at every increment of speed loss to hold the pitch constant. So, in the last 90°, the pitch should remain the same, but the pilot must continue to move the control wheel back in order to maintain this position. Also, as speed bleeds off, torque and P-factor will have a greater effect. The power setting is high and the speed is slow. The turn-and-slip indicator ball should remain in the center at all times during the maneuver, but this will require increasing amounts of rudder pressure. In a left chandelle, even more right rudder is necessary because aileron drag and torque join forces. Torque is already supplying a force to the left; therefore, greater right rudder pressure is needed to stay in coordination. Rolling out of a right chandelle does not require quite as much rudder because the aileron drag will oppose torque. Left rudder probably will not be needed, but a reduction in right rudder pressure should do the job.

If everything is timed out just right, the reference point will arrive on the opposite wing tip just as the wings have reached level and just as the stall horn has sounded. The target speed at the end of the maneuver is 5 knots above the stall speed with flaps up. Because stall warning indicators are supposed to be set to go off 5 to 10 knots above stall, the warning should be going off when the chandelle is completed; if the warning indicator is not sounding at the completion of the maneuver, it is considered bad form to abruptly add back pressure just to hear the horn bump on. The horn should come on naturally at the end of a well-flown chandelle.

Do not allow the airplane to enter the imminent stall at the top of a chandelle. Stalling at any time during a chandelle is incorrect and will cost you a commercial checkride.

LAZY EIGHT

The lazy eight is another maneuver that has no practical application, but the ability to fly one well demonstrates a pilot's mastery of the airplane. The maneuver is not eight shaped. The maneuver consists of two 180° turns in opposite directions (FIG. 12-2). During each turn, a symmetrical climb and descent is accomplished. The name lazy eight comes from the pattern the nose of the airplane follows during the maneuver: a lopsided figure eight lying on its side. During the maneuver, everything is constantly changing. The bank, speed, and pitch of the airplane are never constant. The pilot flies the lazy eight by using subtle control pressures, not movements. If you watched the control wheel while a sharp pilot flew this maneuver, it would be very hard to detect movement of the wheel. Everything is done with slight pressure and as the name implies, it is done slow and lazy. Speed control will again be vital to a successful maneuver; it is not a stalling maneuver. The pilot should never get closer to stall than 5 to 10 knots.

Lazy eights should be flown with enough altitude for a stall recovery. Good visibility is helpful because a reference landmark is chosen to determine position throughout the maneuver. The best situation is to locate a reference point that is upwind of the airplane's position. The maneuver can now be flown into the wind. If the wind is

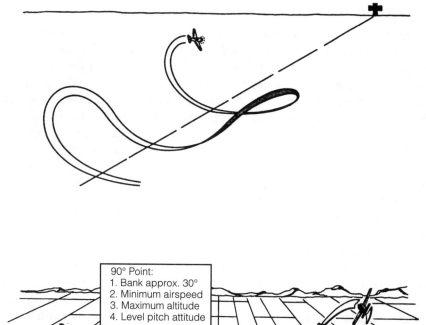

Fig. 12-2. *The lazy eight.*

strong, the turns of the lazy eight will be squeezed together and you can do many turns without moving across the ground very far. Consult the airplane's handbook for suggested entry speed. The entry speed will be the design maneuvering speed or a speed close to it. The power should be set at cruise flight.

To understand the chandelle, we divided the procedure up into two parts: the first and second 90°. To break down the lazy eight, let's look at only one of the 180° turns and divide this 180° into four parts.

Proper entry

The first part starts as the maneuver begins with the wingtip on the reference point. Use a line of rivets down the wing and sight the reference point down that line. The first part ends after a turn of 45° has progressed toward the reference point. During this part, the pitch gradually rises and the bank gradually increases. The pitch and bank changes take place simultaneously, no bank then yank. At the 45° point in the turn, the pitch of the airplane should be as high as it will be throughout the entire maneuver; bank at that point will only be 15° to 20°. The entry to a chandelle is abrupt compared to the slow and easy lazy eight. The amount of pitch up is important. On the way back down, the number of degrees that the nose was above the horizon should equal the number of degrees that the nose falls below the horizon. The maneuver must be symmetrical. In the first part of the maneuver, the airspeed will be reduced from V_A to a speed that is approximately V_{S1} plus 15. The amount of altitude gained is not a criteria for judging the maneuver. The exact altitude gained will be a function of aircraft power and atmospheric conditions.

The second part of the lazy eight begins at the 45° position into the turn and ends at the 90° point. During this portion, the bank will continue to increase to its maximum amount at the 90° position; 30° is the target bank angle to achieve, but greater amounts could be used. During the second part, the airspeed continues to diminish to a speed 5 to 10 knots faster than the clean stall speed. To prevent a stall, the elevator back pressure is released allowing the nose to slowly fall from its highest pitch angle and arrives at the horizon at the 90° position. At the end of the second part of the lazy eight (90° position), the airplane is at its slowest, highest, and greatest bank angle. The nose meets the horizon at the reference point.

The third part begins as the nose slices through the reference point. The bank starts to come out and the nose falls below the horizon. This part ends at the 135° position from the start of the turn with the nose at its lowest pitch. The lowest pitch down should be equivalent to the nose's highest pitch back at the 45° point. The airspeed is increasing as the airplane loses altitude. When the airplane arrives at the 135° position, the nose is as low as it will ever get, and the bank is approximately 15°.

Proper exit

The fourth and last portion of the maneuver continues the rollout of the wings so that the wings are level when the reference point appears on the opposite wing. The nose is gradually brought up from its lowest pitch to the horizon. If all works out, the airplane will arrive at the 180° position with the same altitude and airspeed that began the maneuver. The airspeed indicator needle should start the maneuver at V_A and slowly move to V_{S1} plus 5 before slowly returning to V_A at the conclusion of the lazy eight. The indicator should slow down and speed up at the same rate. This all works on the "what goes up must come down" theory. If the airplane has a certain amount of speed entering the lazy eight, it trades some of the speed for altitude. But the airspeed is replaced when the altitude is given back.

Challenges

Common problems dealing with poor airspeed management plague this maneuver. The first problem might arise if the airplane does not return to the altitude it started from, a result of one of two possibilities; probably the maximum pitch up at the 45° point and the maximum pitch down at the 135° point were not the same. If the climbing and descending turns are not identical, the proper altitude will not be achieved, which adversely affects the airspeed control. If the airplane is too high at the end, and the pilot pushes the nose over at the 180° point simply to reach the entry altitude, the airspeed will race past V_A. If the pilot determines that the airplane will be too low, at the conclusion of the 180° turn, he will pull the nose up to the horizon too rapidly and the speed will never reach the entry speed of V_A. If the pitch angles were the same, yet the entry altitude was not achieved, adjust the power. Do this only after several lazy eight turns.

If the wings-level altitude is increasing after every turn and the pitch angles have been symmetrical, reduce power slightly. Add power slightly if the wings level altitude has successively decreased. Always treat the first lazy eight as an experiment of conditions. On hot summer days, the power required to make the maneuver work will be near the takeoff setting, while on cold days only a low cruise works. Many pilots suspect a power change is needed first and do not look carefully at the up and down pitch angles. It is easy to fix the wrong problem. You troubleshoot your own commercial flight test maneuvers. If you cannot make the proper adjustments to improve the maneuver, an hour of chandelles and lazy eights will be a waste of time and money.

Coordination of the rudder and aileron are once again very important to the successful completion of the lazy eight. More right rudder should be expected in right climbing turns than in left turns because torque favors the left turn and opposes the right turn. In the right climbing turn, the controls might gradually become crossed when left aileron is needed to overcome the overbanking tendency and the right rudder is needed to overcome torque. The pilot's ability to control all these forces and make the airspeed indicator do exactly as intended proves the pilot's proficiency.

STEEP SPIRAL

A steep spiral is not a stalling maneuver and should never be confused with a spin. (Chapter 19 has more on the difference between spirals.) A steep spiral is actually the combination of three maneuvers: steep turns, turns around a point, and power-off glides (FIG. 12-3). Steep spirals can be used in the real world. If an emergency landing is forced upon a pilot, it is always best to land in a field that can be seen well. The best chance of seeing ruts, power lines, and ditches in a field is to look straight down on the field. The spiral provides an altitude loss while maintaining a position over the ground. At the bottom of a spiral it is easy to break off into a downwind, base, and final approach leg to a forced landing.

Before the steep spiral can begin, climb to an altitude that will allow at least three turns and plenty of room to fly out at the bottom. Plan the recovery no lower

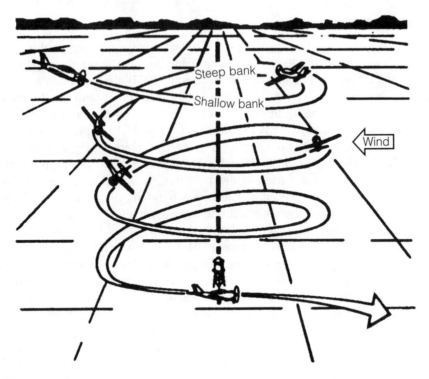

Fig. 12-3. *The steep spiral.*

than 1,500 feet above the ground. All these maneuvers should provide enough altitude so that if an inadvertent stall occurred, there would be sufficient recovery altitude. Watch below for traffic.

Proper entry

Start the steep spiral by locating an object on the ground, below the airplane, that is easily recognizable. Do not use a tower. Spiralling down around a tower will prove your wind drift correction is excellent but will not score points with an examiner. Bring the carburetor heat on and reduce the power to idle. Roll into a bank of up to 55° and allow the nose to fall below the horizon. When the nose is lowered, the angle of attack is also lowered, which produces less lift. The reduction in lift is no problem because the airplane is allowed to descend. The constant altitude loss also means less load factor is present in this turn than in a level turn, but the stall speed will still be faster than shown on the airspeed indicator. Using steady pitch, make the airspeed constant throughout the turns. Changes in airspeed will affect the radius of the turns.

The radius of the turns should be the same from top to bottom. A common error is to start out wide and tighten up as altitude is lost. This makes the spiral look like the shape of a funnel when the proper spiral takes the shape of a cylinder. If the wind is faster than 10 knots, the airplane will begin to drift. This will require steepening and shallowing of the bank angle as if it were the procedure required for a turn around a point. When there is a tailwind, the airplane's groundspeed increases. When the airplane travels faster, it must turn faster to maintain the same radius. This is why steeper banks are required downwind. When the wind comes around to the nose, the groundspeed drops and the turn must slow down. The steep spiral's steepest bank angle must at least reach 50° to 55°, so judgment must be used to keep tight on the point below.

Variation and caution

This maneuver is the most fun when there is little or no wind. In this case, the pilot banks to a constant 50° and sets the pitch for proper glide speed to settle back and enjoy the ride. A little nose-up trim will help maintain the proper pitch. A stable airplane will simply pivot around the point like a corkscrew.

The engine might get too cool during an extended spiral so keep an eye on the cylinder head temperature gauge if you have one. Even if you do not have one, plan to bring the power back gradually. It is also a good idea on any extended glide to move the throttle up and back a few times. This verifies that the engine is indeed still running not just windmilling, and doing this could also avoid fouled plugs and carburetor ice.

The steep spiral should be practiced in both directions. From the left seat a right spiral is tough because it is hard to see the point in the shallow part of the turns. The steep spiral is required by the FAA's practical test standards for commercial pilot applicants but is no longer required for flight instructor applicants.

ON PYLON EIGHTS

This maneuver is greatly misunderstood. First what is its proper name? It can go by "on pylon eights" or "eights on pylons" or simply "pylon eights." Other maneuvers that use the number eight are actually pure "ground reference" maneuvers: eights across a road, eights along a road, and eights around pylons. The eight maneuver that is required on commercial pilot and flight instructor flight tests involves a change in altitude. The pure ground reference eights maintain a constant altitude. For instance, the eights around pylons sounds close to "on pylon eights" but it is actually two turns around a point, in opposite directions, with a common center. The turn around a point is flown at a constant altitude and so is eights around pylons. Lazy eights have nothing to do with any of this.

Perhaps this will sort out all the confusion regarding "crazy eights:"

Private pilot flight test (constant altitude)
- 8s along a road
- 8s across a road
- 8s around pylons

Commercial and CFI flight test (variable altitude)
- On pylon 8s (also known as "8s on pylons" and "pylon 8s")

Pylon definition

Pylons were used years ago as navigation aids to mail pilots. Today checkerboard painted pylons are used to mark the corners of air race courses. For many years, pylon eights were not required for any checkride so an entire generation of pilots came through the ranks not knowing much about them. (I am in that group. When pylon eights were reinstated as a checkride maneuver we all had to learn the maneuver with our students. This has added to the maneuver's acceptance problems.)

The pylon eight does form an elongated figure eight and does use random points on the ground (FIG. 12-4). But that is where all similarity with ground reference eights ends. The pylon eight does not maintain constant radius from the point and has constantly varying altitude.

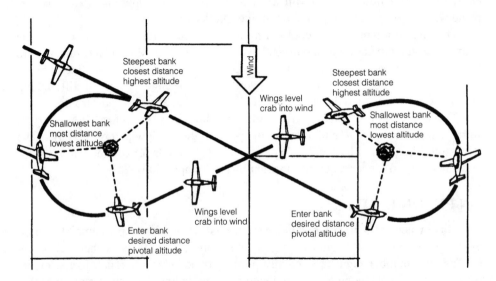

Fig. 12-4. *The pylon eight.*

When the airplane turns around the pylon, a "sight line" must be established. The sight line runs from the pilot's eye to the pylon and is parallel with the lateral axis of the airplane. A row of rivets that runs from the wing root to wing tip is a good sight line. This sight line's position depends upon where the pilot is sitting. If you were to observe a pylon eight from the rear seat of a trainer or four-place airplane, the airplane would not appear to pivot on the pylon.

Maneuver parameters

The actual altitude that the maneuver is flown depends on the airplane's ground-speed. A particular altitude will make the airplane appear to pivot around the pylon; therefore, the altitude is referred to as the "pivotal altitude." A little math determines the altitude: pivotal altitude above ground level is equal to the ground speed in knots squared divided by 11.3 (or ground speed in miles per hour squared divided by 15).

$$GS^2 \text{ (knots)} \div 11.3 = \text{pivotal altitude (above ground level)}$$

$$GS^2 \text{ (miles per hour)} \div 15 = \text{pivotal altitude (above ground level)}$$

The answer to the problem must be added to the elevation of the ground that the pylon eight will be flown over; accordingly, the pilot can use the altimeter to approximate the pivotal altitude. The maneuver should be flown at a cruise power setting and the true airspeed determined. If there is no wind, then the TAS and GS will always be the same, and as a result, the entire pylon eight will be flat. In other words, there will be no need for altitude changes. When groundspeed is constant, the pivotal altitude will be constant. But if a wind does exist, the TAS and GS will not be the same, except in direct crosswinds. When flying the pylon eight, the wind will attack the airplane from virtually every angle except a direct tailwind; therefore, in a wind, GS will be constantly changing as will the need to climb or descend to pivotal altitude. The stronger the wind is, the greater the variance in altitudes.

The next big hurdle is to find two pylons that will help, not hinder, the maneuver. To make everything work out, pylons should be chosen so that the wind blows between the pylons, as if they were football goal posts; if a line were drawn from one pylon to the other, the wind should cross that line at a right angle. The pylons must also be at the same elevation; if one pylon were picked in a valley and one on a hillside, it would be virtually impossible to get the pivotal altitudes correct. The pylons must be close together. The only straight and level part of the maneuver is between the pylons and should only last approximately three to five seconds. One of the hardest things to estimate is the proper distance between pylons before the maneuver begins. The goal of the maneuver is to determine if the pilot can control altitude, airspeed, coordination, and maintain outside reference. The goal is not just to determine pylon distance. I recommend that a pilot choose one pylon to begin with and let the maneuver determine the second pylon.

The general area should have plenty of potential forced landing sites. Because the pivotal altitude is low, an engine problem will not allow much time to select a suitable field. Plan for an emergency before choosing the pylons. Pylon eights are also stall threats. The turns in the maneuver will be low. The turns are not considered steep turns but the load factor of each turn will raise the stall speed. A stall at the pivotal altitude will not allow much room for recovery.

Proper entry and execution

Enter the pylon eight with a quartering tailwind on the left side (FIG. 12-4). Choose something that is in the clear and is easily seen. Recognition of this point will become very important: a single tree in a field, church steeple, house chimney, or stop sign at a highway intersection. When the pylon comes to a position that is on the sight line, begin a left turn. The pivotal altitude should have already been estimated and the airplane at that altitude above ground level. Now the math problems give way to real flying. The bank should be approximately 30°. The bank may be varied slightly to accommodate for a large wind drift, but the more steady the wings are, the better. As the left turn begins, the quartering tailwind changes to a crosswind then a headwind. This means that the ground speed is decreasing and the pivotal altitude is lowering. When the pivotal altitude decreases, the pylon will appear to move forward and ahead of the sight line. When the pylon moves ahead, the airplane is above pivotal altitude.

Power should remain constant and altitude changes accomplished with small pitch changes. When the airplane arrives at the direct headwind position, the groundspeed will be slowest and therefore the altitude should be lowest. If the airplane gets too low, the pilot will see the pylon move backward from the sight line. When the pylon moves behind, the airplane is below the pivotal altitude. As the airplane continues the turn, the wind will change from a headwind to a crosswind and then a right quartering tailwind. The wind should never be a direct tailwind, so the quartering position will produce the fastest groundspeed and the highest altitude. If the pylons and wind are positioned properly, the highest altitude will be in the center of the maneuver and the lowest altitude will be on the outside turns of the eight. If the wind blows in any other direction to the pylons, it will be anybody's guess as to where the altitudes should occur. Keep it simple. Plan to position the wind and pylons early for fewer problems while flying the maneuver.

Look at the directional gyro and notice the direction the wind is coming from. If the DG has a "heading bug," usually used with an autopilot, set the bug on the wind direction. With or without the bug, the pilot must keep track of the position of the airplane in relation to the wind. In the first turn, the wings should be leveled when the wind arrives at the right quartering tailwind position, but the wings do not stay level for long, approximately three to five seconds. As the wings level, start to count. When you reach five, roll the airplane to the right and whatever is there will be your second pylon. Of course, the object down there might not be as recognizable as your first pylon, but it is better to choose a pylon with poor landmark value than to blow the maneuver flying too far between the pylons.

Now, turn right around the second pylon and follow the pivotal altitude to a lower altitude into the wind. As the wind crosses the nose, the altitude will need to increase. When the wind is in the left crosswind position, start looking for the first pylon that you choose. Let the nose cross the first pylon. Roll out only when the nose is approximately 45° to the right of the pylon. This should also place you with a left quartering tailwind and your highest altitude. The level leg between pylons should again be no more than five seconds. This time, after counting to five, the sight line should be back on the first pylon and the maneuver can continue.

DUTCH ROLLS

A Dutch roll is not currently required on any FAA flight tests. Like an airport abandoned by the airlines after deregulation, the Dutch roll is a forgotten maneuver, but it still has a great training value. Every stall and every maneuver discussed so far in this book has had one requirement in common: excellent coordination between aileron and rudder. Unfortunately, our airplanes are so stable that the use of rudder is a lost art. There are pilots who use the rudder only on the taxiway. A Dutch roll can help to teach your feet and hands to work together.

A Dutch roll is not a maneuver, it is a stability term to describe the yaw of the nose during bank transition and it is actually not even a roll. The airplane does not get inverted as would be the case with a real roll.

Begin the exercise by finding a prominent landmark beyond the nose of the airplane; choose something approximately halfway between the airplane and the horizon. Begin at cruise power setting and airspeed with at least 1,500 feet agl. The idea is to roll the airplane from side to side while the nose remains "glued" on the point. First, try it with no rudder at all and bank the airplane left to a 30° bank angle and then immediately right to a 30° bank angle. With ailerons only, the nose will wallow from side to side and cannot stay aimed at the point. The airplane will feel labored and clumsy.

Now try with coordinated aileron and rudder. Apply left aileron and left rudder. Roll to 30°, then apply both right aileron and rudder. Let the airplane roll from 30° left to 30° right. Now apply left aileron and rudder to roll back and forth. The nose will stay on the point when the ailerons and rudder are working together properly. It will take a little practice.

Imagine that the point is a target and your airplane has guns in the nose. Do a Dutch roll and shoot; if you are in coordination, the target will be hit; if you are not in coordination, you will shoot up the entire countryside.

As with other maneuvers discussed, there is no practical application of a Dutch roll. But it will help you to learn to "feel" when rudder is required. The turn and slip indicator ball should not be the only reference of coordination. The proficient pilot will anticipate when rudder is needed and feel when enough rudder is applied.

The commercial flight test maneuvers are not stall maneuvers, but they do involve airspeed control. The chandelle and lazy eight involve wide airspeed swings that must be properly managed. Stall awareness should go beyond maneuvers where a deliberate stall is desired because in real flying, a stall is never desired.

PART 3

Aerodynamics

13
Why it stalls

"ALLRIGHT NOW, RAISE THE NOSE JUST A LITTLE MORE." A FLIGHT instructor is watching a student perform a stall for the first time. "There, you can feel the airplane buffet now. Just a little more back pressure." When the wings stall, the nose pitches down through the horizon. "OK, there it is, now recover."

Flight students are taught that a full stall occurs when the nose falls through, automatically reducing the angle of attack. But is this a true stall? As it turns out, two more definitions of stall are important. To a pilot, a stall is when the nose falls through, but to an aeronautical engineer a stall is the top of the coefficient of lift curve. Both involve raising the nose, but a pilot's stall happens before an engineer's stall. This is due to a built-in airplane design feature that is supposed to keep pilots out of trouble.

Wings do not produce the same amount of lift in every situation. Four main factors come together to produce a lifting force: velocity, wing surface area, air density, and coefficient of lift. Variations in any of the factors will change the amount of lift that is produced.

BACK TO BERNOULLI

The early dreamers of fixed-wing flight learned that curved wings worked better than flat wings. Without knowing it, these designers were putting to use the work of Daniel Bernoulli. Today, Bernoulli's Principle is the basic scientific law of flight. Bernoulli was born in 1700 and became a professor of mathematics like his father. He worked with fluids flowing through pipes to discover the principle of pressure changes. He calculated that the fluid in the pipes would have a lower pressure when the pipe was narrow and the water moving faster. Bernoulli died the year before the first balloon flight in 1783, so he could not have known that his discoveries would open the way to manned flight. But an airfoil is a device that utilizes Bernoulli's calculations.

In many ways, gases, like our atmosphere, act like the water in the pipe; if the air moves fast, the pressure of the air is low; when the air slows down, the pressure increases. This trade-off is due to the conservation of energy idea that says the energy cannot be created or destroyed, it can only be altered. An airfoil produces lift by altering the pressure of the air as it flows over its upper surface. The pressure cannot be changed directly, but the speed of the air can be changed by the shape of the airfoil.

If two air molecules were parted by an oncoming airfoil, one molecule would be forced to flow over the wing and one under the wing (FIG. 13-1). The molecules go their separate ways at the airfoil's leading edge but will meet again at the trailing edge. The molecule on the upper side of the airfoil has a greater distance to travel due to the fact that the upper surface has a hump. The hump is called *camber*. If the two molecules were to meet up again on the airfoil's trailing edge the molecule on the upper camber would have to go faster in order to cover more distance in the same length of time. The accelerated airflow on the upper camber triggers the conservation of energy reaction. The necessary energy that causes the air to speed up must come from somewhere. That energy will come from the air itself.

Fig. 13-1. *Air molecule split up at the leading edge and reunited at the trailing edge.*

PRESSURE'S POTENTIAL

The air has pressure and pressure is a potential energy. Potential energy is a "pent up" force that is poised and ready for release. High pressure air trapped inside a balloon is a potential energy that will exert itself by throwing the balloon around the room if the balloon is released. The atmosphere's air molecules also have a pressure held in by the earth's gravity. This air pressure and its inherent potential energy is released to push the airflow over the camber to a greater speed. As a result, the air pressure decreases. A trade-off of energy takes place. Air velocity goes up and air pressure goes down.

Occasionally, I am asked by nonpilots if I ever worry that the airplane will not take off. This question springs from the idea that flying is some magical, invisible, and unnatural thing. Actually, the airplane must take off because science makes it take off. If you believe in gravity or sunlight or wind, then you already believe in flight. Flight is natural. Flight follows all the physical science rules. Earth-shaking news would result if the airplane did not take off.

An airfoil tricks the air into giving up some of its pressure. If there is less pressure on the top of the wing than on the bottom, a net force is established in the direction from high to low. High air pressure under the wing pushes up from below while low pressure above the wing draws the wing up. This is the basic explanation. But lift is more complex and the actual results depend upon the four factors: velocity, wing surface area, air density, and coefficient of lift.

AIR FLOW VELOCITY

Velocity, then, is the first factor that determines how much lift will ultimately be produced. The faster an airplane moves through the ocean of air, the greater the acceleration that will result on the wings. The over-the-wing airflow will always be faster than the airplane itself in normal flight. This is clearly demonstrated on every airplane takeoff. When a pilot is instructed by a control tower to "taxi into position and hold" the airplane is positioned on the runway centerline, but does not begin the takeoff roll. At this moment, the only airflow over the wings is from whatever wind is present. The wind will pass over the wings and produce a lifting force, but hopefully the lifting force is not enough to offset the weight of the airplane. When an airplane is weighed to determine basic empty weight, it is placed in a hangar with the door closed to ensure that there will be no airflow that could cause the scale readings to be inaccurate.

When the controller issues the clearance, "Cleared for takeoff," the pilot adds power and the airplane moves forward. Throughout the takeoff roll acceleration, the wings are producing lift. When the lift produced equals the airplane's weight, flight is possible and this happens at rotation speed. The ability of the airplane to take off was dictated by the speed of the airflow's velocity.

WING SURFACE AREA

The lift reaction takes place all over the wing; therefore, the more wing, the greater the lift. Airplane designers struggle with how much wing surface area should be used on a particular airplane. Theoretically, the larger the wing, the better; practically, a big wing is heavy and hard to support. The airplane's final wing area is a compromise between the science of lift and the engineering possibilities.

AIR DENSITY

Because the air is used to produce lift, the condition of the air will affect lift. We depend on air molecules to do the job, so the more molecules that are present, the better the job is done. The air density, or *density altitude*, is determined by three factors of its own: temperature, altitude, and humidity.

When the air is hot, the individual air molecules are energized by the heat, become "excited," and fly off in every direction. The air expands and a smaller population of air molecules is left behind. When a wing passes through this sparse population of molecules, there will be less lift because there are fewer molecules passing over the wing. This is why airplanes need more runway and climb slower in August than they do in January.

Lift diminishes as the airplane gets higher above sea level. Air pressure is sometimes hard to imagine because we live our lives without really noticing it. We do not feel the weight of the air because the pressure is inside and outside our bodies. One of the best ways to think about air pressure is to relate it to water pressure. The deeper in the water a swimmer dives, the more pressure is felt due to the weight of the water above; a swimmer in a pool will detect more pressure while sitting on the bottom of the deep end than the shallow end.

Deep or shallow?

An airplane taking off from a sea level airport is in the "deep end of the pool." At sea level, there is more air above the airplane than would be the case if the takeoff was made at 3,000 feet. Gravity pulls the air molecules down and squeezes them at sea level; therefore, the population of air molecules will be much greater the deeper into the atmosphere the airplane goes. When the molecule population (density) is greater, the lift reaction as the air passes over the wings will be greater. Airplanes need more runway and will climb slower taking off from Albuquerque than when taking off from Baltimore. Albuquerque is in the shallow end of the atmosphere (closer to the top of atmosphere), while Baltimore is in the deep end.

Not only the number of air molecules affects lift, but the weight of the molecules involved affects lift. We associate humidity with water and water is heavier than air, so it is tough to understand that a high humidity is bad for airplane performance. The problem is that humidity deals with water in the gas state not the liquid state. Water in the gas state is called *water vapor* and it is always invisible. Steam, fog, and clouds are actually water in the liquid state, but the droplets are too small and light to fall through the atmosphere. Recall from chemistry studies that molecules have weight. The water vapor molecule made up of two hydrogen atoms and one oxygen atom (H_2O) is a lightweight molecule.

The dry air is made up of many other molecules, but mainly nitrogen. The average air molecule is heavier than the water vapor molecule. If the relative humidity is high, this means that heavy molecules have been replaced by lighter water vapor molecules. When an airfoil passes through this atmosphere, there will be a great number of lightweight molecules triggering the trade-off of energy. Lightweight molecules produce a lightweight lift reaction. Airplanes will need more runway and climb slower when the relative humidity is 95 percent than when it is 35 percent.

A takeoff in August from Albuquerque with 95 percent humidity will greatly reduce the wing's ability to produce lift equal to the airplane weight. A takeoff might not even be possible with all the factors working against the pilot. A January takeoff from Baltimore with 35 percent humidity will cause the airplane to leap off the runway and climb like a rocket in comparison.

COEFFICIENT OF LIFT

Velocity is easy to understand. Wing surface can be seen with our eyes. Air density is natural when you think about it. But what is coefficient of lift? The *coefficient of lift* (C_L) is a measure of how well the wings are accelerating the airflow. This factor is determined two ways: airfoil shape and angle of attack.

The airfoil shape causes the initial reaction that triggers lift; if the airfoil has a larger camber, the distance between the leading and trailing edge will be longer. Air molecules flowing over the long camber must accelerate faster to make the trip. The distance is reduced when the camber is smaller (FIG. 13-2A and 13-2B). Anytime the distance is great and the acceleration is fast, a greater effect on lift is produced: *co-*

Fig. 13-2A

Fig. 13-2B. *Thick and thin airfoil cambers.*

efficient of lift. Given the same air velocities, a fat camber airfoil will produce greater C_L than a thin wing. The camber of the wing can be altered by the pilot. Extending the flaps extends the upper surface. This forces upper camber molecules to travel even farther to the trailing edge and therefore even faster. Ailerons do the same thing. In a left turn, the right aileron deflects down, increasing the camber of that part of the wing. That part of the wing is now producing more C_L and therefore more lift so the right wing rises and the airplane turns. All high-lift devices and control surfaces alter the coefficient of lift.

The second determinant of C_L is the angle of attack. The angle of attack is the angle between the airfoil's chord line and the relative wind (FIG. 13-3). The chord line always runs from the leading edge to the trailing edge and the relative wind is opposite the direction of travel. The relative wind has very little to do with the atmospheric wind. If the airplane is traveling south, the relative wind will be north even if the FSS reports winds from the west. If the airplane is diving straight down, then relative wind is straight up. At a low angle of attack, the air molecules go their separate ways on or near the leading edge (FIG. 13-4).

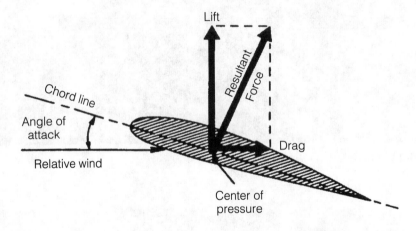

Fig. 13-3

But when the nose of the airplane is raised, the chord line is also raised. This will cause the angle of attack to increase. The relative wind molecules now split up lower on the wing, rather than on the leading edge. The molecules that go over the top now must pass over the leading edge before traveling across the upper camber. This extra distance of travel will cause the molecules to accelerate even faster to reach the trailing edge. Faster airflow has a greater effect in producing lift. C_L increases with an increase in angle of attack, as long as the airflow remains smooth over the upper camber.

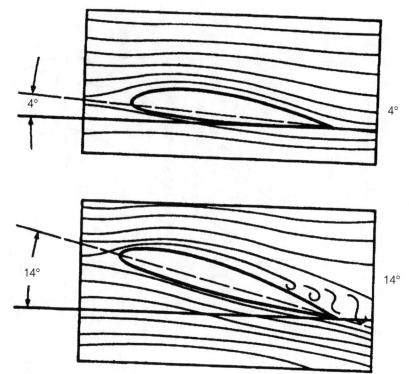

Fig. 13-4

Coefficient curve

The changing coefficient of lift for a particular airfoil can be plotted on a graph called a C_L curve (FIG. 13-5). The horizontal axis of the graph indicates angles of attack; the vertical axis indicates coefficient of lift. The C_L curve slopes upward as the angles increase. The higher the C_L, the faster the airflow over the upper camber. But all good things must come to an end. Eventually, the angle of attack is so high that the air cannot hold the turn. The air then spills over the upper camber and this destroys the pressure differential that was producing lift. The angle that causes the airflow to spill over for the first time is the critical angle of attack.

The actual air molecules are not visible, but if the air is filled with smoke, the direction of the molecules can be seen. Figure 13-6A is a typical airfoil shape in a smoke tunnel. The angle is less than the critical angle of attack because the upper camber airflow is smooth and follows the contour of the airfoil. The critical angle has been exceeded in FIG. 13-6B and it is clear that the airflow on the upper camber is disrupted. Smooth fast airflow yields lift; turbulent airflow destroys lift. The greatest C_L without turbulent airflow is the maximum coefficient of lift, or C_L max. Beyond C_L max, the

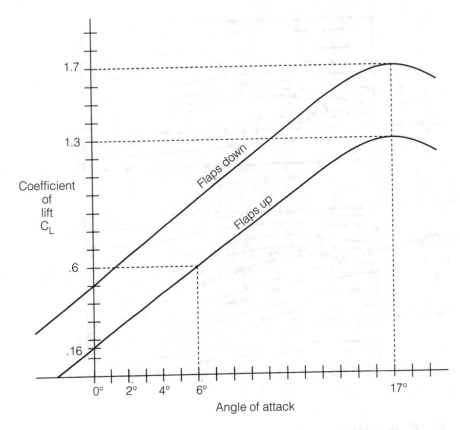

Fig. 13-5. *Coefficient of lift curve.*

lift is diminishing rapidly. The C_L curve climbs to its highest point and then "stalls" out. This is where the term stall originated.

LIFT CALCULATION

Lift can be calculated by considering all the factors that produce lift. Daniel Bernoulli's pressure principle can be updated and applied to aviation. So far, no mathematics has been needed to prove how lift is produced and what changes the force. But it is important to understand how real numbers effect real airplanes. The updated Bernoulli's equation scares most people off because it is long and has stuff in it that is not familiar. But there is nothing new here, just the four factors of velocity, wing surface area, air density, and coefficient of lift (FIG. 13-7A).

Velocity is V; wing surface area is S; air density is represented by the Greek letter Rho; and coefficient of lift is C_L. The answer to the equation comes out in pounds if the proper units are put in the equation. Getting an answer in pounds is easy to associate

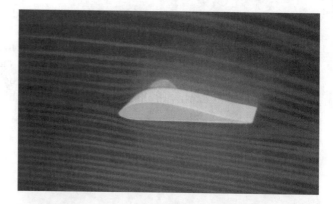

Fig. 13-6A. *Smoke tunnel reveals the airflow around the airfoil. This airfoil's angle of attack is less than the critical angle.*

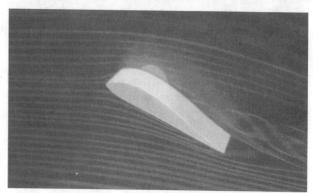

Fig. 13-6B. *The airfoil is inclined past the critical angle of attack and the smoke makes the stall and vortex easy to see.*

because we also calculate the airplane's weight in pounds. The answer from the equation must meet and exceed the weight of the airplane for flight to be possible.

The units that are used in the equation are not as easy to associate because we do not use them everyday. Instead of miles per hour or knots, the velocity in the equation must be in feet per second. The conversion factors for the speeds are:

Miles per hour × 1.468 = feet per second
Knots per hour × 1.693 = feet per second

The wing surface area in the equation is given in square feet. The exact surface area can be found in an airplane's operator handbook. It would be a simple matter to multiply the wing span by the chord length to find the surface area of a rectangular wing, but be careful because most rectangular wings are not exact rectangles. Wing

$$L = C_L \tfrac{1}{2} \rho V^2 S$$

Fig. 13-7A

115

surfaces for wings with tapered, elliptical, or sweptback wings would require some fancy geometry to determine. Consult the handbook for the real numbers.

Perhaps air density has the strangest of all measurement units; air is measured in *slugs*. A slug is a density measure of air molecules in a cubic foot of air. In the equation, the Greek letter Rho (pronounced row) is used to designate the air density (FIG. 13-7B). Standard air density in slugs is 0.00238.

$$\rho$$ **Fig. 13-7B**

The final determinant is coefficient of lift. The C_L number has no units, it is simply a multiplier that influences the rest of the equation just as camber and angle of attack influence the airflow. This multiplier is taken from the C_L curve and is the curve based upon flight testing and wind tunnel testing.

Let's bring the equation out of the math books and onto a real runway. Using the C_L curve from FIG. 13-5, we will attempt to take off in an airplane under the following conditions:

- Airplane weight 1,600 pounds
- Wing surface area 160 square feet
- Air density standard 0.00238 slug per cubic foot
- No wind and wing flaps up

The pilot rolls onto the runway and lines up with the centerline. In order for this airplane to leave the ground, the wings must offset the weight of the airplane; therefore, the first goal of the wings is to produce at least 1,600 pounds of lift during the takeoff roll. While the airplane is standing still, the lift equation is represented in FIG. 13-7C.

The 0.16 C_L comes directly from the C_L curve of FIG. 13-5. The wing will produce some small amount of lift coefficient at zero angle of attack due to the wing's *angle of*

$$L = C_L \tfrac{1}{2} \rho V^2 S$$

$$L = (.16)(.5)(.00238)(0^2)(160)$$

Fig. 13-7C

116

incidence and camber. The angle of incidence is the wing's built-in angle between the longitudinal axis (nose to tail) and the chord line. On FIG. 13-5, the flaps up curve at zero angle reflects a 0.16 C_L.

The problem now is that because the airplane is not moving, the velocity is zero and this is shown in the equation above. (Recall that anytime a zero appears anywhere inside a multiplication problem the answer will also be zero; therefore, the airplane is producing zero lift.)

The pilot adds full power to the engine and the airplane begins to roll forward. The airplane accelerates until 60 knots appears on the airspeed indicator. Freeze the takeoff here and analyze what has changed since the standing start. All the equation's variables, except velocity, remain the same (FIG. 13-7D).

$$L = (.16)(.5)(.00238)(101.58^2)(160)$$

Fig. 13-7D

Sixty knots is the same speed as 101.58 feet per second. To keep the units correct, this conversion is made and inserted into the equation. At this moment, the answer to the equation is 314.34 pounds of lift. The airplane still weighs 1,600 pounds, but the wings are only producing 314 pounds. The pilot will feel a lighter airplane "in the control wheel," but the airplane is not yet ready for flight.

In order to take off, the pilot has three options: allow the airplane to continue accelerating for a longer distance, raise the nose so that a greater coefficient of lift is produced, or a combination of additional acceleration and raising the nose. If the nose is not raised, the airplane will have to accelerate to a speed of 136 knots before enough lift is produced to offset 1,600 pounds; 136 knots on the runway is probably not even possible for this small airplane, even if there was enough runway to attempt it. Because the shape of certain airplane wings yields higher lift coefficients, certain airplanes can be "flown off the runway" without elevator back pressure; however, in this example, the pilot must increase the angle of attack to get in the air.

As the airplane accelerates down the runway, the wings are increasing lift production, plus other control surfaces are becoming more effective. While the airplane is standing still, elevator movement is superfluous; however as the airplane accelerates through 60 knots, the airflow across the elevator will cause a deflection of air and a chain reaction. When the control wheel is pulled back, the trailing edge of the elevator goes up. This causes the air on the underside of the elevator to travel around a greater camber and a "down" force results. The down force on the tail raises the nose and also the wings. This, in turn, increases the angle of attack, which increases the coefficient of lift.

The pilot rotates the airplane and acceleration continues. Now the airplane is traveling 70 knots and has a 6° angle of attack, which changes the lift equation (FIG. 13-7E).

$$\llcorner \;=\; (.6)(.5)(.00238)(118.51^2)(160)$$

Fig. 13-7E

Lift overcomes gravity

The C_L has increased to 0.6 using the C_L curve (FIG. 13-5). The velocity has increased to 70 knots, which is the same as 118.51 feet per second. Completing the multiplication, the lift produced is 1,604 pounds. At this moment, two important forces are acting on the airplane. One force with a magnitude of 1,600 pounds is pulling the airplane down. Another force with a magnitude of 1,604 pounds is pulling the airplane up. The greater force wins the battle and the airplane flies.

The moment that lift becomes more powerful than the airplane's weight, flight is possible. The actual location of lift-off depends upon all the variables. If the air density had only been 0.002 slug per cubic foot instead of 0.00238 slug, the amount of lift at 70 knots would have only been 1,348 pounds; a longer takeoff run that would allow a greater speed is now required for flight. A shorter takeoff run would result if the flaps were lowered, increasing the coefficient of lift, which would increase total lift in pounds. If the pilot used a flap setting that would produce a C_L of 0.82, instead of the 0.6 with no flaps, then the airplane would have produced enough lift for takeoff at only 60 knots. This is why most small airplane manufacturers recommend that flaps be used on a soft-field takeoff because flaps shorten the ground run, but flaps also add to total drag, so they might become a detriment during the climbout.

Variables

Ground effect can change the lift coefficient. Figure 13-8 displays an altered C_L curve when the airplane is flying low over the surface. This advantage to lift is a result of an altered downwash behind the wing and a reduced wingtip vortex. When the airplane is flying at a height above ground level that is vertically higher than the airplane's approximate wingspan, the air flowing off the upper airfoil camber deflects downward and away. But lower than a wingspan's altitude, the downwashing air collides with the ground and piles up. This backup of air changes the airflow around the wing and increases C_L. When the airplane is within ground effect, then the total lift is greater.

Pilots should take advantage of this on soft-field takeoffs. Controlling airspeed very accurately, the pilot can get into the air at a reduced airspeed because of increased lift coefficient. If the pilot then allows the airplane to accelerate to a speed that produces enough lift outside ground effect, a normal climb may follow. If the pilot gets anxious and tries to climb out of ground effect without enough speed, a stall could result. As the airplane climbs, the ground effect goes away and so does the lift coefficient advantage. Now the lift equation has a smaller C_L and the total lift might be lowered below the weight of the airplane. In this case, the airplane will return to earth.

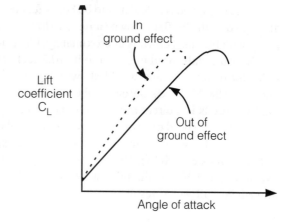

Fig. 13-8. *Ground effect alters the normal lift production.*

All these equations reflect the "engineer's" approach. We pilots certainly do not punch a calculator as we roll down the runway. But understanding the lift equation is important to pilots because it is the loss of lift that is such a threat to safety. The highest value of coefficient of lift is called C_{Lmax}. Any angle of attack greater than C_{Lmax} will produce a partial or complete loss of lift. The pilot is more used to associating stalls with certain airspeeds. The color coding of the airspeed indicator perpetuates this idea because the stall speeds clean and dirty are indicated by a speed value. But the co-efficient of lift curve does not associate a stall with a certain airspeed, instead a stall is associated with a certain angle of attack. The basic lift equation can be rearranged to help pilots understand how angles and speed go together. By solving for velocity in the lift equation at C_{Lmax} a stall speed can be obtained (FIG. 13-9A).

Using the same sample airplane as before, and the coefficient of lift curve from FIG. 13-5, the wings-level stall speeds can be computed. The C_L is different, depending upon whether or not the flaps are up or down. From the C_L curve, we can see that the greatest C_L or C_{Lmax} with the flaps up occurs at approximately 17° angle of attack. This angle yields a C_L of 1.3. Using the same airplane weight, air density, and wing surface, the new numbers can be plugged in (FIG. 13-9B).

Fig. 13-9A
$$V = \sqrt{\frac{2 \times \text{Weight}}{C_{Lmax}\, \rho\, S}}$$

Fig. 13-9B
$$V = \sqrt{\frac{(2)(1600)}{(1.3)(.00238)(160)}}$$

The stall speed is calculated to be 80.39 feet per second, 47.5 knots. If the stall was attempted with the flaps down, an even slower speed should result (from FIG. 13-5, $C_{L_{max}}$ with the flaps down is approximately 1.7) (FIG. 13-9C).

Now the stall speed turns out to be 70.3 feet per second, 41.5 knots. The airspeed indicator of this airplane would show a V_{S1}, the slow end of the green arc, at 47.5 knots, and the V_{SO}, the slow end of the white arc, at 41.5 knots. The difference between the two speeds is a direct result of the increased C_L. The increased C_L is the result of greater airflow speed over the wing when the camber is increased due to extending the flaps. Pilots flirt with this region "in between stall speeds" when flying minimum controllable airspeed (MCA). During the MCA maneuver, the speed should be held between V_{SO} and V_{S1}. If the pilot were holding MCA and then retracted the flaps, an immediate stall would result.

$$V = \sqrt{\frac{(2)(1600)}{(1.7)(.00238)(160)}}$$ Fig. 13-9C

STALL BY THE NUMBERS?

Even though the numbers in this example are hypothetical, they do reflect speeds common to small single-engine airplanes. Speeds of 47.5 and 41.5 seem very slow. Do airplanes actually stall by the numbers? Can math problems really predict real airplane behavior? To answer these questions, we must first decide on which definition of stall to go by. Recall the first of this chapter when two stall definitions were presented: engineer stall or pilot stall. The engineer stall goes exactly by the numbers, but the pilot stall is determined by the downward pitch of the nose and this should take place at a speed faster than the numbers predict. This is due to a design characteristic that many pilots do not really understand. When performing a stall, the nose will pitch down before the wing fully stalls due to a reduction in "tail down" force.

Most pilots never see the correlation between aerodynamics and weight and balance. Aerodynamics is thought of as a science and weight and balance as a calculation. All pilots are supposed to know how to determine the position of the center of gravity. When the CG is known, the pilot checks the CG position against a CG-range chart. We have been trained never to fly unless the airplane is within the proper CG range. But why is this so important? The answer must combine weight and balance with the science of aerodynamics.

As the air flows over the upper camber of the airfoil, lift is produced by acceleration. The air over the upper camber accelerates from the leading edge, reaching its fastest speed near where the wing is the thickest. Past this point, the airflow slows down gradually until the trailing edge. At every position along the chord line from leading to trailing edge, the airflow speed is different. This means that at every point, lift is different. Every point then makes its own contribution to total wing lift. The air-

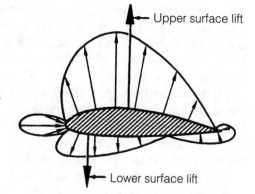

Fig. 13-10. *Airfoil pressure map.*

foil can be "mapped" to determine the lift at all points around the wing (FIG. 13-10). The small lift vectors from all around the wing can be added together to get one large resultant vector of lift. The resultant lift vector is the only arrow that is usually shown in diagrams such as FIG. 13-11.

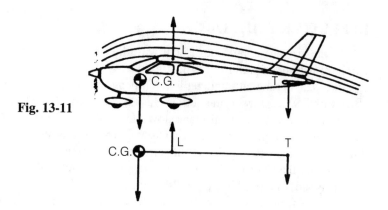

Fig. 13-11

The resultant lift vector is also called the *center of lift* or the *center of pressure*. In FIG. 13-11, the center of lift is placed between the center of gravity and the tail. The center of gravity is also a resultant of weight vectors throughout the airplane. This resultant vector points down to the center of the earth. The tail force vector is all that remains. The tail force is also down, not because of weight, because of air pressure. The tail is never referred to as the "rear wing." This is because the term wing is used to describe something that produces a force opposite the force of gravity; however, the tail force is down and is produced by setting the horizontal stabilizer's leading edge at a negative angle of attack. The lower part of FIG. 13-11 removes the airplane so we can see just the forces.

The one force lifting up (L) is opposed by two down forces (CG) and (T). The tail force (T) is much smaller than the center of gravity force (CG), but the tail force is placed at a greater distance. This greater distance acts as a lever to provide a balanced force against CG. The actual length of an airplane is dictated by how much lever is needed to offset the CG force. The length of an airplane's fuselage is not determined by what looks good, but rather by how much force is needed to hold the nose up. If all goes according to plan, the airplane will be in balance and all will be stable.

If the center of gravity is placed too far aft, the vector of CG will be too close to the center of lift; if this happens, the airplane's tail force will not be in proper balance. This has grave consequences during stalls. If the CG is aft of the safe CG range and the airplane stalls, there will not be enough "nose down" force to lower the angle of attack. This means a stall in an airplane with an aft center of gravity is unrecoverable. This is not to say that if you take off with an aft CG that a stall will automatically happen, but if a stall does occur, the pilot will be helpless. This is basic physics, so read this carefully.

Some pilots might believe that if an aft CG stall occurs, their superior flying skills will allow them to recover one way or another, but they are wrong. It is against the laws of physics to live through an aft CG stall. This should wake up every pilot to the importance of accurate weight and balance calculations. You should determine CG location as if your life depended upon it because it really does.

EFFECTIVE TAIL FORCE

As the airplane approaches a stall with the CG in the proper range, the tail force will be effective. The tail force is not produced by actual weight, but by the force of air pressure. The horizontal stabilizer is actually an "upside down" wing that pulls the tail down with low pressure on the bottom. Just like any airfoil, the faster the airflow is, the greater the force. When the airplane slows down, the tail force is reduced. The force of CG all this time remains the same, so as the airplane gets slower, the tail has a harder time keeping the nose up. When the airflow is so reduced that the tail force can no longer offset the CG force, the nose of the airplane pitches down. This pitch down at extremely slow airspeed is the pilot's definition of stall.

Air flow from off of the wings also affects the tail force. As seen in FIG. 13-11, the downwash from the wings lands on the horizontal stabilizer adding to the tail-down force. When the airflow slows down over the wings, the downwash is reduced and therefore the tail force is reduced. Eventually, the reduced tail force cannot support the nose and the nose "falls through."

As the airplane approaches the stall speed, by raising the nose, the coefficient of lift is getting greater. At the same time, the airflow is diminishing and the tail force is diminishing. As the speed continues to diminish, the C_L gets larger and the tail force gets smaller. The airplane is now on the brink of stall, but the C_{Lmax} has not yet been reached. The angle of attack where the C_L curve "stalls" has not been reached. Then, just before C_{Lmax} is achieved, the tail force gives out. The CG force is no longer offset and because the CG is forward of the center of lift, the nose pitches down. This is when the flight instructor says, "OK, there it is, now recover." However, in reality, the wing was not allowed to completely stall based upon the engineer's definition of the word.

When the nose pitches down, the angle of attack is reduced. The airflow over the wing again follows the contour of the upper camber and the stall, by any definition, is broken. The design of airplanes that provide the tail force is very antistall. Airplanes were not always designed to be antistall, but today's airplanes are the beneficiary of much trial and error. Today's airplanes practically recover from stalls themselves. All the pilot must do is avoid aggravating the situation and making sure the center of gravity is within range.

14
The boundary layer and the golf ball

A FULL STALL OCCURS WHEN THE AIRFLOW ON THE AIRFOIL'S UPPER camber departs the airfoil's contour. When the angle of attack is so steep that the airflow cannot remain smooth, the air spills over the wing and this destroys the low pressure that causes lift. The airflow separates from the camber and the result is high pressure on both the top and bottom of the wing (FIG. 14-1). Without a pressure difference, the wing quits producing lift and causes aerodynamic stall. The angle of attack and location along the wing, where the airflow separates, then is critical to the development of a stall. The position where separation takes place is inside the boundary layer.

As air passes over any object, there is friction between the air molecules and the molecules of the object. If you were able to see a microscopic view of the airflow against the airfoil, you would see the lowest layer of air is stagnant. The molecules of the airfoil retard the molecules of air so that the air does not flow when in direct contact with the surface of the airfoil. This means that a very thin layer of motionless air always surrounds the wing and travels with the wing.

This concept is hard to believe because it cannot be seen, but the effects of boundary layer can be seen. If a cylinder is placed in an airflow, the air molecules will strike the cylinder's leading edge and separate. Some molecules will go over the top of the cylinder and some will go under the bottom. The distance over the top and the distance under the bottom to the trailing edge is the same (FIG. 14-2). The airflow will speed up to go over or under the cylinder but no net lift is produced because the air acceleration will be the same on top and bottom. But a net lift can be achieved by rotating the cylinder in the direction "over the top."

Fig. 14-1. *Stalled airflow.*

Cylinder without circulation

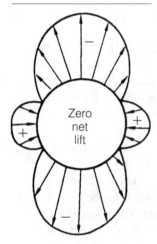

Fig. 14-2. *A stationary cylinder placed in an airflow produces no net lift.*

"OVER AND UNDER" LIFT

Lift is produced due to the existence of the boundary layer. As the cylinder rotates, it carries the boundary layer with it. Over the top of the cylinder, the boundary layer is moving with the "over the top" airflow (FIG. 14-3A). On the bottom, the boundary layer is traveling against the "under the bottom" airflow. This makes the total airflow over the top faster than the retarded airflow under the bottom. Anytime air flows faster, the pressure drops and lift is the result. This lift due to rotation is *Magnus effect*, and also explains why a baseball pitcher can throw a curveball. The pitcher throws the ball with great rotation. The boundary layer around the baseball will cause an increased flow on one side and a retarded flow on the other side. The resulting low pressure on the ac-

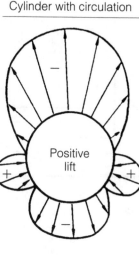

Cylinder with circulation

Positive lift

Magnus effect by
rotating cylinder

Fig. 14-3A. *A rotating cylinder placed in an airflow produces a lifting force due to boundary layer.*

celerated side will pull the ball out of its straight line of flight. The batter, swinging as if the ball flew straight, misses the ball when it veers off line. Major league pitchers make millions of dollars because of boundary layer.

Should airplanes now be outfitted with rotating cylinders rather than wings? No, because the lift produced is extremely inefficient in comparison with standard airfoils. But lift is produced on the cylinder, and curveballs do curve, so the existence of the boundary layer is proven.

LAMINAR AND TURBULENT LAYERS

It is inside the boundary layer that flow separation and stall starts. Boundary layers come in two types, laminar and turbulent, and each type has a different effect on stall. The laminar boundary layer contains a smooth flow of air. The molecules fly in perfect formation as they flow without crossing each other's wake. The turbulent boundary layer, as the name implies, causes individual air molecules to move haphazardly. The molecules churn like water flowing over rocks in a brook.

Now think small. The molecules of air that directly contact the molecules of the upper camber of a wing are stagnant. The friction between these molecules stops the flow altogether. The next layer of air molecules above the stagnate layer has less friction and therefore is allowed to move. The next layer up has even less friction and will move even faster. Layer after layer, the speed increases until the airflow is unaffected by the friction of the surface. The airflow at this layer, and above, is outside the boundary layer.

By analyzing the speed of each layer, a velocity profile can be drawn for airflow inside the boundary layer. The horizontal arrows in FIG. 14-3B get progressively longer as the distance from the surface increases. The arrows represent the molecules' velocity.

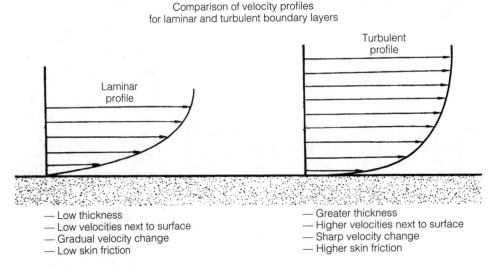

Comparison of velocity profiles
for laminar and turbulent boundary layers

Turbulent
profile

Laminar
profile

— Low thickness
— Low velocities next to surface
— Gradual velocity change
— Low skin friction

— Greater thickness
— Higher velocities next to surface
— Sharp velocity change
— Higher skin friction

Fig. 14-3B. *Boundary layer profiles.*

The longer the arrow, the faster the molecule is moving. If the airflow inside the boundary layer is laminar, the thickness of the boundary layer is reduced. This is good because it reduces the skin friction drag that occurs over the wing. But the molecule speeds are very slow close to the surface. This slow speed will increase the possibility of separation and stall. So, a laminar boundary layer is good for drag, but bad for stall characteristics (FIG. 14-4).

Inside a turbulent boundary layer, the molecules are randomly changing elevations relative to the surface of the wing. As the molecules change from one layer to another, an energy exchange takes place. This makes the turbulent boundary layer thicker and faster. The molecules lower in the boundary layer are moving faster. This means that the turbulent layer as a whole has a greater *kinetic energy*. Kinetic energy is the energy an object has due to its motion. The greater the motion the air molecules have in the boundary layer, the better chance they will have of avoiding separation from the upper camber, which might cause a stall.

As air strikes an airfoil's leading edge and flows over the wing, the air molecules speed up and drop in pressure. This change in pressure is a *pressure gradient*. Anytime the airflow is increasing in speed, the gradient is positive, but when the air slows down, its pressure will start to rise and form an *adverse pressure gradient*. An adverse gradient forms along a wing's upper camber, usually starting from the wing's thickest point and then back to the trailing edge. In this area, the adverse gradient will retard the flow of air in the boundary layer. If the adverse gradient is strong, the boundary layer airflow can be halted and even reversed. If the flow reverses and moves toward the leading edge, airflow above the boundary layer will separate from the airfoil and stall occurs.

A stall then is initiated by flow separation which is triggered in the boundary layer. Two forces oppose each other in the boundary layer: kinetic energy and ad-

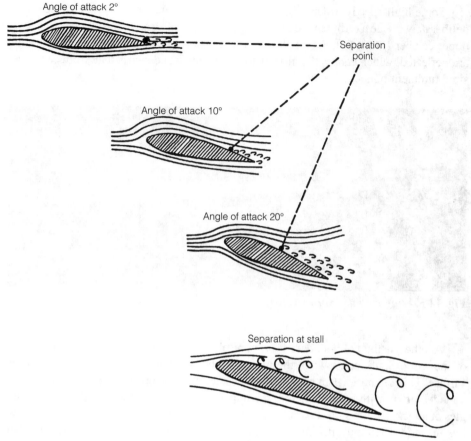

Fig. 14-4. *Attached airflow at low angles of attack and separated flow at high angles.*

verse pressure gradient. If kinetic energy (airflow) is stronger, the molecules in the mid and upper levels of the boundary layer will continue to follow the curvature of the wing all the way to the trailing edge, which is good because the low pressure produced by flowing air is spread out over the entire chord line. In turn, this yields greater total lift. If the adverse pressure gradient is strong, the molecules in the boundary layer will stop flowing and turn around. This breaks up the upper camber's smooth airflow and destroys lift.

BOUNDARY LAYER MANIPULATION

Kinetic energy is favorable in the boundary layer to prevent or put off stall. A turbulent boundary layer has more kinetic energy than a laminar layer. So, even though a turbulent layer causes more skin friction, it also tends to keep the flow on the wing surface longer and a stall occurs later. This makes the critical angle of attack higher and the stall speed lower.

129

Some high-speed airplanes use *vortex generators*, which are strips of metal that deliberately create a turbulent boundary layer. The metal strips stand up on the airfoil's upper camber (FIG. 14-5). As air flows past, the molecules strike the metal strips and are deflected, which causes the airflow to form eddies and swirls that produce the desired turbulent boundary layer.

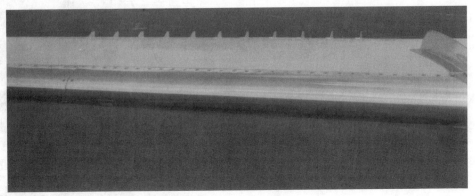

Fig. 14-5. *Wing-mounted vortex generators.*

Another method of boundary layer control is to suck the boundary layer off the top of the wing. Stall occurs when the upper camber boundary layer separates from the surface. This separation can be delayed by vacuuming the upper camber. Figure 14-6 is a model airfoil with holes drilled in the upper camber. When the airfoil is at high angles of attack and the stall separation is about to occur, the vacuum is turned on, drawing air into the wing itself. This keeps the flow attached until an even greater angle of attack. Vacuum pumps in small airplanes, however, simply are not practical. The extra weight of the suction device would overshadow any stall advantages. The method has been used successfully on some military aircraft.

Frost: kinetic killer

If frost is present on the wing it will help slow down the boundary layer and promote early separation. Frost does not weigh much, so additional airplane weight is not the reason frost should be removed from an airfoil before flight. The real reason is that frost produces a very rough surface for the air to pass over. This increases the skin friction drag and kills kinetic energy in the boundary layer. With less airflow energy the molecules will separate sooner and stall will take place at a faster speed. Never take off with any accumulation of frost on the wings.

FLYING GOLF BALLS

The airflow separation from the wing surface is the physical reason that an airplane stalls, but there is another adverse effect: drag. Here is where the golf ball comes

Fig. 14-6. *Airfoil designed to draw off the boundary layer by suction of air through rows of holes along upper camber.*

in. Why are golf balls made with a dimpled surface instead of a smooth surface? What does this have to do with flight dynamics? When a golf ball is hit into the air, the greatest pressure on the ball is on the exact leading edge. This air pressure in front of the ball will prevent the ball from flying as far as would be the case with no air pressure. The differential pressure on the ball increases if the pressure behind the ball decreases.

The airflow behind the ball is mainly a separated and erratic airflow. This erratic airflow is moving quickly, causing the pressure to drop. If any object in flight has a high pressure on its leading edge and a low pressure on the trailing edge, the object will slow down, and in the case of the golf ball, it will fall to earth sooner: *pressure drag due to separation.* This drag can be reduced if the airflow maintains the contour of the ball longer. We now know that a high kinetic energy boundary layer will allow airflow to remain attached longer.

So, a golf ball, in order to stay in the air longer, needs a turbulent boundary layer. The golf ball manufacturer then forms the surface of the ball to produce the turbulent layer with a pattern of dimples (FIG. 14-7). A golf ball without dimples would have a greater pressure drag and therefore less distance. An airplane wing acts the same way. When the airflow is attached to the upper camber, not only is lift created, but pressure drag is decreased. An airfoil in a stall loses lift and increases drag.

Fig. 14-7.

15
Wing planform and stall

TO THIS POINT, AIRFLOWS HAVE ONLY BEEN DISCUSSED IN TWO DIMENSIONS, but real airplanes have three dimensions. Rather than looking at airfoils in cross-section only, we must look at the entire wing. *Planform* is the wing's shape when looked at from above. There are many variations in wing shapes: rectangular, tapered, pointed, and sweptback. Each shape must balance drag effects with stall characteristics.

Several types of drag can be identified on an airplane. The types of drag are divided into two categories: parasite and induced.

PARASITE DRAG

Parasite drag is subdivided into skin friction, form drag, and interference drag (FIG. 15-1).

Skin friction is the parallel retarding force that exists between air molecules and an airplane's surface. Recall that the boundary layer is the retarding force of skin friction.

Form drag is the retarding force that is perpendicular to a surface. Airplanes and even cars are designed to cut down the form drag by streamlining the frontal cross section of the vehicle. The advantage of retractable landing gear is to reduce the surface area presented to the relative wind, which reduces form drag.

Interference drag is the retarding force that exists when air gets caught in pockets and piles up. If air travels into an area and cannot get out, the molecules will begin to

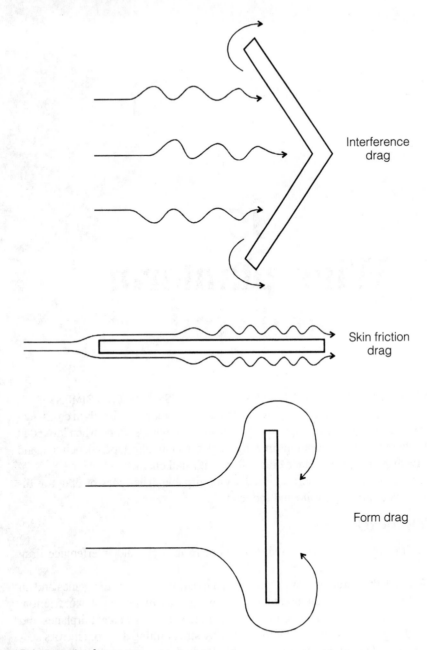

Interference drag

Skin friction drag

Form drag

Fig. 15-1. *Parasite drag types.*

stack up. There are areas around an airplane where this might happen; where the wing meets the fuselage might cup air. Designers fill in these corners with plastic fillets to smooth the airflow. Interference drag makes the airspeed indicator work; air is allowed to flow down a tube and up against a diaphragm; the more air that piles up, the greater the air will push the diaphragm: the greater the push, the higher the indicated speed.

Parasite demonstrations

These three types of drag can easily be demonstrated. While riding in a car or driving on a road with light traffic or no traffic, roll the car window down and hold your hand out into the airflow [clearing turns are unnecessary, but remember that safe driving comes first and the drag demonstration comes second]. Turn your palm down parallel with the ground. You will feel the force of the air trying to push your hand rearward. This is skin friction. Now turn your hand so the air hits straight against your palm. The airflow is now perpendicular to your palm, which has a greater surface area than the edge. Now you will feel a great increase in drag as the air pushes your hand back. This is form drag. Finally, cup your hand forward so that the air is scooped by the palm. Air now has a tough time escaping your grasp and the drag increases even more. This is interference drag.

INDUCED DRAG

Induced drag is a by-product of lift. When lift is generated, an unwanted but unavoidable side effect is also produced that impedes the airplane. The resultant lift vector acts perpendicular to the relative wind. But the production of lift alters the relative wind. Figure 15-2 illustrates how the relative wind's direction is changed by deflection under the wing. The "local relative wind" produces a smaller angle of attack. This changing of the relative wind is also influenced by the "downwash field" that occurs behind the wing. The downwash field is produced by the unequally pressurized air from above and below the wing joining at the trailing edge and by "wingtip vortex." Downwash and the wingtip vortex are both influenced by the wing's planform.

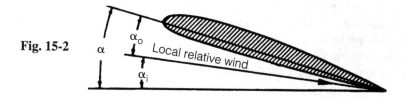

Fig. 15-2

As the local relative wind changes, the perpendicular lift vector also changes. Figure 15-3 depicts the lift vector tilting as the relative wind changes. Lift and relative

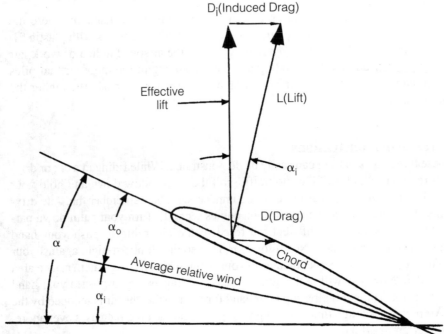

Fig. 15-3. *Induced drag vectors.*

wind are always 90° to each other, so, as the relative wind inclines, the lift vector moves back. When the lift vector leans over, it is separated into components. The "up" portion of the vector is lift. The "back" portion of the vector is induced drag.

When the airfoil produces more lift by increasing angle of attack or changing the airfoil's camber, it will cause more downwash and deflection of the local relative wind. This bends the lift vector back even farther because of greater induced drag. The induced drag can be felt in flight. Without using rudder, turn the airplane to the left. As the control wheel is moving left, the right aileron is moving down. This increases the camber on the right side and accelerates the airflow even faster. The faster airflow produces a greater downwash behind the right wing and this changes the local relative wind. In turn, the inclining local relative wind pushes the lift vector rearward with an increase in induced drag. At this moment, the right wing is producing more lift, but also more drag, than the left wing. This extra drag will hold the right wing back. As the left turn begins, the airplane will momentarily yaw to the right as the right wing's induced drag is produced. This *adverse yaw* is directly related to the amount of induced drag produced.

DRAG REDUCTION

Airplane wing designers try to reduce induced drag with different wing planforms. Adverse side effects become less of a problem if the downwash field behind the wing is less. As we have seen, the production of lift depends upon creating differential pressures above and below the wing. The high pressure below the wing attempts to alleviate the low pressure above. The high pressure cannot relieve the pressure difference because the wing is in the way, similar to blocking high-pressure air inside a balloon from escaping. But out near the end of the wing, high pressure air sneaks around the wingtip to alleviate the pressure imbalance.

Figure 15-4 illustrates the high pressure on the bottom and the low pressure on the top of the wing as seen from behind. The high pressure air escapes the underside and around to the top of the wing. While this is happening, the airplane is moving forward; therefore, the resulting airflow around the wingtip turns into a horizontal whirlwind (FIG. 15-5). The air twists around and down behind the wings to produce the downwash field (FIG. 15-6). This downwash field triggers additional deflection of relative wind and consequently adds to induced drag.

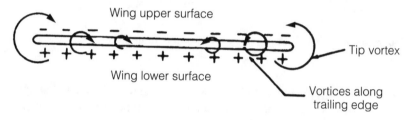

Fig. 15-4. *Wingtip vortex generation.*

One way for defusing the effect of the downwash field is to spread the wingtip vortices out from each other. The wing span must be lengthened. This way the left vortex and the right vortex will not meet in the middle and join forces. An indication of an airplane's vortex separation is the *aspect ratio*. The aspect ratio is a comparison of the wing's span to its average chord line. The higher the aspect ratio, the more

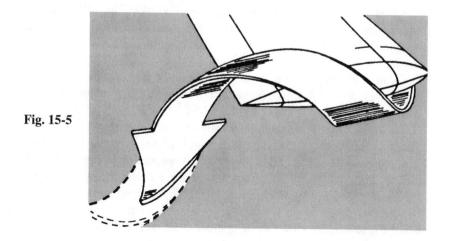

Fig. 15-5

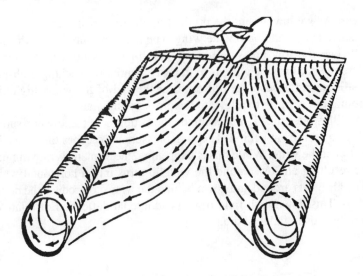

Fig. 15-6. *A downwash field develops between and behind the wings.*

space between wingtips and therefore less drag. High performance sailplanes can have aspect ratios as high as 35:1. Sailplanes have long and narrow wings designed for maximum lift and minimum drag.

The problem is that many wing planforms that are designed to reduce induced drag have very poor stall characteristics. This is just another aviation trade-off. What is gained from drag is lost in stall recovery control.

INCREMENTAL STALL

A better stall situation would be a wing that stalled gradually. The best situation would have that part of the wing with the ailerons stalling last; ailerons would remain effective until the full stall. If the wing stalled at the root first and eventually the stall worked its way out to the tips, the pilot would have an earlier stall warning and better controllability.

If the air becomes stalled and turbulent at the wing root while the wingtip is still flying, the pilot will feel the onset of a stall. The turbulent airflow on the wing root and against the fuselage will shake and buffet the airplane. Hopefully, this buffet will warn the pilot of the imminent stall and a recovery will be made while the control surfaces are all working properly. If the stall progresses out to engulf the ailerons, the directional control in the stall and recovery will be passed on to the rudders. As the stalled airflow churns off of the wing root, it will move rearward toward the horizontal tail. This disrupted airflow will adversely affect the tail-down force, discussed earlier, and the nose will pitch down. The best-case scenario would have the nose pitching down solely due to wing root stall while ailerons were still effective.

Figure 15-7 illustrates the stall progression patterns of various wing planform types. The rectangular wing has a strong wingtip vortex and downwash field that increase drag, but the stall pattern gives favorable stall characteristics. Stall patterns that begin at the tips and work their way in toward the root would give the pilot very little warning of the approaching stall and no aileron effectiveness.

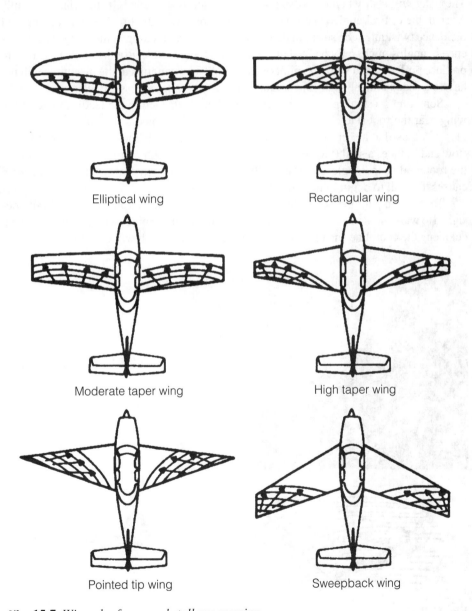

Fig. 15-7. *Wing planforms and stall progression.*

IMPROVED RECOGNITION

To produce favorable stall recognition and recovery characteristics, wing designers have had to be quite creative. The wings can be designed to influence the airflow to trigger the best situation. The most common design feature is *wash-out*. If the wingtips need to stall last, then twist the wing so that the wingtip angle of incidence is lower than the wing root. The wing will stall when its critical angle of attack is exceeded. If the wing is slightly twisted, the critical angle is approached at the root before the tip. The wingtip angle of incidence twist might be so small that it is hard to see by looking at the wing. The difference in angles might only be 3°, but even 3° difference will cause the stall at the root to produce buffeting and warn the pilot of a full stall. The wingtips in the meantime will not have exceeded critical angle and smooth airflow continues across the ailerons.

Sometimes a small piece of plastic or rubber is attached to the leading edge of the wing near the root (FIG. 15-8). The attachment is aptly named a *stall strip*. At high angles of attack that are close to the critical angle, the strip deliberately disrupts the airflow and induces a stall (FIG. 15-9). The stall occurs first behind the strip, which is near the root, and as the angle gets higher, the stall works its way toward the tip. The strip causes the stall to begin in the most favorable position.

To give the pilot the best chance of stall recognition, the airplane is specifically designed to warn the alert pilot. Boundary layer separation determines where the stall will occur along the chordline and planform determines where the stall will occur along the span.

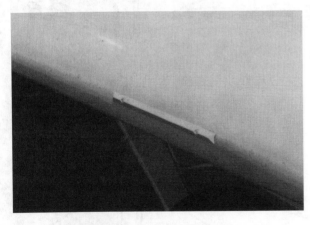

Fig. 15-8. *Stall strips induce the stall along the wing root.*

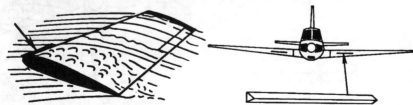

Fig. 15-9

16
High-lift devices

WHEN AN AIRPLANE MUST FLY SLOWLY, THE TOTAL LIFT IS REDUCED simply because the velocity of airflow is low. Remembering the lift equation, it is easy to see that with all other variables equal, a reduction in speed will greatly reduce the wing's ability to produce lift. But the airplane must have sufficient lift during takeoff and landing for safe flight. If speed is reduced, yet lift is to remain constant, one of the other variables must increase to make up the difference. The other variable in the lift equation that the pilot can control is coefficient of lift. At slow airspeed, the pilot must configure the airplane to produce adequate lift despite the low velocity. High-lift devices of all types attempt to maintain lift when airflow velocity alone is not fast enough. High-lift devices all have one thing in common: increase the airfoil's coefficient of lift (FIG. 16-1).

Air molecules that part company on the leading edge will reunite at the trailing edge. The molecules that flow over the top have a longer distance to travel, but the distance must be covered in the same amount of time as the lower camber molecules take to travel under the wing. Because they must go farther in the same elapsed time, they must go faster to arrive on time. The faster airspeed produces the lifting force. If the upper camber distance is extended, the molecules would really have to turn on the speed, resulting in greater lift. Additional speed over the airfoil that is not produced by the airplane's true airspeed (TAS) will show up in the lift equation as an increase in C_L.

$$L = C_L \tfrac{1}{2} \rho v^2 S \qquad \text{Fig. 16-1}$$

SLATS

Devices that increase C_L and consequently increase or maintain lift can be attached to either the leading or trailing edge of the airfoil. Leading edge devices are more commonly found on larger airplanes. The camber of the wing is increased when the leading edge moves out of its normal position and droops forward (FIG. 16-2). These *slats* are lowered when slow speeds are anticipated. On August 16, 1987, a DC-9 departing the Detroit Metropolitan Wayne County Airport crashed during a takeoff attempt. The National Transportation Safety Board determined that probable cause was "the flightcrew's failure to use the taxi checklist to ensure that the flaps and slats were extended for takeoff. Contributing to the accident was the absence of electrical power to the airplane takeoff warning system which thus did not warn the flightcrew that the airplane was not configured properly for takeoff." Without the flaps and leading edge slats deployed, the airplane simply was not able to produce adequate lift at its takeoff speed; 148 passengers and six crewmembers were killed because the coefficient of lift was too low.

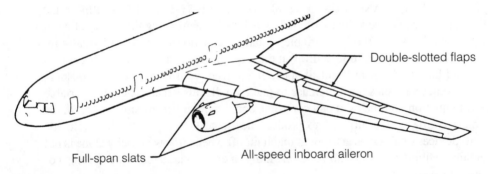

Double-slotted flaps

Full-span slats

All-speed inboard aileron

Fig. 16-2. *Leading edge high-lift devices.*

SLOTS

Another leading edge device that causes stall speed to be slower is fixed or automatic *slots*. A fixed slot can be cut into the leading edge of the airfoil camber. At high angles of attack, air on the underside of the wing flows up through the slot. This directs high energy airflow to the upper camber. This airflow aids the boundary layer in delaying the flow separation. The shape of the camber itself is not changed, but the stall is put off to a higher angle of attack and a slower airspeed. The slot in the wing offers no advantage at low angles of attack where the airflow does not travel through the slot. The slot might even cause additional drag as the air passes over the opening.

To solve this problem, "automatic" slots have been designed. At low angles of attack, a panel is held flush against the leading edge of the airfoil and the shape of the wing is unchanged. At high angles of attack, the upper camber experiences faster airflow and a lower pressure. This lower pressure draws the movable panel out on tracks, away from the leading edge. This forms a slot for the airflow to pass through. Slots may be placed along the entire span of the wing, or just at certain sections. Slots along the wing near the wing tips will produce a better high angle of attack airflow over the ailerons, and this prolongs aileron effectiveness.

TRAILING EDGE FLAPS

The devices more familiar to light airplane pilots are *trailing edge flaps*. Flaps increase total lift by changing the coefficient of lift at every angle of attack. The C_L curve in FIG. 16-3 displays the difference in coefficients with the flaps up (normal airflow) and the flaps down (accelerated airflow). Many flap types are employed on airplanes, each having slightly different characteristics (FIG. 16-4).

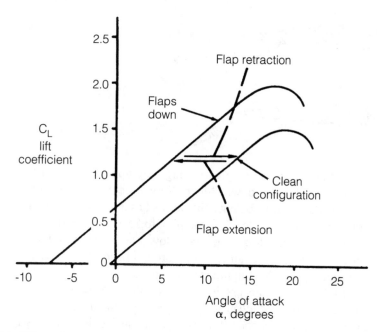

Fig. 16-3. *Effect of wing flaps on coefficient of lift.*

The plain flap is the simplest. A portion of the existing airfoil is hinged and allowed to drop into the airflow. With the plain flap extended, the upper camber distance becomes greater and this produces a large increase in C_{Lmax}.

The split flap is a plate that is held flush against the underside of the wing when not in use. The C_{Lmax} increase with the split flap down is only slightly greater than the

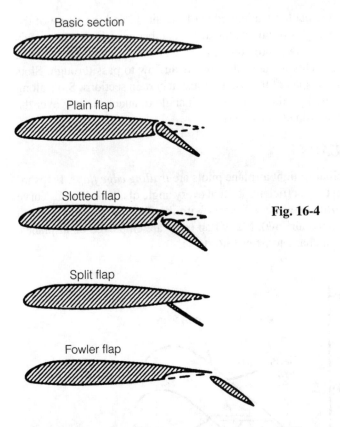

Basic section

Plain flap

Slotted flap

Fig. 16-4

Split flap

Fowler flap

plain flap, but the split flap causes greater drag. The upper camber of the airfoil remains unchanged with this flap down. Air spills over the trailing edge of both the upper camber and the flap. This turbulent spillover makes drag increase dramatically, but this might not be all bad. It would allow the pilot to keep engines running at a higher rpm while the extra split-flap drag keeps speed low. The higher rpm would reduce the power response time from the engine, if a go-around becomes necessary. This technique is best for jet engines that require spool-up time.

The slotted flap employs good science. This flap is hinged like a plain flap, but when the flap panel is lowered a gap is opened between the main airfoil and the flap. Air flowing along the lower camber of the wing is channeled through the gap and over the upper surface of the flap (FIG. 16-5). This extra airflow adds to the kinetic energy of the boundary layer on the flap's upper surface. This additional energy delays the flow separation to a higher angle of attack. As a result, the advantage to C_{Lmax} is greater for slotted flaps than either plain or split flaps.

The Fowler flap also ducts airflow to delay flow separation, and more. The entire flap panel moves aft along a track that lengthens the chord. The total wing surface area is also increased when the flap is extended. This additional surface area contributes to total lift mathematically by increasing the S in the lift equation. The Fowler flap pro-

Fig. 16-5. *High energy airflow passes from underneath the wing through the slot to the upper side of the flap.*

duces the greatest increase in C_{Lmax}. Figure 16-6 compares the flap types and their individual effect on the coefficient of lift curve.

Flaps can provide help during takeoff and landing. First, they may be used on takeoff to shorten the takeoff roll. Second, because of higher coefficients, the landing speed with flaps down may be slower; this allows the airplane to use shorter runways. Third, a steep approach may be made without increasing speed, as would be the case in a dive; this makes approaches over obstructions easier and safer. The last two jobs rely on another characteristic product of flaps and that is drag.

FLAP DRAG

Total drag can be calculated just as total lift. The math used is the same variation on Bernoulli's equation with one exception; rather than plugging in a coefficient of lift, a coefficient of drag is used (FIG. 16-7).

The C_D used in the equation is actually the sum of all the various drag types previously discussed. The total coefficient of skin friction, form drag, and interference drag gives coefficient of drag-parasite (C_{DP}). This is added to the coefficient of drag-induced (C_{DI}) to produce coefficient of drag-total (C_{DT}). C_{DT} is used to find total drag in pounds. Figure 16-8 defines the changing relationship between drag types that yield total drag.

Induced drag is an inescapable side effect of lift. It has now been established that flaps increase lift; therefore, flaps must also increase induced drag. Flaps also add to form drag because they extend down into airflow that goes untouched with the flaps up.

145

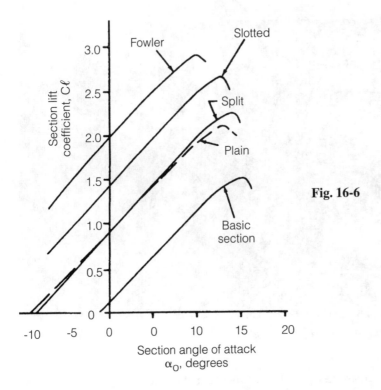

Fig. 16-6

Figure 16-9 illustrates the drag production of the various flap types. The curves shown are *drag polars*. A polar chart is a plot of coefficient of lift versus coefficient of drag. As the airplane's angle of attack is increased, the C_L increases, so you travel up the C_L side of the chart. The greater the C_L, the greater the corresponding C_D will become and the line bends away. The slotted and Fowler flaps offer low drag at low angles of attack but high drag when lift production is high. These flaps would provide the pilot with a slower, steadier approach speed and steeper glide angle.

The effect the flaps and other high-lift devices have on stall speed can be calculated by changing the variables in the stall equation. In chapter 13, the difference in speeds was illustrated by merely changing the C_{Lmax} max in the equation. The type of high-lift device that an airplane deploys will determine the degree of C_{Lmax} change and, therefore, the slower stall speed.

$$\boxed{D} = C_{D(total)} \; \tfrac{1}{2} \; \rho \; V^2 \; S \qquad \text{Fig. 16-7}$$

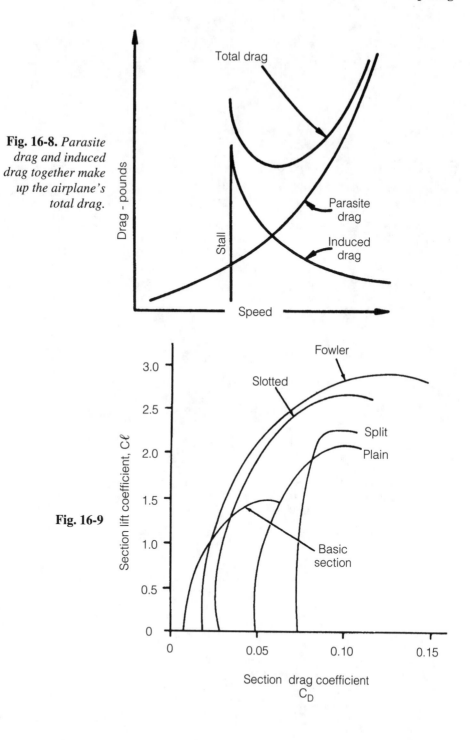

Fig. 16-8. *Parasite drag and induced drag together make up the airplane's total drag.*

Fig. 16-9

17
Pushing the outside of the envelope

THE STALL EQUATION WAS ALTERED IN CHAPTERS 13 AND 16 TO MODIFY lift. C_{Lmax} was changed to obtain different results, but the coefficient of lift is not the only variable in this equation that pilots must be concerned about. In the top part of the equation, the airplane's weight is multiplied by 2. This means that changes in weight will change stall speed drastically. In FIG. 13-5, the stall speed was calculated to be 47 knots when the airplane's weight was 1,600 pounds. What if the weight of the airplane had been a mere 100 pounds heavier, 1,700 pounds? (FIG. 17-1A)

Stall speed is now 83 feet per second, or 50 knots. Nothing else changed but the weight and a stall speed increase was the result. The color coding on the airspeed indicator only tells the truth when the airplane is operated at 1 G at maximum allowable gross weight. If the weight is higher or lower than gross weight, the stall speeds will be somewhat different than indicated by the slow end of both the green and white arcs.

When the airplane is heavy, more lift by the wings is required. More lift is provided with greater angle of attack, but this places the wing closer to the critical angle of attack. The critical angle will be reached while, at a faster speed, the airplane is heavily loaded.

LOAD FACTOR II

Chapter 9 discussed load factor, the "false weight" that the wings must overcome to remain in flight. Load factor is really a ratio of the load supported by the wings to the actual weight of the airplane. The weight that is supported, in addition to the airplane's actual weight, comes from other forces of flight. The most common of these

$$V = \sqrt{\frac{(2)(1700)}{(1.3)(.00238)(160)}}$$ **Fig. 17-1A**

forces is centrifugal force of a turn. Increased stall speed occurs anytime the actual weight increases or the load factor increases.

Figure 17-1B illustrates what effect a level coordinated turn has on the load factor. When the pilot makes a steep power turn of 60° bank, the load factor increases to 2 Gs. A 70° level turn would produce 3 Gs. During these turns, the wings are asked to produce sufficient lift to support the airplane's real weight, plus the extra turning effect of centrifugal force. The wings cannot tell the difference between gravity and centrifugal force. The wings just provide lift against all forces. But, of course, the wings have limitations. The "W" in the stall equation is the "effective" weight, not just the real weight. If the load factor goes up, the effective weight goes up and so does the stall speed.

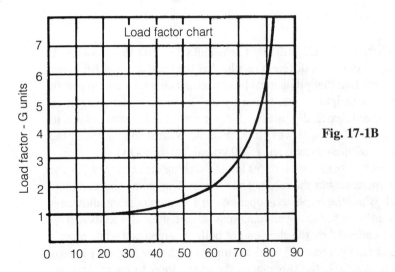

Fig. 17-1B

A pilot places an airplane in a level 60° turn. What effect does this have on stall speed? Assume the variables from previous examples are the same: C_{Lmax} 1.3, air density 0.00238, wing surface area 160 square feet. If the airplane's real weight is 1,600 pounds, the 60° 2-G turn will produce an effective weight of 3,200 pounds (1,600 × 2 = 3,200 pounds). Now look at the equation and the new stall speed (FIG. 17-2A).

The new stall speed is 113.7 feet per second, which is 67 knots. This is a 20-knot increase. Using the same equation, but solving the problem for a 70° 3-G turn, would cause the stall speed to skyrocket to 82 knots. Many small single-engine airplanes have a hard time doing 82 knots in cruise, yet that would still not be fast enough to avoid a stall under this condition.

$$\text{Fig. 17-2A} \quad V = \sqrt{\frac{(2)(3200)}{(1.3)(.00238)(160)}}$$

DESIGN MANEUVERING SPEED

A stall, even an accelerated stall, is not really dangerous to the structure of the airplane. When the airplane stalls, the lift disappears and the airplane is unable to produce load factor. The G force returns to 1 G. This means that a stall is the ultimate protector of the airplane. But is there a speed where a stall would not occur before damage to the airplane occurs? Yes, *design maneuvering speed*, designated V_A, the fastest speed in which an airplane can be safely stalled. If a stall is approached at a speed beyond V_A, the airplane might be damaged and even structural failure could occur before a stall intervenes and saves the airplane. Structural failure is the engineering term that really means "stuff tearing off the airplane." The maneuvering speed is vitally important to the pilot because it offers a sense of peace of mind. At a speed below V_A, the pilot can do just about anything stressful to the airplane and know that damage should not occur; however, those speeds below V_A do not give the pilot protection from a stall. In fact, the stall is the safety cushion that prevents a pilot who is flying below V_A from harming the airplane.

Maneuvering speed can be calculated using the same stall speed equation. The "W" in the equation must be the total effective weight that the airplane is built to handle. This amount occurs when the weight is multiplied by the airplane's greatest positive G allowance. Chapter 3 discusses the FAA's regulations regarding aircraft categories: normal, utility, and acrobatic; the calculation of V_A would be different for each category.

Using the same example as before, assume the airplane is certified as a utility category airplane. The greatest positive G loading allowed is 4.4. If the airplane weight remains 1,600 pounds and a force increased the effective weight by a factor of 4.4, the total weight the wings must support would be 7,040 pounds (1,600 × 4.4 = 7,040). Now plug in the new numbers into the stall equations (FIG. 17-2B).

$$\text{Fig. 17-2B} \quad V = \sqrt{\frac{(2)(7040)}{(1.3)(.00238)(160)}}$$

The stall speed with the force of 4.4 Gs, which is V_A in this case, would be 168 feet per second or 99.6 knots. Past this speed, any additional G-force will cause damage to the airplane. Any speed slower than 99.6 knots will produce a stall prior to stress damage. V_A simultaneously represents the greatest coefficient of lift and load factor that the airplane can handle. This speed/stress figure also determines the safety limit of a tight turn and how fast the rate of turn may be.

V-G DIAGRAM

The range of speeds and stress that any airplane can take is graphed on a V-G diagram. The V is for velocity and the G is for the G force. The safe zone has six boundary lines. The lines make up the "envelope" that the book *The Right Stuff* made famous. Figure 17-3 is a V-G diagram for our sample airplane from chapter 13. The slow end of the green arc (V_{S1}) which is the flaps up, 1 G stall speed is 47 knots. This boundary line extends from positive 1 G down to negative 1 G. This line represents a speed that is as slow as the airplane can fly without flaps or the slow end of the envelope. The fast end of the envelope is represented by the airplane's speed limitations.

The *never-exceed speed* (V_{NE}) is the fastest speed that the airplane can fly without damage. In this example, V_{NE} is 140 knots. This speed is indicated by a vertical line on the chart and with a red line on an airspeed indicator. The airplane stress loading goes up when flying in turbulent air. A second slower speed should not be exceeded when the ride is bumpy, the maximum structural cruise speed is designated V_{NO}. The yellow arc *caution range* on an airspeed indicator begins at V_{NO} and runs to the red line of V_{NE}. The green arc's slow end is V_{S1} and its fast end is V_{NO}, where the yellow arc begins.

Green arc: normal operating range, V_{S1} to V_{NO}
Yellow arc: caution range, V_{NO} to V_{NE}

These numbers define the extreme fast and slow speeds of the envelope and are graphed on the horizontal scale. Load factors that the airplane is stressed to handle are depicted on the vertical scale. The example is a utility category airplane. The top of the envelope is +4.4 Gs and the bottom of the envelope is –1.76 G.

The envelope is not a rectangle. The line between V_{S1} and V_A is a sloping line. This sloping line is the very line between flight and an accelerated stall. As discussed before, the stall speed increases with weight or load factor. The sloping line is simply a "schedule" of stall speeds at various load factors.

Flap envelope

Another envelope lies within the envelope: *flap envelope*. The slow end of this envelope is the stall speed in a *landing configuration* (flaps down), designated V_{SO}. The fast end of this envelope is the *maximum flap-extended speed*, designated V_{FE}. The distance between V_{SO} and V_{FE} is the *flap operating range* and is depicted on airspeed indicators as a white arc. The top and bottom of the flap envelope is determined by the load factor that is safe for the airplane with flaps down. This example depicts a safe flap stress region from 0 G to +3.5 Gs. The sloping line of the accelerated stall with flaps down actually crosses the flaps-up stall line because, with flaps down, more lift is produced and this extra lift will provide a slower stall speed even in an accelerated situation.

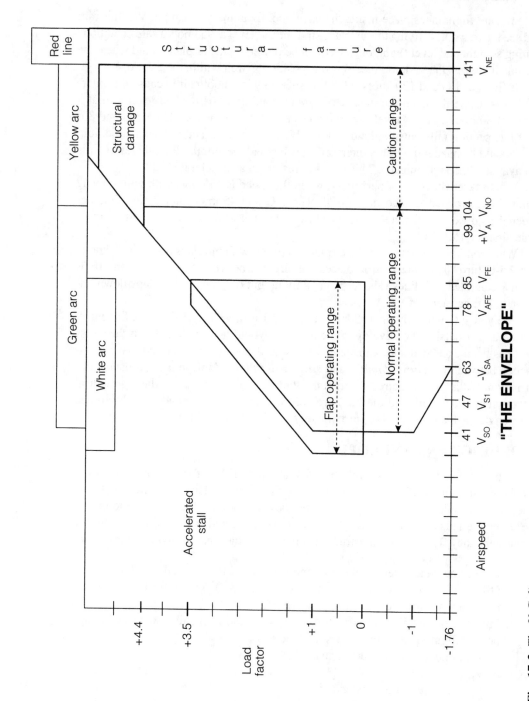

Fig. 17-3. *The V-G diagram.*

ENVELOPE EXAMINATION

All safe flight takes place inside the envelope. Examine this sample V-G diagram and see for yourself. Is flying this airplane straight and level at 95 knots a safe condition? During straight and level flight, only 1 G will be placed on the airplane. Find where the l-G line intersects the 95-knot line. Yes, this position is well within the envelope.

Is flight at 1 G and 120 knots safe? It is safe only in smooth air because this intersection is inside the caution range. How about making a 60° banked level turn at a speed of 80 knots? A 60° level turn produces a load factor of 2 Gs. The 2-G and 80-knot intersection falls outside the envelope. If this were your actual flying condition, what would be happening? This intersection is beyond the sloping line; therefore, it is not available aerodynamically. This position results in an accelerated stall.

What maneuver is being performed when the speed is 45 knots with wings level? Wings-level produces a load factor of 1. The 1-G and 45-knot intersection falls between the slow end of the green and the slow end of the white arcs: minimum controllable airspeed (MCA).

What condition exists when the airplane is flying with the flaps down at 70 knots, in a 2.5-G turn? This intersection places the airplane between the flaps up and flaps down accelerated stall lines. The airplane is flying but only due to the flaps-down addition to lift: accelerated MCA.

Are you safe when flying 105 knots and under a stress of 4.5 Gs? No, this intersection is just outside the envelope. The airplane would not be stalled, but the stress limit has been exceeded and damage could result. Airplane designers do make a distinction between *structural damage* and *structural failure*; damage is a permanent deformation of the primary aircraft structure; failure is the condition where structural parts (wings, flaps, tail, and the like) are detached from the fuselage. The difference between damage and failure is approximately a safety factor of 1.5.

"FOLDING" AN ENVELOPE

This example might be helpful, but what about real flying? Most pilot operating handbooks do not include a V-G diagram for the airplane. How are pilots to know where the "outside of the envelope" is when they do not have the envelope to examine? Every serious pilot should take the time to calculate and draw a V-G diagram for the airplane they fly most. To construct the diagram, gather the following information:

1. Determine what category the airplane is certified for: normal (+3.8 to −1.52), utility (+4.4 to −1.76), and acrobatic (+6.0 to −3.0). This information can be found on the airplane's airworthiness certificate.
2. Find the following speeds from the pilot operating handbook, the FAA-approved flight manual, or the airspeed indicator:
   a. V_{NO}, maximum structural cruise
   b. V_{NE}, never-exceed
   c. V_{FE}, maximum flaps-extended

3. Find the airplane's wing surface area from the pilot's operating handbook.
4. Find the airplane's maximum allowable gross weight from the handbook or from the airplane's weight and balance papers.
5. Find the coefficient of lift: maximum with flaps up plus maximum with flaps down. This information must come from the C_L curve. These curves are not usually provided in pilot handbooks, but may be obtained from the manufacturer.
6. Find the maximum flaps-down load limits in the pilot's operating handbook.
7. In order to keep it simple, make all calculations based upon the standard air density value or 0.00238 slug per cubic foot.

With this information in hand, get a pencil, a calculator, and a sheet of graph paper. Start by drawing out the scales. In the lower left of the graph, start with zero airspeed and mark off increasing increments of airspeed from left to right along the horizontal axis. Again, starting in the lower left corner, draw the load factors. Begin with −3.0 and mark up along the vertical axis through zero and on toward the positive numbers until reaching +6.0.

Next, start boxing in the envelope. Draw the horizontal lines on the scale for the maximum positive and maximum negative allowable G force (load factor). Then draw the vertical lines of V_{NE} and V_{NO}. The gap between these two lines forms the yellow arc. The upper limit, the lower limit, and the speed limits are now in place.

To develop the slow end of the graph, you will need your calculator. First, determine the stall speed in a clean configuration at 1 G. Use the stall equation 13-9A and plug in the numbers: airplane weight, C_{Lmax} from the coefficient of lift curve, wing surface area, and air density. Remember, the answer comes out in feet per second; to convert to miles per hour or knots per hour, use the conversions (feet per second × 1.468 = mph or feet per second × 1.693 = knots). Draw a vertical line from +1 G to −1 G at the proper speed for a clean stall (V_{S1}).

Now, determine the design maneuvering speed (V_A) by multiplying the airplane weight by the maximum allowable positive G load for your airplane. By multiplying weight by maximum +Gs, you have the greatest load factor the airplane can support. This figure is the airplane's greatest effective weight. Use this figure in the stall equation to find V_A. Place a dot on the graph at the intersection of the maximum positive G load and the calculated maneuvering speed.

Do the same calculation on the negative side. Multiply the airplane weight by the maximum negative G load. Take that figure and place it in the stall equation for weight. Place a dot on the graph at the intersection of the maximum negative G load and the calculated speed. This is essentially the negative V_A speed.

Connect some dots. First, draw a line from V_{S1} at +1 G to the dot representing +V_A. Then draw a line from V_{S1} at −1 G to the dot representing −V_A. These two lines close the envelope. The actual slope of each line might not be straight; if you wanted the actual curve of these lines, you could select intermediate load factor positions and find the correct speed by calculating for stall using the same stall equation.

Internal flap envelope

The flap envelope can be drawn using the same method. First, draw the horizontal lines at the maximum positive and maximum negative load factor limits with the flaps down; the lower limit is often zero G for the flaps-down envelope. Then, draw a vertical line at the maximum flap extended speed (V_{FE}). With these three lines drawn in, the load factor limits and high-speed envelopes are determined, but again it takes a calculator to close the envelope.

Calculate the stall speed with flaps down at 1 G, which will be V_{SO}. Use the same equation as before, but use the C_{Lmax} with flaps down from the C_L curve. Take the answer to this problem and draw a vertical line on the graph at that speed from the +1 G position to the –1 G position.

Now find the "flaps down V_A." Multiply the greatest positive load factor with flaps down by the airplane's weight. Take this number and plug it into the stall equation and compute. When you arrive at an answer, place a dot on the graph at the intersection of this G load and this newly calculated speed. Connect the dots. Draw a line from the V_{SO} at +1 G to the "flaps down V_A." This line closes the flap envelope.

No pilot goes through the calculation of a V-G diagram as part of their routine preflight planning, but if you want to get more familiar with your airplane, a V-G diagram is a great way to do it. It is also a great way to prepare for an FAA checkride because in order to complete the diagram, you must really know the airplane's V speeds and understand load factors. Every checkride's practical test standards require test applicants to know their airplane. Beyond the test, the basic knowledge of the envelope leads to greater understanding of how and why your airplane acts the way it does.

EFFECTS OF TURBULENCE

One more major factor affects stall speed: air turbulence. If the airplane is hit by a vertical gust of air, this will significantly alter the relative wind; if the relative wind shifts while the angle of attack remains constant, the airfoil will move closer to the critical angle. While flying in turbulence, the stall horn might bump on from time to time, indicating that the shifting relative wind is causing the critical angle to be momentarily exceeded. The V-G diagram can be used here also.

Look at FIG. 17-3 one more time. What would be the effect of a vertical gust on this airplane while flying with wings level at 80 knots? This condition is well inside the envelope. Wings level means only 1 G and 80 knots is in the heart of the normal operating range (green arc). But if the gust places a stress on the airplane equal to 3.5 Gs, a stall will occur anyway. Find the intersection of 80 knots and +3.5 Gs and notice that this point lies outside the envelope in the accelerated stall region.

This means that the pilot cannot go too slow in turbulent air for fear that the bottom will drop out during gusts. But the pilot cannot fly too fast either. The "real" never exceed speed becomes the fast end of the green arc when the going gets rough. The envelope gets smaller when the air gets more turbulent. The best way to stay out of trouble is to know the envelope.

18
Multiengine
stalls and V$_{MC}$

WHEN WORKING TOWARD THE MULTIENGINE RATING, APPLICANTS MUST perform various stalls in a multiengine airplane. Although the basic aerodynamics that apply to airfoils hold true with multiengine airplanes, there are several additional considerations. First, it is very important to recognize the imminent stall in multiengine airplanes because that is the recovery point. Pilots try to set the throttles so that power is exactly equal from both engines, but this equality might never actually be reached. As a result, there will be uneven thrust as a stall is entered. The uneven thrust will yaw the airplane and unwanted yaw in a full stall can produce a spin. Full stalls are not required on the FAA's multiengine checkride. Some airplane manufacturers recommend that stall recovery be initiated when the stall warning system goes off, which of course, is prior to aerodynamic indications of a stall. Unless otherwise noted, the stall recovery should begin no later than the first indication of buffeting.

Both power-on and power-off stalls are performed in twins. The exact step-by-step method for setting up the stalls is different from one airplane to the next, so read the pilot's handbook carefully before any stall practice. The recovery in multiengine airplanes can be somewhat different than in a single-engine because of the engine configuration. Very little of a single-engine's propeller wash passes over the wings, but conventional multiengine airplanes have the engines on the wings. This means that high energy, fast moving air is blown over the airfoils and this alone creates lift.

The natural reaction for stall recovery in a single-engine airplane is to lower the nose to reduce the angle of attack. The lower angle of attack produces a smooth upper camber airflow and that produces lift. In a multiengine airplane, less nose-down pitch is needed for stall recovery because the engines will supply smooth airflow over the upper camber. When a stall is recognized, a full-power recovery should begin. When engine rpms rise, an "accelerated slipstream" or "induced airflow" develops over the airfoils. As the stall is approached, airflow over the wing will become turbulent and churn under. When the accelerated slipstream is then produced, the propwash blows across the airfoil smoothly and replaces the turbulent air. For this reason, most multiengine airplanes have the ability to "fly out" of a stall. The total amount of lift produced is directly related to the power produced. Power should always be reduced slowly in multiengine airplanes because "chopping" the power will stop the induced airflow and this will cause a loss of lift or even a stall.

SAFER OR NOT?

Many pilots believe that having two engines means the airplane is twice as safe. This is certainly not true. On a dark IFR night, at high altitude, with plenty of airspeed, having an extra engine will be great, but two engines are twice as dangerous at slow airspeeds. If one engine were to fail in a slow airspeed condition, the problem might not be stall recovery but simply aircraft control.

Conventional twins have one engine on each wing. Neither engine pulls the airplane through the center of gravity. When one engine fails the engine that is still operating produces thrust that will yaw the airplane. The side of the airplane with the operating engine will try to outrun the side with no thrust. This causes the entire airplane to yaw toward the bad engine. Figure 18-1 depicts the uneven forces that are present in an engine-out situation. The pilot cannot allow the airplane to yaw uncontrollably, so a counterforce to the yaw must be applied. That force will come from the rudder. In order to keep the nose of the airplane straight, the pilot of the airplane in FIG. 18-1 must hold the left rudder pedal. That will cause the trailing edge of the rudder to move left. The vertical tail and rudder combination is just a symmetrical airfoil. When the rudder's trailing edge moves left, the camber on the right side is increased (FIG. 18-2). This increases the airflow on the right side and lowers the air pressure. The higher pressure on the left side pushes the entire tail to the right.

Remember all this movement was the direct result of airflow. When the tail swings right, the airplane pivots on its center of gravity and the nose swings left. This left yaw will hopefully counteract the right yaw produced by the good engine's uneven thrust. While there is sufficient airflow over the rudder to produce the counterbalance yaw force, the airplane can be flown with safety to landing with only one engine. The pilot's leg will be very tired from holding the rudder, but this would be better than an off-airport emergency landing.

A real problem takes place when the airspeed gets so slow that the airflow over the rudder becomes too weak to produce the counterbalancing yaw. This is the reason why a stall in a multiengine airplane is a bad idea while one engine is out. Control of airspeed is essential while practicing engine-out procedures in multiengine airplanes. Never let the airspeed get too slow while one engine is out or even with reduced thrust

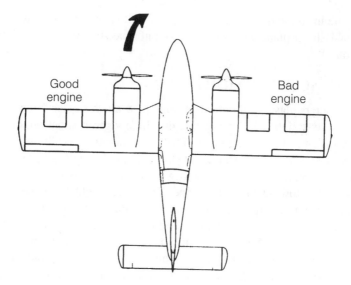

Good engine

Bad engine

Fig. 18-1

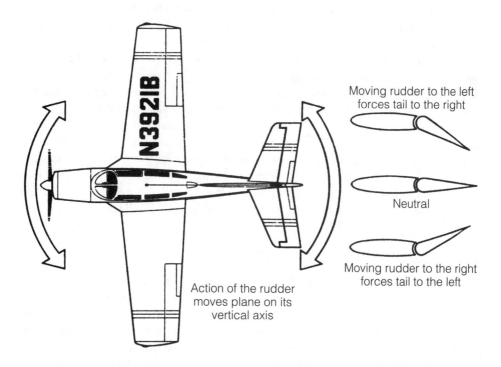

Moving rudder to the left forces tail to the right

Neutral

Moving rudder to the right forces tail to the left

Action of the rudder moves plane on its vertical axis

Fig. 18-2. *Rudder movement pivots the airplane around the center of gravity to move the nose.*

on one engine in simulation of engine-out. If a stall is entered, the yawing forces present can make the airplane uncontrollable and normal stall recovery techniques might not save you.

KEEP THE NOSE STRAIGHT

Several factors play together to determine how much rudder force will be needed to keep the nose straight with one engine out. In any given situation, there will be an airflow speed that is just enough to fight the engine-out yaw: the minimum control speed that is designated V$_{MC}$. Any speed slower than V$_{MC}$ will not provide the needed opposition force and the engine yaw will win the battle. This means that the airplane will yaw and roll toward the bad engine. The pilot might have the correct rudder pushed all the way to the floor, but the force provided by the rudder is just too small. The airplane will soon be inverted and out of control. This situation must be avoided, so it is vital to understand how the minimum control speed is determined.

Power from an engine is usually a good thing. But when one engine is dead, the more powerful the good engine is, the more yaw there will be to overcome. It would be to the pilot's advantage to have less power on the good engine. One situation will automatically reduce the power of an engine: altitude. Every engine needs both fuel and air to operate. When either fuel or air is reduced, the engine(s) will lose power. As the airplane climbs up into the atmosphere, the air will become less dense and that means there will be a reduction of engine power. As the power from the good engine is reduced, the minimum control speed (V$_{MC}$) is also reduced because less rudder airflow is needed when there is less yaw to overcome. Figure 18-3 graphs the reduction of required airspeed for control (V$_{MC}$) against increasing density altitude. At a low density altitude, the good engine is powerful and a fast V$_{MC}$ is required to keep the nose straight and under control.

Refer to FIG. 18-3 again. At 1,000 feet of density altitude, the force to overcome dead-engine yaw will require 70 knots to maintain control. If a pilot experienced an engine failure at a speed of 100 knots, there would be no problem maintaining control. But if the speed were allowed to diminish to 69 knots, it would be beyond the pilot's ability to control the airplane. The airplane will lose control, but it will not stall in this example. The stall speed shown here is 60 knots and indicated stall speed remains constant while V$_{MC}$ reduces with altitude.

A DANGEROUS MISCONCEPTION

It seems then that the higher the airplane is, the better, because the V$_{MC}$ will be slower, but this is a dangerous misconception. The problem is compounded by stall. Refer to FIG. 18-3 once more. If one engine failed while flying at a density altitude of 5,000 feet at a speed of 100 knots, there would again be no problem controlling the airplane. The V$_{MC}$ speed is greatly reduced at 5,000 feet because the power from the operating engine has been greatly reduced. The speed gap between 100 knots and V$_{MC}$ is wider at 5,000 feet than it was at 1,000 feet. The pilot might feel that because there is a wider cushion of airspeed before reaching V$_{MC}$, that this is room to "play with."

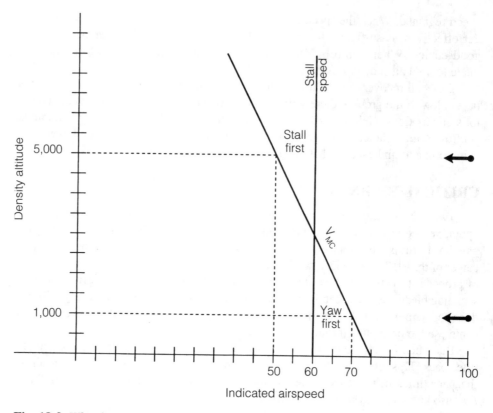

Fig. 18-3. *What happens first, stall or yaw? The density altitude decreases, but indicated stall speed remains the same.*

The problem is that the airplane will stall at the same indicated airspeed regardless of density altitude. If this airplane is allowed to slow down below 60 knots, searching for V_{MC}, the airplane will stall before V_{MC} is reached. A stall in this situation could be extremely dangerous. Because one engine is operating while the other one is not, yaw is present in the stall. Also, there will be uneven lift produced. One wing has engine-induced airflow producing lift, while the other wing has no such lift. This stall will have violent roll tendencies. A spin probably will be the result with recovery uncertain.

TWIN TECHNIQUE

To prevent the spin and execute a safe recovery from this stall, a new procedure must be used. All previous training in stall recovery has involved the use of full power to prevent a great deal of altitude loss. Unfortunately, when a multiengine airplane stalls with one engine dead, you do not have the luxury to hold altitude in the recovery. Rather than going full power, the pilot must reduce the power on the operating engine in order to stop the unwanted yaw. Then the nose must be lowered and speed regained. When the speed is well above the single-engine stall speed and rudder effectiveness sufficient for control, it will be safe to add power back into the good engine. When control effectiveness is regained, then every effort should be made to hold altitude or climb.

This stall recovery procedure requires a large amount of altitude. If this situation occurs low to the ground, there will be very little chance for a safe recovery. The pilot's only options might be strike the ground out of control or strike the ground under control. Neither choice is any good. The determinants of V_{MC} and stall are linked, so it is important to understand what other factors alter the V_{MC} speed.

CRITICAL ENGINE

Two factors determine how much yaw force results when one engine becomes inoperative: the power output of the good engine and the length of *yaw lever arm*. The yaw lever arm is the distance from the airplane's center of gravity and the propeller's center of thrust. Theoretically, when the airplane is flying straight and level the center of propeller thrust would be at the prop spinner. If, while the prop is turning, the descending blade and the ascending blade have the same angles of attack, they will produce the same thrust. Equal thrust on both sides produces a resultant vector in the center, so the prop pulls through the spinner.

But when the airplane's nose is raised, the propeller disk is also raised, actually tilted back. This tilt causes the descending prop blade to take a bigger bite of the air. At the same time, the tilt reduces the bite that the ascending blade takes, which is *P-factor*, also known as *asymmetrical thrust*.

With the nose high, the right side (descending blade) grabs the air more and the resultant vector shifts from the spinner to a position to the right of the spinner. With more thrust coming from the right side, the airplane will tend to turn left. This is why right rudder is usually required during climbouts. This is also why the left engine is the *critical engine* on most twin-engine airplanes. The critical engine is the engine whose failure would most adversely affect the performance and handling of the airplane. When both engines are running and the airplane has a nose-high attitude, the thrust vectors from both engines move to the right. This means that the left propeller's thrust vector moves closer to the airplane's center of gravity while the right propeller's vector moves away from the center of gravity.

The farther away a force is from its pivot point, the longer the lever arm. A lever is a simple machine that can create a mechanical advantage. The longer the arm, the greater impact the force will have. In this case, the force in question is the yaw force that must be opposed with rudder; if the yaw force is multiplied by lever arm, there will be an even greater need for rudder pressure. This rudder pressure must be supplied by airflow. Greater airflow (airspeed) will be required when the lever arm is long; if the left engine quits, the only remaining thrust would come from the right shifted vector of the right engine. The right engine has the greater lever arm and therefore will require a faster V_{MC} (FIG. 18-4A). If the left engine failed, the arm would be shorter and the V_{MC} slower.

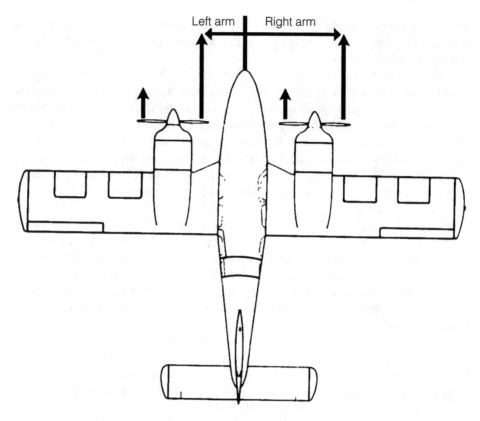

Fig. 18-4A. *The distance from center of gravity to center of thrust shifts to the right due to P-factor.*

ROTATIONAL COMPENSATION

Some airplane designers have eliminated this critical engine problem by using *counterrotating props*, which means that the propellers and the entire engine run in opposite directions. The left engine propeller would turn clockwise as seen from the pilot's seat and the right engine would turn counterclockwise. The P-factor of the right engine would shift the thrust vector toward the inside, closer to the center of gravity. This configuration means that the lever arm on both sides is the same length. Being the same length, the adverse effects of engine failure would be equal, no matter which engine failed.

PROPELLER DRAG

When one engine fails, it is incorrect to assume that only 50 percent of the power has been lost. Drag plays a large part in engine-out aerodynamics. Unfortunately, several factors increase drag when one engine fails. With the power cut in half and the drag increasing, the net power loss from a failed engine can reach 80 percent. How many airplanes could climb while fully loaded on a hot day using only 20 percent of their power? Not many.

In a multiengine airplane, when one engine fails, the pilot must do everything possible to decrease drag over the entire airplane if there is any hope of climbing out of trouble. Pilots should follow their airplane operating manual exactly. The procedure will probably include raising the flaps and landing gear. If the airplane is close to the ground and in a descent, then, of course, you would rather have the gear down to help absorb the collision with the ground but when the altitude is stabilized or in a climb, the gear must come up.

Raising the flaps and landing gear will not change V_{MC} because the drag reduction is symmetrical (unless only one flap or one main gear comes up). Drag will not be the same on both sides because of the dead engine. When one engine fails, you cannot identify the failed engine just by looking at the two propellers. The prop of the dead engine will continue to turn, *windmill*, due to the relative wind. A windmilling prop that is producing no thrust produces great drag. The drag comes from the entire disk that makes up the area swept out by the blades: holding a trash can lid out in the airflow. This drag swings the wing with the dead engine back; meanwhile, the good engine is pulling its wing forward. These two forces work together and pivot around the airplane's center of gravity (FIG. 18-4B).

To overcome these two forces a great deal of rudder force will be needed. Large amounts of rudder pressure require greater airspeeds and therefore a faster V_{MC}. To reduce the two forces in opposition to the rudder, most propellers of multiengine airplanes can be *feathered*. When feathered, the constant-speed prop blades are angled into the relative wind so that only the leading edge of the blade is struck by the relative wind. Blades at a near-normal pitch angle turn as if a pinwheel in the wind, but with no wind deflection angle, the propeller will stop turning. When the prop stops, the "drag disk" disappears and is replaced by the thin leading edge of the blades. This greatly reduces the backward swing of the dead engine's wing and less airspeed is required to hold the nose straight. This means the airplane could get slower without losing directional control: V_{MC} is slower.

AIRCRAFT WEIGHT

The airplane's weight and balance play a part in the minimum control speed calculation. In this case, a heavy airplane is better than a light airplane. This fact seems backward at first because almost all airplane performance factors are adversely affected by an increase in weight. But V_{MC} is not a performance speed, it is only a control effectiveness speed. A heavy airplane has more inertia; it takes a great force to move a great mass; therefore, a heavier airplane will not yaw as quickly. But a light airplane can be pushed around with ease. This is also why a lighter airplane has a slower maneuvering speed (V_A). When the plane is heavy, the yaw force present when only one engine is operating will be less effective. Less rudder force will be required and this would lower V_{MC}.

Not only the amount of weight, but the position of weight is important. As the airplane's center of gravity moves aft, the distance between the CG and the rudder is re-

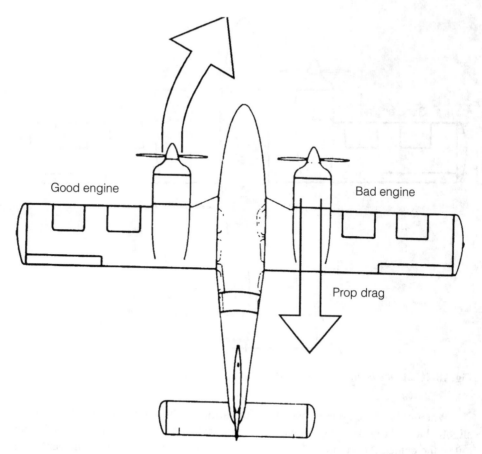

Fig. 18-4B. *A windmilling propeller produces drag that will help swing the airplane around the center of gravity.*

duced. This shortens the lever arm that exists to yaw the airplane in opposition to single-engine yaw (FIG. 18-4C). The rudder's ability to yaw the airplane's nose is reduced as the lever arm is reduced. More speed is now needed to match the engine yaw and maintain control: V_{MC} is yet faster.

COORDINATION

Drag is also reduced by how the airplane is flown. We pilots try very hard to fly with coordination. Using the ailerons and rudder properly, so that the ball of the turn-and-slip indicator remains centered, is a primary goal when learning to fly. Every flight student has heard their flight instructor squawk when the ball swung from the center during a turn, takeoff, or stall. But, just like other things that do not sound correct with engine-out aerodynamics, the airplane should be flown so that the ball is not in the center.

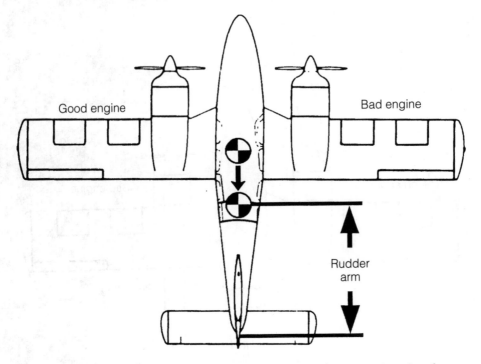

Fig. 18-4C. *As the center of gravity moves aft, the rudder effectiveness is reduced.*

When only one engine is operating, the airplane should be flown with the wings slightly banked toward the good engine and the ball approximately one-half ball width out of the center. Approximately a 3°–5° bank with the ball just out of the center will produce a "zero side slip." Because the airplane's net thrust is not coming through the center of gravity with one engine dead, the turn-and-slip indicator lies to the pilot. In this situation, when the ball is centered, the airplane is actually in a slip. When in a slip, the relative wind strikes more of the airplane's fuselage and drag goes up. Also, the wind flows more parallel to the deflected rudder and this reduces the ability of the rudder to do its job (FIG. 18-4D).

When the rudder loses effectiveness, the force must be replaced with greater airspeed: V_{MC} gets faster. Banking the wings toward the good engine also helps out. The vertical lift vector is tilted when the wings are banked; the vector then has a small horizontal component that helps the rudder. When the wings are level, this extra aid is missing and must be replaced with greater airspeed, so V_{MC} would be faster with wings held level.

POWER PRODUCED

The last factor that affects V_{MC} is the available power from the good engine. Ordinarily, the higher the power output, the better, but not in this case. The more power

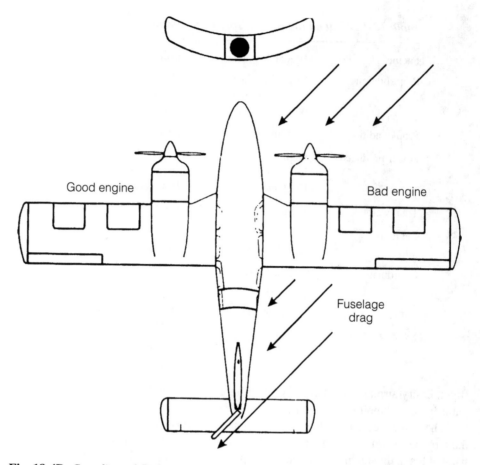

Fig. 18-4D. *Coordinated flight actually hinders performance. By flying with one wing low and the ball one-half width out from the center, "zero side slip" will result.*

coming from the engines the more yaw will be present when one engine fails. When yaw is strong the rudder force will also have to be strong to match and offset the force. Anything that will cause an engine to produce more power, such as low altitude or cold temperatures, is bad for V$_{MC}$. Greater engine performance requires faster speeds to overcome single-engine yaw so when power goes up V$_{MC}$ goes up. All the factors are represented in TABLE 18-1.

V$_{MC}$ DEMONSTRATIONS

Every pilot that flies a multiengine airplane should experience the flight characteristics at V$_{MC}$ airspeed. By performing a V$_{MC}$ demonstration, the pilot can be even more familiar with the airplane and truly understand what V$_{MC}$ is all about. With a qualified flight instructor and plenty of altitude, experiment with engine-out slow

Table 18-1. What changes the airplane minimum control speed?

Factor	Higher V_{MC} (bad)	Lower V_{MC} (good)
Prop rotation	Critical engine; props turn same way	No critical engine; counter rotating props
Prop condition	Windmilling	Feathered
Power produced	High Low altitude Cold temperature	Low High altitude Hot temperature
Total weight	Light	Heavy
Center of gravity	CG aft	CG forward
Coordination	Ball centered Side slip	Ball ½ out Zero side slip
Bank	Wings level	Banked to good engine

flight. Every airplane will have slightly different set-up procedures, so consult the airplane handbook before attempting a V_{MC} maneuver.

The maneuver usually begins by reducing power on both engines to start slowing the airplane down. Go through a GUMP (gas, undercarriage, mixtures, props) checklist, but leave the landing gear and flaps up. Then push both throttles to full power. After full power is reached, reduce the power of the left engine to idle. Going to full power on both engines first will simulate the worst possible situation of a critical engine failure on takeoff. Full power will also produce the greatest yaw and require the quickest pilot reaction. Doublecheck your airplane's recommended procedure.

Failing the left engine simulates the critical engine's failure. With the right engine running at takeoff power and the left engine windmilling, the pilot must hold right rudder to control the airplane. Now, raise the nose of the airplane gradually, losing about one knot of airspeed per second. Bank to the good engine and hold the ball one-half width out from the center. As the speed diminishes, more and more rudder will be required to hold the nose straight. One of three things will happen next: the airplane could stall, the nose could start to slice off to the left, or the rudder pedal could hit the floor. A recovery should be made when the first of these symptoms happens. The recovery is made by reducing the power on the operating engine and lowering the nose. The power reduction will reduce the asymmetrical thrust and as the nose pitches down, speed will increase. The power of the good engine does not need to be reduced to idle. An intermediate power setting should be used so that altitude loss is kept to a minimum.

Practice V_{MC} demonstrations with variations to see the difference that drag and density altitude can make. Try V_{MC} with wings level and the ball held in the center. This will prove that a "zero side slip" allows for slower control speeds. Practice a V_{MC} demonstration during good (low) density altitude conditions and later during poor (high) density altitude conditions. The higher the density altitude is, the better chance that the airplane will stall in a V_{MC} demonstration.

Recover at the first buffet of the airplane. A stall near V_{MC} will not only have a yaw tendency, but a roll tendency as well. When holding a bank to the right, toward the good engine, the left aileron will be down and the right aileron up. The "down" aileron creates lift to raise the wing, but it also produces induced drag. This means that the left wing will have greater drag than the right wing and this can cause a violent roll toward the dead engine during a full stall.

Like any stall, practice and knowledge lead to safety. The greatest safety in multi-engine airplanes can only be achieved with an understanding of single-engine aerodynamics and practice in the airplane. There is no requirement for recurrent training of stalls and V_{MC} demonstrations in multiengine airplanes, once rated in those airplanes. But safe pilots stay sharp with practice without being prodded by regulations.

19
Why it spins

LET'S ADMIT IT. A SPIN CAN BE VERY FRIGHTENING. ONE MOMENT THE VIEW out the front of the airplane is beautiful, with everything in place. All is right with the world. Then, in the next moment, the view out the front is a blurred, whirling, confusion. One of the reasons that a spin can be so dangerous is that it can look so bad from the pilot's seat. If the pilot is shocked by what he sees, he might panic. In the midst of a spin-panic, pilots forget what to do in order to recover and a fatal accident can occur. A spin can cause pilot paralysis. If a spin is entered, the pilot must keep his head because the recovery technique that will save the situation might take a little thought. Recovery from an unintentional, unexpected spin will put the pilot to a test that cannot be failed.

In reality, there should never be an unintentional, unexpected spin. A spin is an aggravated stall. Good piloting involves a constant awareness of the airplane's condition. If the airplane nears a stall, the pilot should know what is happening and take corrective action. Prevention of the imminent stall is simultaneously the prevention of the imminent spin. If you do not want to spin, then do not stall. If an intentional spin is performed, it must begin with a stall. Spin accidents usually involve some other outside factor that turns the pilot's attention away from the primary job of flying the airplane. When interference breaks the pilot's situational awareness, the airplane can gradually move toward stall and spin.

OVERALL AWARENESS

The pilot of a Beech 65 multiengine airplane was involved in an fatal spin accident on a flight from Houston, Texas. Witnesses said they saw the airplane and assorted parts spin out from the base of a cloud layer and hit the ground. The investigation found that one set of gas tanks was empty while another set was full. The exact situation is not known, but it was theorized that the pilot mismanaged the fuel and allowed the tanks supplying fuel to the engines to run dry. The pilot was flying in the clouds and both engines started to run rough or even stop. The pilot might have remembered that there was plenty of fuel in the auxiliary tanks and began the process of switching valves and turning on pumps. But this panic situation inside the cockpit stole the pilot's attention away. The plane was now pilotless. The trim, or balance, or even turbulent air could have caused the nose to rise until a stall occurred. The stall was followed by a spin and the pilot was caught completely off guard. The pilot, not knowing his exact condition, tore the airplane apart in the air during the attempt to right the situation. The fuel mismanagement did not cause the spin, the distraction did.

A check airman and simulator instructor for a commuter airline company stresses cockpit crew coordination during training; he let me in on a technique that he uses with his newly hired pilots. In the simulator, the new pilot/employee is given an instrument approach to fly. During the approach, an equipment malfunction is presented. When the malfunction alarm goes off, the check airman, who is sitting in the copilot's seat, looks at the new pilot's eyes. If the pilot starts looking around the cockpit for the malfunction, he is in trouble. "If the guy looks up at the overhead panel, then I have him...," the check airman said. "What he should do is continue to fly the airplane and say to the first officer, "Turn off that alarm and tell me what the problem is." Unfortunately, small airplanes do not always have a second pilot that can step in and share the workload. In most general aviation flying, the single pilot must do everything. With or without a copilot, the priority must be to fly the airplane and prevent an unwanted stall.

INSIDE THE SPIN

If a spin were unintentionally entered, the pilot must wake-up fast to what is happening. The pilot must immediately recognize what is taking place. The following is a sequence of events that could happen to you if you were caught off guard. A spin happens fast and is very hard to analyze as it happens. To slow down the spin, the photos were taken using a camera with a motor drive taking photos in rapid succession without stopping. The actual time lapse between photos is less than a half second. Cameras were placed in a Cessna 150 and also in an observation plane. The photos allow us to see and discuss what happens in a spin.

The airplane was a Cessna 150 utility category airplane approved for intentional spins. The spin was entered by simulating a typical stall maneuver. The center of gravity was in the middle of the allowable CG range.

The Cessna in FIGS. 19-1A and 19-1B is slowed to near-stall speed to perform a

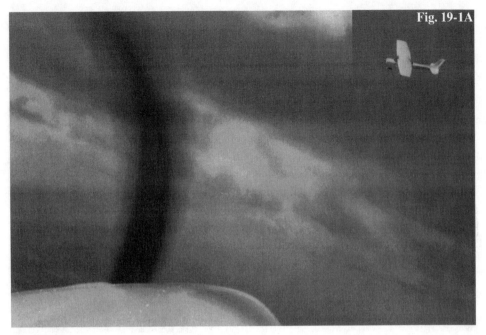

Fig. 19-1B

clean stall. The flaps are up and the airplane's nose is gradually raised. The stall warning horn comes on, and the wings are level.

At the first indication of aerodynamic stall (FIGS. 19-2A and 19-2B), the left rudder is pushed to the floor and the control wheel is brought all the way back. This deepens the stall and causes the plane to be uncoordinated. Looking out from the airplane, everything still looks normal: sky up and ground down.

A combination yaw and roll begins (FIGS. 19-3A and 19-3B). The left rudder is being held to the floor and the elevator is held all the way back, a "pro-spin input." The horizon can now be seen by the pilot slicing away at an ever increasing angle. The nose and the tail of the airplane begin to trade places. The direction of travel is also changing. During the stall entry, the airplane was slow, but it was still moving forward or parallel to the ground. Now the airplane is in transition to a flight path that is perpendicular to the ground.

Disappearing horizon

Autorotation takes over (FIGS. 19-4A and 19-4B). Both wings are stalled but not to the same degree. The right wing is producing slightly more lift so the roll motion is sustained as long as pro-spin inputs are held. The horizon is disappearing up and to the right.

The airplane is not completely inverted (FIGS. 19-5A and 19-5B), but it certainly looks as if it is from the pilot's seat. The airspeed indicator on the panel still is showing

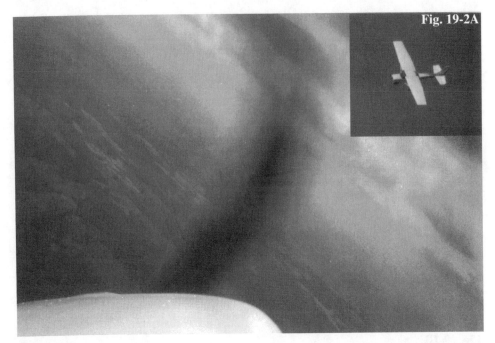

Fig. 19-2A

Fig. 19-2B

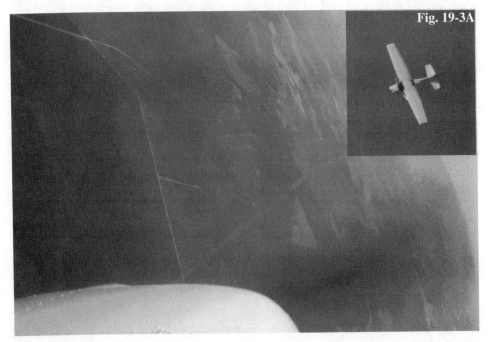

Fig. 19-3A

Fig. 19-3B

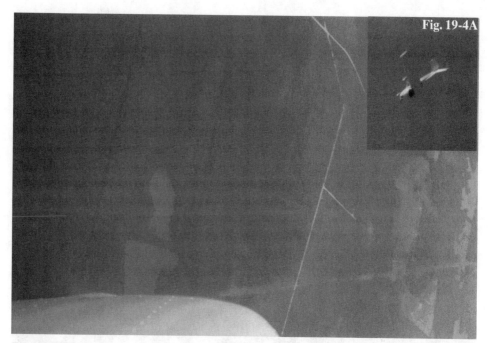

Fig. 19-4B

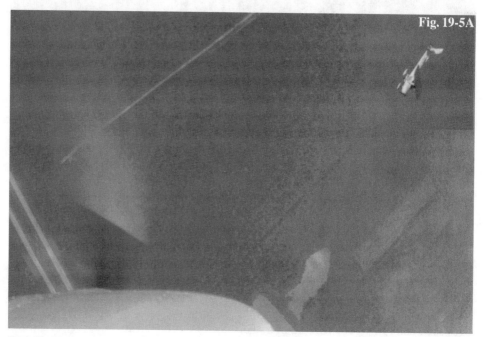

Fig. 19-5B

a stall. The airspeed is less than the slow end of the white arc. You have always heard that a stall could occur at any attitude and any airspeed. This photo proves that a stall can occur even when the nose is aimed almost straight down.

The first one-half turn of a spin entry is completed (FIGS. 19-6A and 19-6B). The nose is down and the window is filled with earth. The elapsed time between FIG. 19-1 when everything was looking normal, to FIG. 19-5, when we are looking straight down at the ground, is slightly more than one second. Think about that for a moment. In less time than it takes to read this sentence you could be in a spin if you were not paying attention to the airplane. Seeing this in the window, especially if it is unexpected, can unnerve any pilot. This is the real reason pilots react improperly to a spin: surprised, scared, and unglued. This was a planned spin.

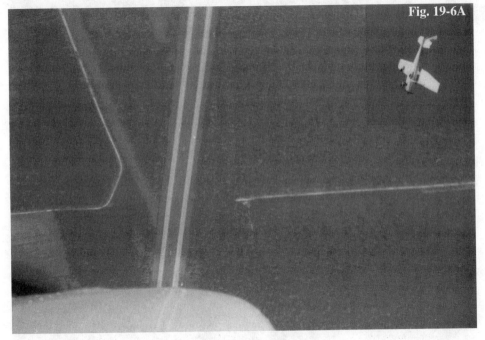

Fig. 19-6A

Fig. 19-6B

I began the maneuver by flying over a highway. When a spin develops, the rotation can be so fast that it is hard to keep up with where you are. By using the highway as a reference, the position in the spin can be determined. The photos were taken at a camera shutter speed of 1/500 second. This extremely fast shutter speed stops the motion, even the propeller, in the pictures. But to the pilot, the motion does not stop and the images seen can run together into a blur. This is a real problem for recovery because it might not be easy to exactly determine which way the spin is turning just by looking out the window. An out-the-window photo might not actually be seen by the pilot be-cause things are happening so fast.

Spinning faster

The rotational speed of the spin begins to increase (FIGS. 19-7A and 19-7B). Figure 19-6 photos were taken at approximately one-half turn. Less than a half second later, FIG. 19-7 was taken and the airplane has progressed to three quarters of a turn. The stall horn has been sounding all this time and the airspeed indicator still rests on the peg showing no airspeed.

Fig. 19-7B

The angle of FIGS. 19-8A and 19-8B is important because it can be seen what the true pitch down angle in a spin actually is. The first several photos were taken in transition during spin entry, but by the time this photo was taken, the spin had "set-tled in," the *incipient* spin. From the pilot's viewpoint, the nose looks as if it is straight down (FIG. 19-8B), but actually it is not straight down. The angle is actually closer to 50° below the horizon (FIG. 19-8A). The pilot can easily get the wrong per-ception here. To recover from any stall, even a spin/stall, the nose must be lowered. But if the pilot believes that the nose is already straight down, he/she will be reluc-tant to push the nose over even farther. This false impression in the pilot's mind can

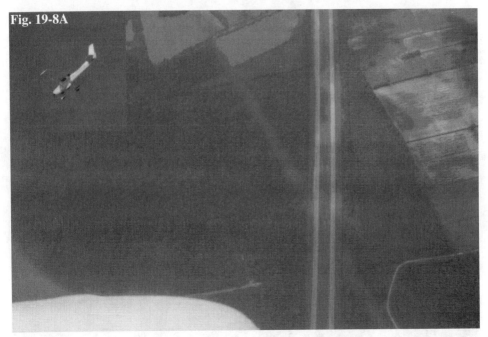

Fig. 19-8A

Fig. 19-8B

delay or prevent recovery. Study FIGS. 19-8A and 19-8B because this is a point of decision for the pilot.

RECOVERY

Almost one turn is complete and the recovery begins (FIGS. 19-9A and 19-9B). Recovery cannot take place without reducing the angle of attack on the wings. Even though the airplane looks as if it is falling straight down, the pilot must use some discipline and push forward on the wheel anyway. Compare the nose-down angle in 19-8A with 19-9A. Clearly, in the time between photos, the nose has been lowered from 50° below the horizon to approximately 70°. This change in pitch has broken the stall and the airplane starts flying again. Looking out the window, the nose-down angle change from FIG. 19-8B to FIG. 19-9B can be detected. When the stall is broken, the airspeed will leap off the peg and accelerate rapidly. The airflow sound around the airplane changes and the stall horn stops screaming. Simultaneously, the opposite rudder has been applied. In this spin, right rudder was needed to stop the rotation. Pushing the wheel forward and using rudder opposite of the spin direction is an "antispin input."

As the speed increases and the rotation stops, (FIGS. 19-10A and 19-10B), the nose is gradually raised back to the horizon. Figure 19-10 photos show the nose coming up through approximately 45° nose-down pitch on its way to a position level with the horizon. Care must be taken here not to overspeed the airplane by not raising the nose

178

Fig. 19-9B

Fig. 19-10B

fast enough or to reenter a stall by pulling the nose up too quickly. This is the only part of the entire maneuver where G loading can be detected by the pilot.

Normal flight resumes after the FIG. 19-10 photos. More photos were taken during the recovery; the entire one-turn spin took approximately three seconds; 1,200 feet of altitude was lost during the turn.

Experiencing a spin for the first time in an airplane will make a big impression on you. The sheer surprise at the radical attitude a spin takes you to, and the speed in which it takes you there, can paralyze a pilot. This is one of the strongest arguments for spin training. If you were to see the FIGS. 19-1 through 19-8 sequence out your window for the first time while alone and untrained, the shock could prevent you from executing a recovery as seen in FIGS. 19-9 and 19-10. At least with spin training, the initial shock would be reduced and you could turn your attention to solving the problem.

SPIN DISSECTION

A spin is an aggravated stall, but how does it get aggravated? To understand the aerodynamics of a spin, we must start with the stall. As the angle between the relative wind and the airfoil chordline increases, the coefficient of lift increases. Due to this, the total lift increases until the critical angle is reached. Past the critical angle, portions of the wing experience separated upper chamber airflow and the lift produced diminishes. This is a normal stall. A spin is produced from this circumstance when one more force is applied: yaw.

If the stall is entered while uncoordinated, one wing might rise while the other falls. This means that the wings are subjected to different and changing relative wind. Remember that the angle of attack is the difference between the wing's chordline and relative wind. Ordinarily it is the angle of attack that is discussed when explaining the onset of a stall, but in this case, it is the changing relative wind that causes the problem. Relative wind is always in the opposite direction of the travel path. Usually the airplane and its parts travel on the same path, but not when the airplane rolls. When entering a left spin, the right wing must go up. This produces a complicated vector problem. Now the right wing is not only moving forward with the rest of the airplane but is also moving up. The path taken by the right wing is actually a raised diagonal line. The relative wind then changes because it is always opposite of the path taken. The new relative wind direction is closer to the chordline and effectively reduces the angle of attack.

Figure 19-11 illustrates the normal condition between relative wind and chordline. Figure 19-12 illustrates what happens when the right wing moves up. This reduction of angle of attack shifts the right wing to a new position on the coefficient of lift graph. Assume that the right wing is stalled and has the angle of attack represented by position A of FIG. 19-13. When the left roll begins, the angle of attack on the right wing gets less and shifts to position B. At this moment, the right wing might not be exceeding the critical angle of attack.

Meanwhile, the left wing is rolling down and the left wing's relative wind is changing as well. This time the changing relative wind increases the angle of attack

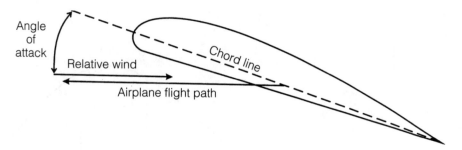

Fig. 19-11

and aggravates the problem. Figure 19-14 shows how the descending wing produces a much greater angle of attack and therefore a much worse stalled condition. As before, this rolling motion affects the ability of the wing to produce lift. Assume the left wing has the angle of attack represented by position A of Figure 19-15. When the wing moves down, the angle of attack gets larger and moves to position C, which is a much more severe stall condition.

In this instant, the right wing is less stalled and the left wing is more stalled. This situation produces *autorotation*, which is where a spin gets its name. The left wing will continue to drop and the right wing will continue to rise; the airplane is both yawing and rolling and autorotation starts to feed itself; turning velocities perpetuate the situation. The outside wing in any turn is moving faster. Remembering the lift equation, we know that any velocity increase will increase lift. This lift increase on the right side will be matched by a lift decrease on the left side. And then there is drag.

Drag sustains the autorotation. Figure 19-16 is a typical coefficient of total drag curve. When the right wing's angle of attack is reduced from position A to position B the total drag of that wing is reduced. The right wing now has less resistance and swings forward freely. Figure 19-17 illustrates the left wing's increasing drag. When

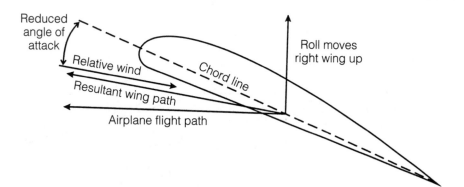

Fig. 19-12. *In a left spin entry, the right wing will rise, which shifts the relative wind and decreases angle of attack.*

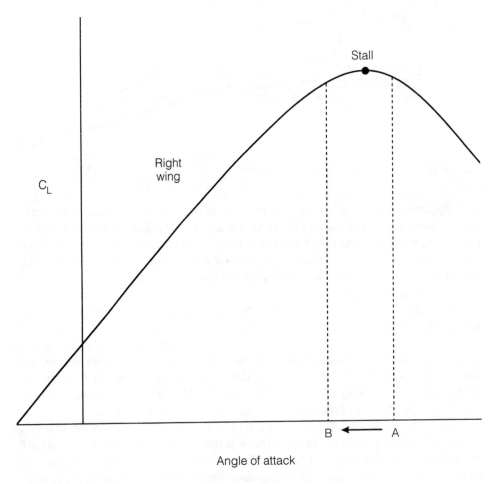

Fig. 19-13. *Right wing will be "less stalled" in a left spin.*

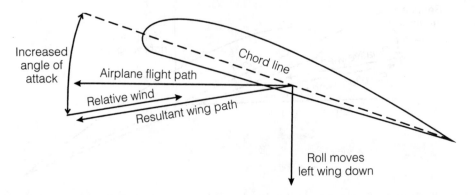

Fig. 19-14. *In a left spin entry, the left wing will fall, which shifts the relative wind and increases angle of attack.*

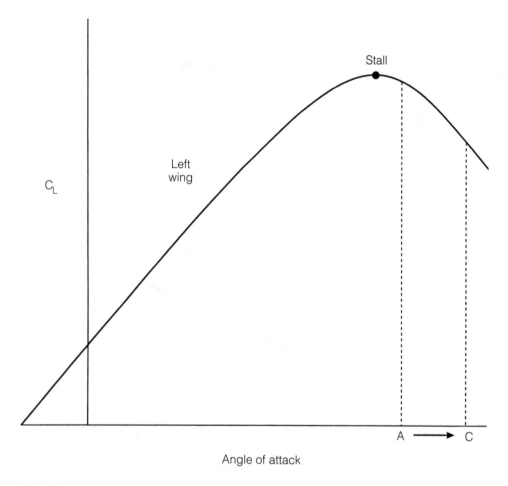

Fig. 19-15. *Left wing will be "more stalled" in a left spin.*

the angle of attack increases from position A to position C the total wing drag increases. This means the left wing has more resistance and is held back.

ROUND AND ROUND

The life cycle of a practice spin has four stages: entry, incipient, developed, and recovery. (Unfortunately, an unintentional spin might not have a recovery....) The spin entry begins like an approach to stall. If full power is used, the spin is usually entered more quickly. Once in the spin, a high power setting will further aggravate the spin and greater altitude loss on the recovery will result. When practicing spins, the entries should be made with power on and power off. The spin entry is accomplished with prospin control inputs. The rudder should be deflected to its greatest amount of travel and simultaneously the control wheel aggressively brought all the way back to the greatest elevator deflection. The entry can look worse from the pi-

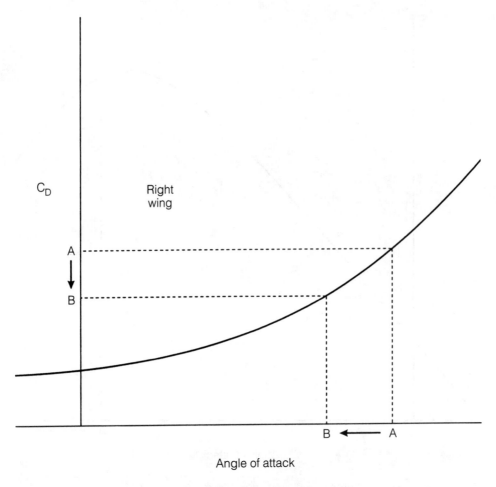

Fig. 19-16. *In a left spin, the right wing produces less drag.*

lot's viewpoint than the rest of the spin. The radical attitude achieved is seen in FIGS. 19-5A and 19-6A. The airplane is not inverted, but looking out the window you do get the sensation of being on your back.

Incipient

The definition of incipient is "beginning to exist;" therefore, the incipient spin is a transitional time when the airplane stops moving across the ground and starts moving toward the ground. The autorotation forces are starting to take effect on the airplane. The rate of rotation is increasing. The view out the front of the airplane gets blurred. Most small airplanes go through this transition within the first two turns.

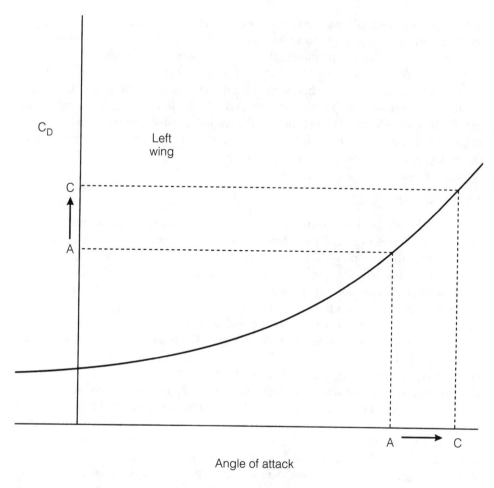

C_D

Left
wing

C

A

A ——→ C

Angle of attack

Fig. 19-17. *In a left spin the left wing produces more drag.*

Developed

The developed spin condition is reached when the rate of rotation stabilizes. Airplanes spin differently, so the fastest rate of rotation might be anywhere between 150° and 300° per second. Also, the nose-down attitude will stabilize at approximately 50° to 70° below the horizon. If the prospin inputs are continued, the nose-down pitch of the airplane could oscillate. The nose might rise up closer to the horizon, then pitch back down toward the ground. The angle that the nose is pointed down is the airplane's *spin mode*. The closer the nose comes to the horizon, as it spins, the "flatter" the spin mode becomes. Common sense would have you believe that pointing the nose at the horizon would be a good thing. But once again a spin is a confusing paradox. The spin developed in the first place by exceeding the critical angle of attack. The only way to get out of a spin is to retrace the steps that lead you in. The nose must be lowered to a position less than the critical angle of attack.

The earth's position in relation to the airplane's position has nothing to do with it. You cannot afford to worry about what is up and what is down in a spin. You only worry about what is above or below the airfoil's critical angle of attack. If the nose points at the horizon in a spin, then the attack angle is a long way past the critical angle. As the nose is lowered to aim more at the ground, the distance between the current angle of attack and the critical angle is reduced and recovery is closer. This is why a flat spin is so deadly, because recovery is so far away.

FLAT SPINS

While in the developed spin, two forces are doing battle on the airplane. All the aerodynamic forces that produce autorotation tend to lower the nose into a steep spin mode. But as the spin progresses, centrifugal force tends to throw the wings out and this raises the nose to a flat spin configuration. The fight between aerodynamic and inertial forces causes the nose to oscillate up and down as you go around and around. If the inertial forces ever win the battle, the airplane will go into a flat spin. Because the flat spin's angle of attack is so far past the critical angle of attack, the recovery might be delayed or even impossible. When in the spin, the physical laws of angular momentum apply to the airplane. When figure skaters finish a routine on ice, they often skate into a spin. When the skaters hold their arms out from their bodies, the speed of their rotation is slow, but when they bring their arms in, the momentum increases and their rotation speed turns them into a blur of color. The speed creates a dramatic finale to the performance.

The airplane's rotational speed is affected the same way. When the nose is low, the spin will be fast; when the nose is high and the wings widened out, the spin will be slow. Once again, the spin paradox. You would think that a slow spin would be good, but actually a faster spin is safer because it is produced by a steeper spin that is closer to the recovery angle.

The rotational velocity of the spin is determined by the distance between the airplane's center of gravity and the spin's axis of rotation. (The earth turns on an axis that runs from north to south.) The airplane's spin also turns on an axis. The farther the spinning object gets from the axis, the faster the rotational speed will become. A propeller is a good example of this principle. The prop spinner is the axis of rotation for the prop blades. The blade tips move much faster than the blade hub because the tips are farther out from the axis. In a spin, the axis of rotation starts just ahead of the nose, and as the spin develops, the axis of rotation will move in closer to the center of gravity. If the spin mode goes flat, the axis moves closer to the CG, causing the rate of rotation to slow down.

The altitude loss per turn of the spin depends upon the mode of the spin. In a small trainer airplane, the first turn will waste more altitude than subsequent turns. Due to the entry and incipient spin, the first turn will lose between 1,000 and 1,500 feet of altitude. Turns to follow might only lose 500 feet per turn.

SENSORY RESPONSE

As with most piloting techniques, more than one of the senses should be used to detect when the spin mode begins to go flat. If the pilot sees the nose pitch up toward the horizon while spinning, this is the first indication that the spin mode is going flat. As the mode goes flat there will be less roll and more yaw. This yaw should be felt "in the seat of the pants" by the pilot just like in an uncoordinated turn. And because the flat mode produces a slower rate of rotation, the sound of the airflow around the airplane will change and lessen. Changes in sight, feel, and sound that alert a pilot to a spin mode change to flat means recovery should be initiated immediately. If the spin is allowed to move to a flat condition, as stated before, the recovery will take longer or might not even be possible.

INVERTED FLAT SPINS

I've always heard through hangar flying that the worst possible situation a pilot could ever find himself in while piloting an airplane was an inverted flat spin. I did not even know what that was, but it sure sounded bad. Well, it is bad, but there is some good news. By using the proper prospin control inputs the spin will not end up upside-down. I was fortunate enough to fly once with William Kershner, the noteworthy aviation author. Kershner pointed out that even if you enter the spin upside-down, the spin that develops will be rightside-up if you pull back on the control wheel during the entry. We promptly began a loop and when we reached the top and were inverted, we went prospin with full rudder deflection and full-back elevator. The airplane tumbled end over end for a while, then rolled, then yawed, and eventually it settled down into a normal spin.

You know you are in a real bad situation when you are hoping for a spin to develop. At least you know what a spin looks like and can get out of one with training. An inverted spin could only be created by stalling with a forward motion on the control wheel, and although this is possible, it is not likely.

GAUGING A SPIN

Some airplanes have one more way of determining the developed spin: fuel gauges. The fuel quantity indication that is read off the instrument on the panel gets its information from a float that rides on top of the fuel in the tank. If the float is mounted in the tank closest to the fuselage, the fuel level will read empty in a developed spin (FIG. 19-18). The centrifugal force that builds up during the spin will slosh the fuel to the outside of the tank. The float on the inboard side of the tank will have no more fuel to support it and will fall to the bottom of the tank. This will read on the fuel gauge as an empty tank.

It is unlikely that you will have time during a spin to watch the fuel gauges. When I do spin training for flight instructor applicants, I always do one spin where I ask them to look only inside at the airspeed indicator, turn coordinator, inclinometer (the ball),

Fig. 19-18. *Centrifugal force throws the gas in the fuel tanks to the outside of the spin. If the fuel gauge sending unit inside the tank is mounted close to the fuselage, the fuel tanks will read empty during a developed spin.*

and fuel gauges. They very seldom are able to really look at those instruments with all that is going on outside.

One last item. The port where the fuel leaves the gas tank on its way to the engine might also be located on the inboard side of the tank. If this is the case, the fuel will swing out away from the fuel line. When this happens only the fuel remaining in the carburetor keeps the engine running; eventually, this fuel will be used up and the engine will stop. In the Cessna 150 that I use for flight instructor training, the time it takes for the fuel to run out is about the same amount of time it takes to complete a nine-turn spin; time shall vary among different airplanes and engines. This means that if the spin recovery is not executed in a short amount of time, the pilot must contend with one more problem, restarting the engine during recovery.

20
Spin recognition and recovery

WHEN TEACHING SPINS I ALWAYS TRY EXTRA HARD TO COMMUNICATE TO the student exactly what I am doing and what to expect. I explain the control movements that will put us into a spin and also the procedure to get us out. It is very easy to lose your train of thought when distracted by the swirl before your eyes, but obviously the pilot must overcome the surprise and fly the airplane out of the spin.

Exceeding the critical angle of attack that produced a stall is the first step in spin entry. For spin exit, it will be necessary to break the stall by returning the nose to an angle that is less than the critical angle. But at the same time, the pilot must stop the autorotational forces, and then protect the airplane from excessive dive speeds.

Before spinning any airplane, you should read and understand the manufacturer's recommended spin recovery techniques. The recovery procedure will be somewhat different from one airplane to the next. There is no substitute for thoroughly knowing your airplane. The FAA now requires flight instructor applicants who fail their CFI checkride due to lack of spin knowledge, to actually take the FAA inspector for a spin demonstration; however, as pointed out in chapter 2, this does not actually happen very much because the inspectors do not want to place themselves in a position where they must spin an unfamiliar airplane. I do not blame them. The more you know about what to expect from a particular airplane in a spin and in the spin recovery, the safer you will be.

The basic spin recovery technique has three steps: stop autorotation, stall recovery, dive recovery. Depending upon the configuration of the airplane when the spin was entered, a recovery might require more action to protect the airplane, but the basics will remain the same.

STOP AUTOROTATION

The pilot must take steps to overcome the forces that brought on the spin. The autorotation began when the upgoing wing and the downgoing wing began to produce asymmetrical lift. That took place when the rudder's yawing force was introduced. To stop the rotation, the wings must return to a condition where they are both equally stalled by applying rudder in the direction opposite the rotation. When practicing intentional spins, this is easy. To sustain the airplane in the spin, the pilot is holding the rudder pedal down. To recover, you start holding down the other pedal. Using opposite rudder lowers the wing that is on the outside of the spin. As the wing comes down, its relative wind changes; therefore, the wing's angle of attack is increased. The wing on the inside of the spin will rise while applying opposite rudder; therefore, that wing's angle of attack decreases. When the wings are level, they will have the same angle of attack and they will be equally stalled.

Which direction?

If the spin is entered by accident, it might not be clear at first which direction the airplane is turning. First, if the spin was inadvertent you simply will not be thinking about spin direction and recovery. Watching an unexpected spin develop from the pilot seat means that the pilot has become just a spectator. Theoretically, the pilot who is doing his job properly will never spin unexpectedly. If it does happen, the pilot must quickly switch from spectator to participant, but this switch might not happen without panic. In a panic, the pilot might not be able to read the spin. Reading the spin means regaining your situational awareness by determining which way you are going and initiating the proper recovery.

A spin's rotational speed is very fast. The outside world is doing things that you never wanted to see from an airplane. It might be difficult to decide in that moment which rudder to push to stop the rotation. If you push the wrong rudder, the spin will tighten up; if you still have enough altitude, you can always correct your mistake and still make the recovery. Once the correct rudder is applied, hold it down. The autorotation might not stop immediately. How far you progressed into the developed spin will determine how long it takes to get the rotation stopped. (The spin's direction may also be determined by using flight instruments, which is explained in this chapter.)

If the spin was entered with power on, it will be important to reduce the power to idle during this step in the recovery. The thrustline of most airplanes is positioned in relation to the center of gravity so that when power is added, the nose pitches up; when power is reduced, the nose pitches down. We want the nose to come down in spin recovery in order to break the stall. Power-on will oppose the stall recovery, so pull back the throttle all the way.

If the spin is entered with the flaps down, they must be raised. The recovery characteristics might be different than expected with the flaps down, and the pullout dive speed will probably be faster than the maximum flaps extended speed. Flaps should always be up when practicing spins; however, a spin might be entered unexpectedly while the flaps are down. This could happen while practicing minimum controllable airspeed maneuvers or approach to landing stalls or even on a real approach to the airport.

Ailerons

Not much has been said about the ailerons during spins and recoveries. During the recovery, the ailerons should be neutral. Pilots seem to react faster with their hands than they do with their feet. When the spin happens, the natural tendency will be to stop the rotation with the ailerons, but this might not do anything. Remember, the wings are stalled and the ailerons are part of the wing. The ailerons might be completely ineffective during the spin. As the recovery is made, a deflected aileron will have unknown effects on drag and rotation. Stopping rotation depends upon placing both wings in the same condition, but if the ailerons are deflected, the wings will remain asymmetrical and recovery could be prolonged. Ailerons should be neutral in the entry as well. It is even possible to cause a spin with ailerons because ailerons produce adverse yaw and yaw can cause a spin. It is wrong to think that spins can only be entered by pushing on a rudder pedal.

The time it takes to stop autorotation depends upon two things: how fast the airplane is spinning and how effective the flight controls are. The speed in which the airplane rotates depends upon many factors, but where the weight is placed in the airplane is critical. The more weight that is placed away from the center of gravity, the more tendency the airplane will have for spinning. A suitcase in the far aft baggage compartment will do more to sustain the spin than a person who is sitting on the center of gravity. The airplane becomes a spinning gyro and will resist recovery.

This is another reason to calculate weight and balance and assure that the airplane is properly loaded. But the airplane design itself might be very progyro. Wingtip fuel tanks, long fuselage, and aft baggage compartments extend the weight distribution and add to the problem. Multiengine airplanes are especially progyro because wing-mounted engines add great amounts of weight out from the center of gravity.

Rudder

During normal spin recovery, the rudder is used to stop rotation, but the rudder must have adequate airflow to produce the recovery force. If the air is thin, the rudder will not get a good "bite" and recovery will be delayed. It would take an airplane at 15,000 feet longer to recover than an airplane at 5,000 feet because the airplane at the lower altitude simply has more air to work with. The thicker the air, the faster the response time of the airplane to rudder deflection. The ratio between the mass of the airplane and the mass of the air is *relative density*. The lower the ratio, the faster the recovery. The ratio is determined with the following equation:

Relative Density = Airplane Mass/(Air Density) (Span) (Wing Area)

Airplane mass is determined by taking the airplane's total weight and dividing it by the acceleration of gravity, which is 32.2 feet per second squared. An airplane weighing 1,600 pounds is spinning at sea level on a standard day (density is 0.00238 slug per cubic feet). The airplane has a wing span of 33 feet and a wing area of 160 square feet. The ratio would be:

Relative Density = 49.69/(0.00238) (33) (160) = 3.96

Now, spin the same airplane at 18,000 feet where the atmospheric density is half that of sea level. The ratio now becomes: 7.91. The higher the ratio, the less effective the flight controls. This example is an extreme case, of course, but time to stop autorotation will be adversely effected by hot, high, humid conditions.

STALL RECOVERY

This procedure is physically like a stall recovery, but mentally it is different. The physical mechanics of recovery call for the control wheel to be pushed forward with as much pressure as required to lower the nose to an angle below the critical angle. But remember, this forward motion on the wheel must take place while the pilot is already looking at the ground. The natural tendency is to pull the wheel back because we are more comfortable when the airplane is aimed at the horizon rather than straight down. This might be the primary reason that spins are fatal. In an attempt to bring the nose to the horizon, a panicked pilot might pull the airplane into a deeper and deeper stall.

Figure 19-8A showed that the nose is down in a spin, but not straight down. This is something that you must tell yourself before the spin because in the spin it will look as if you are looking straight down (FIG. 19-8B). Regardless of the fact that the front window is filled with ground rather than sky, you must push the nose even farther forward to break the stall. This does not seem correct, but remember, the travel path of the airplane is now down, so relative wind is up. To recover, you must lower the airfoils into that upcoming relative wind.

After Autorotation stops, the airplane is essentially in a free fall. The manufacturer recommendations are extremely important here. It might be required that steps one and two be executed simultaneously. The rudder's airflow might be interrupted during the free fall by the placement of the horizontal stabilizer or fuselage. With reduced rudder airflow, the ability of the rudder to stop the autorotation would be reduced as well. Figure 20-1 depicts the "dead-air region" that develops downstream of the airflow. The dead air can shield the rudder and inhibit recovery. The actual steps for recovery might be simultaneous opposite rudder and forward elevator, followed by dive recovery.

DIVE RECOVERY

After rotation has been stopped and the stall broken, the plane is returned to normal flight. Figure 20-2 is the last shot in the sequence of spin photos from the previous

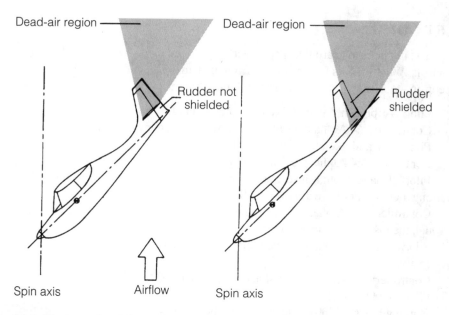

Fig. 20-1. *Horizontal stabilizer placement might reduce rudder effectiveness in a spin and alter recovery techniques.*

chapter. (Compare FIGS. 19-9A and 19-10A with 20-1.) The nose is coming up. This means that the stall has been broken and the airplane is flying again. When the control wheel is pushed forward in order to get the plane flying again, the airplane will be at its greatest nose-down attitude. The idea now is to raise the nose to the horizon with minimum altitude loss, but without overstressing the airplane. Once the stall is broken, the airspeed indicator will move rapidly. If there is no turbulence, the airplane should not be damaged by accelerating into the yellow arc.

Turbulence might have been encountered in the first place that contributed to an inadvertent spin, so recovery in that case should be made remaining in the green arc. Pilots might be anxious to return to level flight and apply too much elevator back pressure. This could induce a secondary stall as well as bending the airplane.

Fig. 20-2

LET GO?

You might have heard that a spin recovery can be made by simply letting go of the controls. What follows is a transcript from an actual air traffic control recording. The recording took place during a stall/spin fatal accident.

Pilot: "Approach, I would like clearance to land."
Controller: "64 Alpha the field is IFR, what are your intentions?"
Pilot: "I would like clearance to land."
Controller: "64 Alpha, are you equipped and qualified for IFR flight?"
Pilot: "I have enough instruments on board and I have about eighteen hours of training, but I do not have a rating for IFR as of yet."
Controller: "64 Alpha, are you requesting an emergency authorization to descend through the instrument meteorological conditions?"
Pilot: "Ah. . .I am request an emergency. . .if I could get down."
(pause)
Controller: "64 Alpha descend and maintain 4,000 feet."
Pilot: "4,000, roger."
(pause while 64 Alpha descended into the clouds)
Pilot: "Having difficulty. Having difficulty."
Controller: "64 Alpha, ah. . .level off 64 Alpha."
Pilot: "Help, help, help. . . ."
Controller: "64 Alpha, if you are in a spin, release your controls."
Pilot: "Controls released, roger."
(longer pause)
Controller: "64 Alpha, radar contact lost."

The pilot of this airplane became spatially disoriented (vertigo) in the clouds and accidentally entered a spin. The pilot did not know which end was up and had no hope of making the spin recovery himself. The controller did all he knew to do. From his position at the radar scope, the controller could not tell which way the spin was rotating so he could give no advice on which rudder should have been applied. "Release your controls," was the best he could do. Was this good advice?

First of all, let's hope that pilots will not put themselves in such a disoriented situation. Pilots should have a plan of action that is better than just letting the control wheel go. But when the pilot is unaware of what is taking place, their attempts to correct the situation might very well aggravate the situation. In this case, the pilot would be better off simply releasing the controls and let the airplane's stability serve him well.

ASAP

If a no-hands/no-feet recovery is attempted, do it early. If the airplane is allowed to move from the incipient to developed stage of the spin, the chances of successful no-controls recovery are greatly reduced. From the accident transcript above, the pilot's last transmission confirmed that the controls were released, yet recovery did not follow. Enough time had passed for several turns to have taken place before the pilot released the controls. This means that he probably was in a developed spin and the airplane's built-in stability forces just could not overcome the spin forces prior to impact. No-hands/no-feet recoveries can be practiced, but only attempt them within the first two turns (incipient stage) of the spin.

If a no-hands/no-feet spin recovery is successful, it will be because the airplane's designed stability takes over. Stability comes in two forms: *static* and *dynamic*. Static refers to an object in equilibrium; dynamic refers to an object already in motion. If an object in equilibrium is disturbed, but returns itself back to its original state of equilibrium, it would have positive static stability. But this is only part of the picture because static stability is the object's initial reaction to being disturbed. Dynamic stability is the airplane's overall reaction to being disturbed. After the airplane is disturbed, if the aerodynamic forces dampen the disturbance so that eventually the airplane returns to its original state, then the airplane has positive dynamic stability. If the controls are released in a spin and if the airplane has positive stability, the natural tendency will be for the nose to drop and the rudder to return to neutral.

Today's airplanes are designed to be stall/spin resistant. Stability (absence of rudder and elevator pressure) will eventually stop the rotation and break the stall. As the airplane dives in the natural recovery, the airflow and lift increases. This excess lift will raise the nose. As the nose comes up, the airspeed will slow down and correspondingly, lift will be reduced. From this, the nose will pitch down again, but not to the same degree as before. The airplane will oscillate up and down, each cycle being less severe than the one before (FIG. 20-3). The airplane, if trimmed neutral, should eventually return to level flight. If you were relying on this process to make a full spin recovery, you would need plenty of altitude.

IFR

The accident transcript brings up one more problem. Spins and instrument flying. Unfortunately, most IFR flight training consists of repeated instrument approaches and

Fig. 20-3. *Positive static and dynamic stability will return the airplane to its original position.*

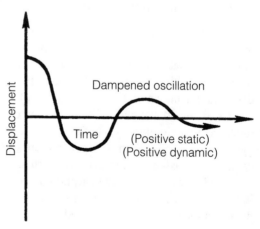

usually the same approaches at the same airports over and over again. (The pilot actually gets an approach rating, not a true instrument rating. More emphasis needs to be placed on working in the real IFR system and on emergency situations.)

Instrument flying has all the ingredients that can produce a spin. A pilot can become disoriented in the clouds. Turbulence makes vertigo worse and more likely. Gusts from the turbulence can induce an unexpected stall and that is just one step away from a spin. The scariest thing about a spin in the clouds is that you cannot tell by looking outside which way the spin is rotating. Because the first recovery step is to stop autorotation, determining the direction of spin is required for survival. The condition of the airplane in the clouds can only be determined by flight instruments, so, what are the flight instruments telling us in a spin?

Pitot-static instruments

The altimeter, vertical speed, and airspeed indicators all work just fine during a spin. Rate of altitude loss in a spin is dizzying. Depending upon how steep or how flat the airplane is spinning, the rate of descent can be anywhere between 6,000 to 8,000 feet per minute. The standard rate of climb or descent used in instrument flight is 500 feet per minute, so you are coming down much faster than you ever do in any other IFR maneuver. Most vertical speed indicators do not have a scale that goes all the way to 8,000 feet per minute, so during a spin, the VSI will be pegged out. The VSI is working, but it does not give you any more information other than the fact that you are going down.

The altimeter is unwinding in a spin. The aneroid bellows inside the altimeter really get a workout. As the airplane sinks into the atmosphere, the pressure increases and this squeezes the bellows. The altimeter usually keeps up with the spin very well.

The airspeed indicator shows zero during a true spin. Some airspeed indicators have a peg that prevents the needle from moving all the way to zero, but the indication should be the slowest possible reading. If any airspeed is showing, then the airplane is transitioning to a spiral rather than a spin.

Gyroscopic instruments

The directional gyro (heading indicator) and attitude gyro (artificial horizon) will probably not work well in a spin. All gyros spin inside a bracket. The bracket itself is allowed to rotate on gimbals in order to give the proper instrument readings. But the brackets have limitations. The bank and pitch limits of the directional gyro vary with design and manufacturer, but usually 55° of pitch or bank is all they can handle. If the limit is exceeded, the gyro will tumble and cannot be trusted until it is reset. Repeated tumbling will slowly degrade the instrument's accuracy. (I will not fly IFR using a gyro that I know has been spun several times.) During the spin entry, the DG limits will certainly be passed and the gyro will turn at random.

The DG cannot be used to accurately determine recovery heading. When spinning in the clear air, ground references should be used to determine spin position. The spin photos in the previous chapter used a highway to establish position. In the clouds, this reference would be missing. If you are actually spinning in the clouds, the recovery at all costs is the most important thing. You really do not care which heading you come out on. Also, when the gyro tumbles, it might not turn in the correct direction. The DG should not be used to determine the direction of spin rotation.

The attitude gyro has limits as well. Usually, the attitude gyro will reach its limits from 100–110° of bank and from 60–70° of pitch. These limits will also be exceeded in the spin entry and the attitude gyro will wallow around its dial aimlessly. This instrument cannot be relied on either.

The turn coordinator is actually two instruments in one. The gyro portion operates the turn needle. The ball (inclinometer) is a completely separate indicator that just happens to be on the turn coordinator's face. The fact that the two are together is no accident because they should work together to provide coordinated maneuvers. The ball itself is unreliable in a spin. The ball swings back and forth in the curved glass tube, dampened by fluid that is in the tube. The ball reacts to any force that will push it around, such as centrifugal force. In a spin, centrifugal force changes the way we ordinarily would read the ball. Your flight instructor has definitely told you to "step on the ball," in order to fix coordination problems. But while in a spin "stepping on the ball" will work only 50 percent of the time.

Recall that the spin revolves around an axis. The axis is not always exactly at the airplane's center of gravity, but the axis is close enough to use for this demonstration. What the ball does in the spin depends upon where the turn coordinator is mounted on the instrument panel. Most turn coordinators are on the far left side of the cockpit. Figure 20-4 illustrates the position difference between the ball and the center of gravity. If

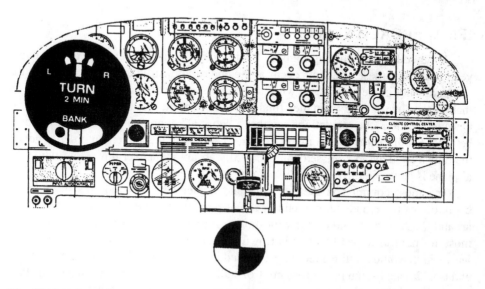

Fig. 20-4. *Enlarged turn and slip indicator illustrates the position of the ball. The ball will swing out regardless of the direction of the spin. Note that the turn indicator is not deflected...you determine which way to spin the paper.*

you were to cut this diagram out of the book you could easily see what will happen (for those of you who do not want to cut up your book, use your imagination or make a photocopy). Lay the diagram on a table and place the point of a pencil on the center of gravity symbol. Now, twirl the entire diagram around the pencil. As you can see, no matter which way you turn the paper, the turn coordinator is on the outside and centrifugal force would throw the ball to the left. If the plane is in a developed right spin, the ball will be to the left. Stepping on the ball is correct in this situation, but the ball will also be on the left in a developed left spin and stepping on the ball during a left spin will make things worse. This demonstration proves that the ball cannot be used to determine direction of spin in the clouds.

So far, we have not found a single instrument that could help us decide which rudder to push to stop autorotation. Forget the magnetic compass. Remember, the fuel gauges can tell you that a spin is taking place but not what direction it is going. The only instrument on the panel that can be of any service is the turn coordinator's airplane wings or the turn and slip indicator's needle indication.

The direction that the indicator is leaning is the direction of spin.

To successfully recover from a spin in the clouds, the pilot will have to have an excellent instrument scan and know which instrument to rely on. If the airplane has a turn coordinator, step on the rudder on the side of the indicator's raised wing. If a turn and slip indicator is used, step on the rudder opposite of the needle deflection. The indication will not represent the true rate of rotation because the indicator will be pegged out, but the true direction can be discovered.

IFR APPROACH STALLS

Another danger involving spins and instrument flying causes fatal accidents every year. Ironically, these accidents occur at the end of an instrument approach while the airplane is not in the clouds and with the danger supposedly past. Most IFR pilots let their guard down a little when they finally break out of the clouds and spot the runway. Once in the clear, the regulations say that a "normal" approach to the runway should be used. But in reality, pilots might border on acrobatic maneuvers in order to get on the runway and avoid a missed approach. Any abrupt maneuver down low, while the airplane is slow and dirty, is a stall/spin threat.

The most common is the circle-to-land maneuver. This requires the pilot to break out of the clouds on one end of the airport, then, typically, the pilot must fly around the airport to land on the wind-favored runway. This maneuver is lower than most normal traffic patterns and is flown tighter to prevent losing sight of the runway, which would require executing a missed approach procedure. The turn at the far end is a classical setup for a cross-control stall that leads to a spin accident. The best way to avoid this situation is to fly the approach as a teardrop rather than a rectangle, if cloud conditions permit. This gives you more room to make the turn (FIG. 20-5) and a greater margin of safety.

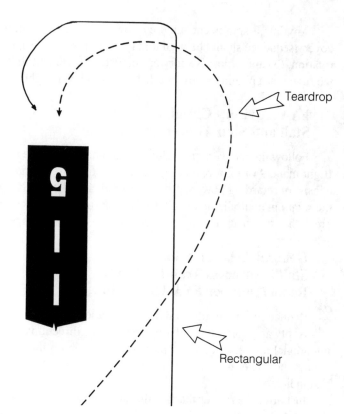

Fig. 20-5. *Allow extra room to make the circle-to-land maneuver. This will avoid a final approach overshoot and reduce the danger of a low-level stall.*

BASIC RECOVERY PROCEDURES

Part Four of this book examines spin research and recovery techniques, including a review of how to recover in select specific airplanes. Spin recovery might vary from one airplane to the next, but basic techniques are similar. Several documents have already established basic recovery procedures.

FAA Flight Training Handbook

The first corrective action taken during any power-on spin is to close the throttle. Power causes an abnormal loss of altitude in the recovery.

To recover from the spin, the pilot should first apply full opposite rudder; then after the rotation slows, apply brisk, positive straight forward movement of the elevator control. The control should be held firmly in this position.

Slow and overly-cautious control movements during spin recovery must be avoided. In certain cases, it has been found that such movement results in the airplane continuing to spin indefinitely.

Anytime a spin is encountered, regardless of the conditions, the normal spin recovery sequence should be used to: (1) retard power; (2) apply opposite rudder to slow rotation; (3) apply positive forward elevator movement to break the stall; (4) neutralize rudder as spinning stops; and (5) return to level flight.

FAA Advisory Circular
Stall and Spin Awareness Training

Follow the recovery procedures recommended by the manufacturer in the airplane flight manual or pilot operating handbook. In most aircraft, spin recovery techniques consist of retarding power (if in a powered aircraft), applying opposite rudder to slow the rotation, neutralizing the ailerons, applying positive forward elevator movement to break the stall, neutralizing the rudder as the spinning stops, and return to level flight.

General Aviation Pilot
Stall Awareness Training Study
Report number FAA-RD-77-26

Reduce throttle to idle and neutralize ailerons.

Apply and hold full rudder opposite to the direction of rotation. If the spin was unintentional and disorientation prevents determining the direction of rotation, refer to the turn needle or turn coordinator to establish direction of rotation. Do not refer to the ball indicator.

Just after the rudder reaches the stop, move the control wheel briskly forward far enough to break the stall. Full down elevator may be required.

Hold these control inputs until rotation stops.

As the rotation stops, neutralize rudder and smoothly recover from the resulting dive. Retract flaps before exceeding flap extension speed.

FAA Flight Test Guide for
Certification of Part 23 Airplanes

(Spin) recoveries should consist of throttle reduced to idle, ailerons neutralized, full opposite rudder, followed by forward elevator control as required to get the wing out of stall and recover to level flight, unless the manufacturer determines the need for another procedure.

NASA Stall/Spin Research for
General Aviation Airplanes

Move the rudder briskly against the spin, followed by forward stick about one-half turn later while maintaining neutral ailerons.

PART 4

Spin characteristics
of
trainer airplanes

21
Spin research

THE NATIONAL TRANSPORTATION SAFETY BOARD COLLECTED DATA ON general aviation stall/spin accidents for a study to determine accident frequency of common light airplanes. Thirty-seven light aircraft were chosen for the study over a three-year period. Thirty of the airplane types were single-engine and seven were multiengine. The study was not conducted in order to pass judgment on the relative safety of any of the airplanes, but rather to identify airplanes that would merit further stall/spin research.

The number of stall/spin accidents that each airplane was involved in was recorded. The number of accidents alone did not yield any good information because some airplane types are exposed to more stall/spin threats than others and would naturally have more accidents. To make the numbers more meaningful, accident totals were compared with the total hours that a particular type of airplane had flown during the three-year study. The numbers were further restricted to accidents that took place during flights classified as either pleasure, practice/instructional, or private business.

For example, during the study, Cessna 150s were involved in 140 stall/spin accidents. It was also determined that the Cessna 150 was used in pleasure, instructional, and business flights for a total of 10,460,395 flight hours during the same three years. Do not ask me how those flight hours were actually counted, but that is approximately 75,000 hours of Cessna 150 flight hours per stall/spin accident. Few modes of transportation have such a good accident rate.

All 37 airplanes were calculated the same way, then measured in relation to each other. When all the numbers were in, five categories were established for stall/spin accident frequency: very low, low, average, high, and very high:

Very low
- Piper PA-28 series
- Cessna 182 series
- Cessna 210 series
- Beech 35/35-33 series

Low
- Piper PA-24 series
- Cessna 172 series
- Cessna 180 series
- Cessna 206 series

Average
- Cessna 120/140 series
- Cessna 310 series
- Mooney M-20 series

High
- Beech 95/95-55 series

Very high
- Cessna 150 series
- Cessna 177 series
- Piper J-3/PA-11 series
- Piper PA-30 series

If the airplane you fly is on this list, that does not necessarily mean that it is practically spin-proof or extremely spin-hazardous. The study cautions readers to consider that a stall/spin accident is complex and factors, including "pilot judgment and proficiency, aerodynamic characteristics, effectiveness of installed stall warning equipment, phase of flight relationships," and the like, that could have been a more important cause of an accident than the airplane itself. The study points out that the method of stall/spin accident frequency calculation only defines "what" airplanes are involved most often, but does not define "why" the accident occurred. The value of the study should tell manufacturers, researchers, and pilots which airplanes should be examined more closely for stall/spin characteristics.

RESOLUTION

This sounds great. We have isolated the problem, now it is simply a matter of solving the problem; unfortunately general aviation aircraft spin testing that can be used by the general public is rare. This problem is the result of two situations: lack of money and product liability.

The manufacturers do not seem to have the dollars to spin test airplanes past that which is required for FAA certification. Most of the single-engine airplane training fleet is old. Companies want to work on new projects that will produce profits in the short term, not spend money on 15-year-old airplanes that have already run their economic course toward corporate profitability.

The manufacturers also fear lawsuits. Product liability litigation has driven most aircraft companies from the trainer airplane market altogether. Extensive stall/spin data on light aircraft does exist in many cases, but the manufacturers will not give over the data to the public for fear it would invite more lawsuits. NASA has done important work in the past on light general aviation airplanes, but NASA is very seldom allowed to test production airplanes. Instead, they test a "modified" Cessna or a "modified" Yankee. The testing facilities of NASA belong to the American taxpayer; therefore, the facilities are often rented by manufacturers for testing and the tests are conducted by company employees, rather than NASA employees. When the company-conducted tests are complete, the data received is considered "top secret" by the company. Any results from the tests that might help pilots would only appear in changes to future models. Beechcraft, for instance, conducted spin tests on the Skipper at the NASA spin tunnel, but the results were retained by the company.

This is not to imply that the manufacturers are at fault here, or are trying to hide something that would make flying safer. The system is broken. Today I teach people to fly in airplanes that time and technology has passed by. Tremendous strides have been made in almost every field in the last 15 years, but I will have students this year who are younger than the airplanes they fly solo in. Of course, during those same 15 years, lawsuits brought to the courts have scared off the manufacturers from innovation. The public should certainly be protected from flawed and dangerous products; unfortunately, pilots are less safe because a balance has not been achieved.

I wish this chapter were filled with valuable information that will produce safer pilots through stall/spin research knowledge, but the truth is that such data is just not widely available. The information about stalls and spins that is let out to the flying public is contained in the airplane's operating handbook or airplane flight manual. (Chapters 22 and 23 have single-engine and multiengine airplane recovery recommendations.) To their credit, Cessna has published a booklet entitled *Spin Characteristics of Cessna Models 150, A150, 152, A152, 172, R172, and 177*. This book goes beyond the pilot's operating handbook to discuss what a pilot can expect from these airplanes in a spin. If you fly any of these airplanes, I highly recommend that you obtain a copy from the Cessna publications department.

NASA RESEARCH

Spin testing in America takes place at a relatively small and out of the way facility at the Langley Research Center in Hampton, Virginia. Every year I take a group of college aerodynamics students to Langley, the home of aerodynamics. Several times my students and I have had the pleasure of touring the NASA spin tunnel with Dr. Raymond D. Whipple, who is the spin research group leader, NASA's "Spin Doctor." The facility is extremely unique with only two others like it in the world. The facility is also old and historic. Every United States military airplane from World War II to the present has been tested there and even spacecraft going back to the Mercury Project were spun inside the tunnel.

Scale-model tests

Unlike most wind tunnels with horizontal airflow, the NASA spin tunnel airflow is vertical (FIG. 21-1). A large fan draws air up through the test section of the tunnel.

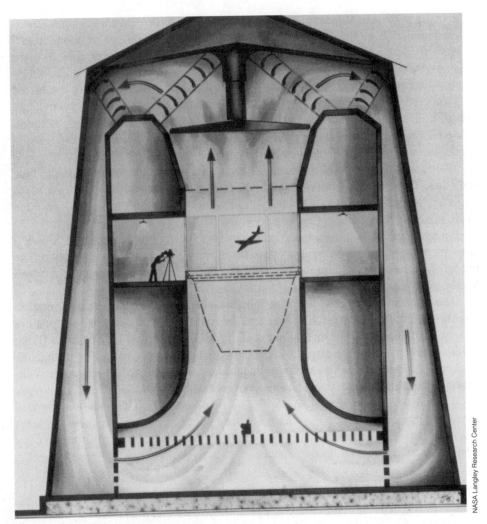

Fig. 21-1. *NASA's 20-foot vertical spin tunnel.*

NASA Langley Research Center

The air is then channeled around the outside of the thimble-shaped building. The air passes down and then is once again draw in and up though the test section. The speed of the fan blades is altered to match the descent rate of the model being tested. In 1992, the fan blades were replaced with a more efficient five-blade arrangement.

Scale models of aircraft are tossed into the vertical gale and observed during spins and recoveries. But these are no toy store models. I was holding an F-4 Phantom model once while at the tunnel and a student asked one of the technicians how much a model like that would cost. The man calmly said that that particular one cost more than $50,000. I carefully put the model down. They cost so much because they are "real."

All the control surfaces work and can be controlled from outside the tunnel by radio (FIG. 21-2). The model is a perfect match of the larger airplane; you would expect it to look like the real airplane, but these models are also proportionally weighted just like the real airplane.

Fig. 21-2. *Radio control unit for spin tunnel testing.*

When the model is flung into the test section of the tunnel, it starts off spinning. The remote-control pilot then attempts to fly the airplane into a spin recovery. If the spin recovery is successful, the model will dive into a safety net (FIG. 21-3).

Ordinarily, the models are free spinning (falling) in the center of the tunnel, but NASA uses another method to measure forces on the model during a spin. The model is mounted on a *rotary balance* device that holds the model in place and allows the model to spin at a predetermined rate (FIG. 21-4); therefore, changes in aircraft configuration and the resultant forces on the model can be measured.

NASA Langley spins models in the actual atmosphere by dropping them from the side of a helicopter. The helicopter has a special model dropping attachment that hangs over the side. Once dropped, the spin recovery is attempted by radio remote control.

Real-model tests

And finally, NASA spins real airplanes. The fleet of typical general aviation airplanes that has been tested includes the Yankee (FIG. 1-7), a Beechcraft Sundowner, a Cessna 172 (FIG. 21-5), and a prototype Piper T-tail airplane. The spin test aircraft were outfitted with various gear to assist in the experiments. The Yankee was equipped with a spin parachute that was used to stop a spin when normal control movements failed to stop the spin. The Sundowner had hydrogen peroxide rocket engines on the wings to stop spins or to speed them up. The airplanes had external cameras, instrumentation to calculate rotation rates, and wingtip booms that provided extremely accurate airspeed, angle of attack, and slip information. The results of NASA-conducted tests are available to the public.

Fig. 21-3A. *Airplane model during spin test.*

Fig. 21-3B. *NASA spin test of modified Grumman trainer airplane.*

Fig. 21-4. *Flow visualization test using model on the rotary balance apparatus.*

Fig. 21-5. *NASA-modified Cessna 172 spin test airplane.*

22

Single-engine airplane spin recovery techniques

AIRPLANES THAT ARE DESIGNED DIFFERENTLY WILL RECOVER FROM A SPIN differently. The following are samples from manufacturer recommendations of single-engine general aviation airplanes. (The pilot in command is responsible for safe operation of the aircraft during any training maneuver. Refer to current operating handbooks to help ensure safety.)

Cessna 150M, 152, A152 Aerobat, 172N, 177B, and 210R

1. Retard throttle to idle position.
2. Place ailerons in neutral position.
3. Apply and hold full rudder opposite the direction of rotation.
4. Just after the rudder reaches the stop, move the control wheel briskly forward far enough to break the stall. Full down elevator may be required at aft center of gravity loadings to assure optimum recoveries.
5. Hold these control inputs until rotation stops. Premature relaxation of the control inputs may extend recovery.
6. As rotation stops, neutralize rudder, and make a smooth recovery from the resulting dive.

Cessna has also published basic guidelines for intentional spins in Cessna airplanes:

- Know your aircraft thoroughly.
- Prior to doing spins in any model aircraft, obtain thorough instruction in spins from an instructor fully qualified and current in spinning that model.

- Be familiar with the parachute, airspace and weather requirements of FAR 91 as affect your flight.
- Check the aircraft weight and balance to be sure you are within the approved envelope for spins.
- Secure or remove all loose cockpit equipment prior to takeoff.
- Be sure the area to be used is suitable for spins and is clear of other traffic.
- Enter each spin at a high altitude. Plan recoveries to be completed well above the minimum legal altitude of 1,500 feet above the surface.
- Conduct all entries in accordance with the procedures recommended by the manufacturer. Limit yourself to 2-turn spins until completely familiar with the characteristics of your airplane.
- Use the recommended recovery procedure.

Cessna also recommends:

For the purpose of training in spins and spin recoveries, a 1 or 2 turn spin will normally provide all that is necessary. All of the characteristic motions and control inputs required will be experienced. Longer spins, while acceptable as a maneuver in appropriately certified airplanes, provide little additional insight to the student in the area of spin recovery since the prime reason for conducting a spin is to learn how to avoid an inadvertent entry in the first place and then how to recover if one should develop.

It is recommended that, where feasible, entries be accomplished at altitudes high enough to complete recoveries 4,000 feet or more above ground level. At least 1,000 feet of altitude loss should be allowed for a 1 turn spin and recovery, while a 6 turn spin and recovery may require somewhat more than twice that amount for the Cessna models 150, A150, 152, and A152.

Piper PA-38-112 Tomahawk

1. Neutralize the ailerons.
2. Apply and maintain full rudder opposite the direction of rotation.
3. As the rudder hits the stop, push the control wheel full forward. As the stall is broken, relax forward pressure to prevent an excessive airspeed buildup.
4. Close the throttle.
5. As rotation stops, neutralize the rudder and ease back on the control wheel to recover smoothly from the dive.
6. Retract the flaps if they have been extended.

Piper PA-28-161 Cadet

1. Throttle—idle.
2. Ailerons—neutral.
3. Rudder—full opposite to direction of rotation.

4. Control wheel—full forward.
5. Rudder—neutral (when rotation stops).
6. Control wheel—as required to smoothly regain level flight attitude.

Piper Cherokee 140

1. Throttle—idle.
2. Rudder—full opposite to direction of rotation.
3. Control wheel—full forward.
4. Rudder—neutral (when rotation stops).
5. Control wheel—as required to smoothly regain level flight attitude.

Piper PA-28-161 Warrior II

Immediately move the throttle to idle and the ailerons to neutral.
Full rudder should be then applied opposite to the direction of rotation followed by control wheel full forward. When rotation stops, neutralize the rudder and ease back on the control wheel as required to smoothly regain a level flight attitude.

Piper Arrow II

1. Throttle—idle.
2. Rudder—full opposite to directions of rotation.
3. Control wheel—full forward.
4. Rudder—neutral (when rotation stops).
5. Control wheel—as required to smoothly regain level flight attitude.

Mooney M20K (252) and M20J (201)

1. Rudder—apply full rudder opposite the direction of spin.
2. Control wheel—forward of neutral in a brisk motion. Additional forward elevator control may be required if the rotation does not stop.
3. Ailerons—neutral.
4. Throttle—retard to idle.
5. Hold anti-spin controls until rotation stops.
6. Flaps (if extended)—retract.
7. Rudder—neutralize when spin stops.
8. Control wheel—smoothly move aft to bring the nose up to a level flight attitude.

Beechcraft Skipper 77, Bonanza V35B and F33A, and Sundowner 180 C23

Immediately move the control column full forward and simultaneously apply full rudder opposite to the direction of the spin; continue to hold this control position until the rotation stops and then neutralize all controls and execute a smooth pull out.

Ailerons should be neutral and throttle in idle position at all times during the recovery.

Bellanca Decathlon

1. Throttle—closed.
2. Ailerons—neutral position.
3. Elevator—positive forward to neutral (free release of elevator control is not adequate for recovery).
4. Rudder—full deflection in opposite direction to the rotation.
5. Rudder—neutralize when rotation stops and positive control and flying speed is restored.
6. Nose attitude—raise smoothly to level flight attitude.
7. Throttle—only after recovery from diving attitude, then as required.

[Notice elevator before rudder in this recommendation.]

Bellanca Citabria

1. Throttle—closed.
2. Rudder—full deflection opposite direction of rotation.
3. Elevator—slightly forward of neutral.
4. Ailerons—neutral position.

When rotation stops (½ to 1 turn after recovery is initiated).

5. Rudder—neutralized.
6. Nose attitude—raise smoothly to level flight attitude.

Grumman American Cheetah

1. Throttle—idle.
2. Ailerons—neutral.
3. Rudder—hold opposite of rotation, full rudder.
4. Elevator—full forward, simultaneously with rudder application.
5. Hold controls in these positions until rotation stops.
6. When rotation stops, neutralize rudder and recover from the dive.

23
Multiengine airplane spin recovery techniques

THE FOLLOWING ARE SPIN RECOVERY RECOMMENDATIONS FOR MULTI-engine airplanes provided to pilots from the manufacturer. Realize that current FAA regulations for multiengine airplane certification do not require spin and spin recovery tests; several of the recommendations refer to this. If you spin a multiengine airplane, you really do become an instant test pilot.

Piper PA-44-180 Seminole

1. Throttles—retard to idle.
2. Rudder—full opposite to the direction of spin.
3. Control wheel—release back pressure.
4. Control wheel—full forward if nose does not drop.
5. Ailerons—neutral.
6. Rudder—neutralize when rotation stops.
7. Control wheel—smooth back pressure to recover from dive.

Note: Federal Aviation Regulations do not require spin demonstration of multiengine airplanes; therefore, spin tests have not been conducted. The recovery technique is based on the best available information.

Piper PA-34-200T Seneca II

Immediately retard the throttles to the idle position. Apply full rudder opposite the direction of spin rotation. Let up all back pressure on the control wheel. If the nose does not drop, immediately push the control wheel full forward. Keep the ailerons neutral. Maintain the controls in these positions until spin rotation stops, then neutralize the rudder. Recovery from the resultant dive should be with smooth back pressure on the control wheel.

Piper Pa-23-250 Aztec

If a spin occurs, retard both throttle controls to idle. Apply full rudder opposite to the direction of the spin and place the control wheel forward of neutral, full forward if necessary to effect recovery. Leave ailerons neutral. Neutralize rudder when rotation stops. Smoothly recover from the dive when the spin is arrested.

Cessna 310

1. Cut power on both engines.
2. Apply full rudder opposing the directions of rotation.
3. Approximately ½ turn after applying rudder, push control wheel forward briskly.
4. To expedite recovery, add power to the engine toward the inside of the direction of turn.
5. Pull out of dive with smooth steady control pressure.

Cessna 337 Skymaster

1. Retard the throttles to idle position.
2. Place ailerons in neutral position.
3. Apply and hold full rudder opposite to the direction of rotation.
4. As the rudder reaches the opposite stop (approximately ¼ turn), move the control wheel briskly full forward.
5. Hold these control inputs until rotation stops.
6. As rotation stops, neutralize rudder and make a smooth recovery from the resulting dive.

Cessna 421 and 441

1. Throttles—close immediately.
2. Ailerons—neutralize.
3. Rudder—hold full rudder opposite the direction of rotation.
4. Control wheel—forward briskly, ½ turn of spin after applying full rudder.
5. Inboard engine—increase power to slow rotation (if necessary).

After rotation has stopped:

6. Rudder—neutralize.
7. Inboard engine (if used)—decrease power to equalize engines.
8. Control wheel—pull to recover from resultant dive. Apply smooth steady control pressure.

Note: The airplane has not been flight tested in spins, thus the above recommended procedure is based entirely on the best judgment of Cessna Aircraft Company.

Beechcraft Duchess 76 and Baron 58

Immediately move the control column full forward, apply full rudder opposite to the direction of the spin and reduce power on both engines to idle. These three actions should be done as nearly simultaneous as possible; then continue to hold this control position until rotation stops and then neutralize all controls and execute a smooth pull-out. Ailerons should be neutral during recovery.

Note: Federal Aviation Administration regulations do not require spin demonstration of airplanes of this class; therefore, no spin tests have been conducted. The recovery technique is based on the best available information.

[Author's note: No spin tests were performed on a production Beechcraft 76, but NASA did conduct extensive spin tests on a modified Beechcraft 76. The NASA spin test project on the Duchess resulted in more than 150 spins including fully developed spins.]

Douglas DC-3

Approaches to stalls are performed at a minimum altitude of 5,000 feet above the terrain at various operational gross weights. They are performed in the clean configuration and landing configuration while straight and level and in a 15 degree banked turn. Speed is reduced until buffet onset occurs, at which time a recovery is effected. The objective is to regain a safe climb speed (84 knots) with minimum loss of altitude commensurate with safety.

Characteristics:

General buffeting warns of an impending stall.

When stalled, the aircraft has no tendency to roll and recovery is normal.

Maintaining the aircraft at a stall results in severe tail buffeting.

The aircraft will stall with power on at speeds considerably below those given in the stall speed chart, and has a definite tendency to fall off on one wing or snap roll.

Recovery:

Normal procedure is used for corrective measures. Accomplish the recovery gently but firmly.

Spins:

If an inadvertent spin occurs, recovery is normal.

[Author's note: A "normal" spin recovery is not defined, but remember the DC-3 is from an era when every pilot was required to spin as a requirement for certification.]

Boeing 727

Pilot performance is judged on the ability to recognize the approach to stall, prompt action in initiating recovery, and holding the heading and smooth recovery without excessive loss of altitude. [Same as in a Cessna 150.]

The Boeing 727 was certified with an operable stall warning device for all flights. This will not be deactivated in flight. Consequently, pilots will be trained to initiate recovery at the earliest identifiable warning even though this is caused by an artificial device.

Configuration—clean stall

Initial conditions:
Flight director—off
Altitude—above 8,000 feet AGL
Set EPR bugs—go-around EPR
Primary airspeed bug—V ref
Secondary airspeed bug—V ref + 15 knots
Trim to—200 knots
Recover at—190 knots

Entry procedure:
Power off above [faster than] 210 knots
210 knots call for 55% N1
Rate of climb 100 to 300 fpm
Hold heading

Recovery procedure—stick shaker:
Start recovery at earliest warning and no less than V ref + 33 knots. Advance power levers and call for max power.
Two hands on yoke.
Lower nose slightly below horizon.
Call for flaps 2 degrees.
Call—Speed Brakes Down.
Accelerate to 190 knots.
Zero rate of climb.
Keep wings level with ailerons.
Clean up on flap/speed schedule.
Call for climb power.

Grumman Aerospace Corporation's F-14A Tomcat

The Tomcat is very forgiving when flown into out-of-control maneuvers and is highly spin-resistant except for a small region around 17 units of angle of attack (AOA) when not using slats.

It will spin if pushed hard enough—a very fast, flat spin, with loading nearing 6 G's which is extremely difficult to get out of.

Departing controlled flight (spin): This can occur during maneuvers in which roll is combined with increasing AOA, and is caused by adverse yaw generated by the differentially moving tailerons.

Recovery is effected by neutralizing rudders and lateral stick, then pushing the stick slowly forward to reduce the AOA to 17 units or less. If the yaw and roll motion does not cease, it should be controlled by using the stick in the direction of, and the rudders opposite to, the direction of the roll/yaw, neutralizing both controls when the motion stops. Level flight is then regained by holding 17 units AOA until speed increases enough to permit a harder pullout.

[Author's note: It seems that the basic spin recovery procedure is common: (1) power to idle, (2) rudder opposite the spin, (3) elevator forward to break the stall, (4) hold controls until spin stops, and (5) smooth pullout to level flight. Very few differences are found between single-engine trainers, multiengine businessliners, airliners, and carrier-based fighters.]

PART 5

Flight proficiency

24
Regulations

THE CURRENT FEDERAL AVIATION REGULATIONS DICTATE WHAT PILOT applicants must learn in order to be eligible for pilot certification. The flight instructor is responsible for teaching the required topics and allowing the student to practice until they meet the FAA test standards. There comes a time when all the logbook requirements are met and the flight instructor debates in his or her mind whether or not the student is truly ready to pass the checkride.

Before the checkride can begin, the flight instructor must sign a legal endorsement that certifies that the requirements have been met and in the opinion of the instructor the applicant can complete the test. When an instructor signs that endorsement, they put their reputation on the line. If an applicant fails the checkride they can always get additional instruction, then go back and pass the test on the second attempt.

Years later nobody will ever know if an applicant passed on the first try or not. The only long-term record of a student's success or failure on the checkride goes on the instructor's record. The flight instructor certificate is the only pilot certificate that is issued with an expiration date. When the instructor comes up for renewal, the FAA often looks at their percentage of students who pass on the first attempt versus those who fail the first time. Good flight instructors never give out their signature very quickly and without being sure that what they sign is the absolute truth.

The following is a list of regulations (and translations from legal jargon to English) pertaining to stalls and spin education. Every pilot should know exactly what the FAA expects at all levels of flight.

The regulations are constantly changed and updated. As you progress through pilot training and career as a pilot, it will be important to check these regulations from time to time to catch any changes, whether a new regulatory paragraph number or text change.

Is learning about stalls required prior to the first solo? Yes. FAR 61.87 is the "first solo" regulation. A flight instructor must write a legal endorsement in the student's logbook and also sign the back of the student pilot certificate (third-class medical certificate) that attests to the fact that all required training has been accomplished. To fly solo in an airplane for the first time, the student must "have received presolo flight training in stall entries from various flight attitudes and power combinations with recovery initiated at the first indication of a stall, and recovery from a full stall," according to 61.87(e)(5).

FAR 61.87(c) defines how well the student should perform a stall: "student must have demonstrated proficiency to an acceptable performance level as judged by the instructor who endorses the student's pilot certificate."

The wording of this part of the regulation has changed. The word proficiency has replaced a mere reference to flight training given. Apparently, a legal difference exists. It was possible to show a student a stall and say that they received the required stall training even though the student could not perform a stall demonstration. This new wording specifically calls for the student and instructor to go beyond demonstration and practice until the student is proficient.

Does a recreational pilot certificate require stall training to become eligible for solo? Yes. The requirements of FAR 61.87 pertains to anyone who flies solo as a student pilot regardless of what certificate they are working toward.

Are applicants for the recreational pilot certificate required to demonstrate stalls on the checkride? Yes. FAR 61.98 is the recreational pilot flight proficiency regulation: 61.98(a)(5), "an authorized flight instructor has found the applicant competent to perform...flight at slow airspeeds with realistic distractions and the recognition and recovery from stalls entered from straight flight and from turns."

Are applicants for the recreational pilot certificate required to demonstrate spins on the checkride? No. Spins are not required under 61.98; however, spins are a part of a recreational pilot's ground school curriculum. FAR 61.97(h) states that an applicant for a recreational certificate must have aeronautical knowledge of "stall awareness, spin entry, spins, and spin recovery techniques." In other words, you do not have to actually spin in an airplane, but you must talk about spins.

Are applicants for the private pilot certificate required to stall during flight training or on the checkride? Yes. FAR 61.107 spells out what flight proficiencies private pilots are supposed to display; 61.107(a)(4), pertaining to airplanes, says that applicants must be competent to perform "flight at slow speeds with realistic distractions, and the recognition and recovery from stalls entered from straight flight and from turns." This is exactly the same requirement for recreational pilots.

Are applicants for the private pilot certificate required to spin during flight training or the checkride? No. But the same requirement exists for stall and spin awareness. FAR 61.105 outlines what private pilots need to know in order to pass a checkride; 61.105(a)(6) states that an applicant must have knowledge of "stall awareness, spin entry, spins, and spin recovery techniques." Once again, real spin training is not required but the topic is no longer taboo in ground school.

Are stalls required for the instrument pilot checkride? Possibly. FAR 61.65 has instrument rating rules. No mention is made in this regulation about stalls or spins specifically. But, 61.65(c)(5) says that applicants for the IFR rating must be found competent in "simulated emergencies, including the recovery from unusual attitudes." It would be easy for an examiner to consider a stall under the hood as an "unusual attitude" and ask the applicant to either perform stalls under the hood or recovery from a stall that the examiner has placed the airplane in. Carrying this a little further, a spin is a very unusual attitude. Does this mean that the examiner could cause the airplane to enter a spin during unusual attitude recoveries and expect the applicant to recover under the hood? This probably will not happen, but the regulation does not rule it out.

What about commercial pilot applicants? Are they required to stall while preparing for the checkride and also on the checkride? Yes. FAR 61.127(a)(2) lists the same requirement as recreational and private pilots.

Are commercial pilots required to spin? No. The requirement is aeronautical knowledge of spin entry, spinning, and spin recovery.

What are flight instructor applicants required to do regarding stalls and spins? FAR 61.187(a)(6) states that CFI applicants must be competent to pass a practical test that "shall include the satisfactory demonstration of stall awareness, spin entry, spins, and spin recovery techniques in an aircraft of the appropriate category that is certified for spins." All the pilot certificates so far have required the demonstration and proficiency of stalls but this is the first time spins have been required "in an airplane."

Are flight instructor applicants required to spin on their checkride? Maybe. According to FAR 61.183(e), the FAA inspector has the option to "accept the spin training logbook endorsement OR require demonstration of the spin entry, spin, and spin recovery maneuver on the flight portion of the practical test." If the checkride is failed and the reason for the failure is the lack of knowledge about stalls, spin entry, spins, and spin recovery, then there is no option: the applicant must spin for the FAA inspector. The spin training logbook endorsement referred to in this regulation is another legal statement that spin training and applicant proficiency has been accomplished. FAR 61.187(b) also stipulates that the person who makes this written statement must themselves have been a flight instructor for the previous 24 months and has given at least 200 hours of flight instruction.

Are airline transport pilots required to do stalls? Yes. Appendix A of Part 61 outlines all the maneuvers that constitute the ATP checkride;

"Inflight Maneuvers—Approaches to Stalls" (IV(b)) states that ATP applicants must perform at least three stalls: "(1) one must be in the takeoff configuration (except where the airplane uses only a zero-flap takeoff configuration); (2) one in a clean configuration; and (3) one in a landing configuration."

By this rule's definition, the approach to stall is accomplished when "there is a perceptible buffet or other response to the initial stall entry." One of these stalls must be performed while "in a turn with a bank angle between 15 and 30 degrees." One more requirement is that all stalls must be performed in "simulated instrument conditions," which means under the hood.

When intentional spins are performed, are parachutes required? This answer depends upon why the spins are executed. According to FAR 91.307(c), "Unless each occupant of the aircraft is wearing an approved parachute, no pilot of a civil aircraft carrying any person (other than a crewmember) may execute any intentional maneuver that exceeds (1) A bank of 60 degrees relative to the horizon; or (2) A nose-up or nose-down attitude of 30 degrees relative to the horizon." A spin will certainly exceed both of those no-parachute limits. But like all good FARs, there is an exception: 91.307(d) says that the parachute requirement is waived when it takes place during a "(1) flight test for pilot certification or rating; or (2) for spins and other flight maneuvers required by the regulations for any certificate or rating when given by a certificated flight instructor." So any spinning done without a flight instructor must be done with parachutes. (Speaking as a flight instructor, this seems a little odd. If a situation arises where a parachute is needed the danger will not be reduced just because a CFI is on board. This is not to increase safety but to create a loophole. If parachutes, parachute training, and actual jumping from airplanes was required to teach CFIs, economics would drive even more instructors from the business. By allowing this exception the extra parachute expense is eliminated. But is this loophole in the law the best for flight safety? You decide that one. I personally have a bias based upon the fact that I am another pilot who is afraid of heights and I have no intention of jumping from an airplane.)

25
Checkride standards

IN THE LATE 1980S, THE FAA CHANGED THE FORMAT THAT CHECKRIDES follow. Designated pilot examiners formerly used a flight test guide that outlined various maneuvers that could be used to make up the checkride. The examiners used their own judgment as to what exactly would be on the test. This meant that checkrides became very different from one examiner to another. The FAA began to realize that with everyone taking a different test for the same pilot certificate, the quality of the pilot product would be different from one pilot to the next. The FAA then took steps to standardize the checkrides in hopes of making them more uniform.

Theoretically, the same test should be given by any examiner, anywhere in the country. To do this, the FAA published the *Practical Test Standards* (PTS) that made the old test guides obsolete. The practical test standard plainly spells out exactly what the examiner will do and what is expected of the applicant. In other words, they have published the checkride.

WRITTEN TESTS

Years ago the FAA did the same thing with the written test. You do not have to be too old to remember when all written tests were given at the general aviation district office (GADO), which are now called flight standards district offices (FSDO). When I went to the Nashville GADO to take the private pilot written exam in 1972, I was first given an oral exam. That's right, there was a time when inspectors actually quizzed students to determine if they were prepared enough to take the written test. I remember what the inspector said to me: "I'm not sure how well the information has sunk in, but I'll go ahead and let you take the test." He then lead me into the testing room where I filled out a bunch of paperwork.

The room had metal tables lined up and one wall was a long window so that GADO personnel could watch you take the test. On each table was a Wichita sectional and a yardstick. We all knew that there would be several cross-country planning questions asked on the test from the Wichita sectional. The yardstick was to make the "across-the-chart" true course line easier to draw. Above all was the fact that nobody knew what questions were on the test. The tests were kept in a safe.

Then somebody stole the tests and began passing them around. After that, the FAA went to the format where all test questions were published. Now all pilots buy the 1,000 questions knowing that they really only need to know the answer to between 50 and 100 of them. For questions that involve a long calculation, students simply memorize which selection is correct and move on. The test is no longer a test of aeronautical knowledge, but a test of how to take a test, and the FAA knows this. More emphasis is now placed on the practical test because the written test is less effective. The actual determination of a pilot's knowledge and skill is made on the checkride and that is why the practical test standard is so important.

TESTING CONTROVERSY

The practical tests have also come under some controversy. FAA inspectors do very few checkrides. Most of the checkrides are done by private citizens who have been given the power to issue pilot certificates: designated pilot examiners. Designees receive no money from the FAA, they only make money by charging applicants for the checkride; giving checkrides can be big money. As we have seen in so many other walks of life, wherever there is the potential for big money, corruption is soon to follow. Flight instructors have the option of choosing which examiner they will send their students to for the test.

If an examiner gets the reputation as being very tough and many applicants are failed on their first try, the flight instructors will soon be sending their students elsewhere. This is human nature. If the examiner sees his business and income falling off because of his or her reputation, there will at least be the temptation to ease up a bit. If an examiner is known among flight instructors as being a "Santa Claus," that examiner can get rich. The vast majority of examiners are uncorruptable and are doing the job in the best interest of aviation, but there are still plenty of stories about examiners taking the money and issuing the certificate without ever flying with the applicant.

One examiner was caught giving away ATP certificates three at a time: one applicant in the left seat and two in the back seat. The applicants in the back never flew the airplane. Once the FAA gives a person examiner status, it is tough for them to take it back. Hard proof would be required to strip an examiner, but checkride evaluation is just the examiner's opinion.

The FAA has come up with one plan that would eliminate the examiner profit motive and more completely standardize the tests. When a flight instructor decides to send a student on a checkride under this plan, he would not contact an examiner directly, but would call the FSDO first. The FSDO would then assign an examiner to give the test. The problem is that the assignment would be made on a rotation basis and the student might be forced to fly across the state to take the test while other examiners are closer. The examiner would have a steady flow of students regardless of his or her reputation. Examiners could give the test knowing that the outcome would not affect their revenue.

PTS PRESCRIPTION

The FAA suggests that flight instructors introduce the *Practical Test Standards* to the student pilots early in the training. This is probably a good idea because the student can see what is expected from the beginning. Springing the PTS on a student the night before a checkride is considered bad form. But teaching from the PTS also fosters the "only-teach-to-the-test" problem. The best situation is when students learn to fly to standards greater than what the test requires and then the test becomes just another step in the learning process.

My first aviation instructor was Bill Gehres, affectionately called Big G. I remember Big G telling us what he had asked his flight instructor to do, "teach me to fly, and oh yes, a license would be nice too." He was very proud of that statement. He meant that learning to fly was more important than to aim low at some words in a book.

Nevertheless, the PTS is the gate-keeper to pilot certification. I advocate learning to fly for all the right reasons, but I am practical as well. Practical test applicants had better read and understand the PTS. Standards pertaining to stalls and spins for every pilot certificate finish this chapter.

OVERVIEW

Each PTS has a catchall paragraph in the introduction. The layout of the PTS with its objectives and tasks is explained and then it gives the examiner some latitude when it says that in addition to the tasks that are clearly spelled out in the PTS certain areas that might "not be shown under each task, but are essential to flight safety will receive careful evaluation throughout the practical test." These additional areas are listed: "The examiner will also emphasize stall/spin awareness, spatial disorientation, collision avoidance, wake turbulence avoidance, low-level wind shear, use of checklists, and other areas as directed by future revisions of this standard." These areas of knowledge apply to recreational, private, instrument, and commercial certificates.

The "use of distractions" as a test evaluation tactic is also covered in the PTS introduction: "Many accidents have resulted from engine failure during takeoff and landing where safe flight was possible if the pilot had used correct control techniques and divided attention properly." The PTS then lists examples of distractions that examiners might attempt when evaluating the student's division of attention training:

- Simulate engine failure
- Simulating radio tuning and communications
- Identifying a field suitable for emergency landing
- Identifying features or objects on the ground
- Reading the outside air temperature gauge
- Removing objects from the glove compartment
- Questioning by the examiner

Recall that the distraction or distractions can lead to a stall and a stall to a spin. Students should always remember that their most important job is to fly the airplane. Flying the airplane by properly controlling airspeed is still the most effective stall prevention.

RECREATIONAL PILOT CHECKRIDE STALL STANDARDS

V. Area of operation: flight at critically slow airspeed

A. Task: stall - power on
Objective. To determine that the applicant:
1. Exhibits knowledge of explaining the aerodynamic factors and flight situations that may result in stalls - power on, including power recovery procedures, and hazards of stalling during uncoordinated flight.
2. Selects an entry altitude that will allow a recovery to be completed no lower than 1,500 feet above ground level.
3. Establishes takeoff or normal climb configuration.
4. Establishes takeoff or climb airspeed before applying takeoff or climb power (reduced power may be used to avoid excessive pitch-up during entry only).
5. Establishes and maintains a pitch attitude straight ahead that will induce a stall.
6. Establishes and maintains a pitch attitude that will induce a stall in a turn with a bank angle of 20 degrees, plus or minus 10 degrees.
7. Applies proper control to maintain coordinated flight.
8. Recognizes the indications of a stall and promptly recovers with a minimum loss of altitude by simultaneously decreasing the angle of attack, leveling the wings, and adjusting the power as necessary to regain normal flight attitude.
9. Avoids a secondary stall.
10. Retracts the wing flaps and establishes straight and level flight.

B. Task: stall - power off
Objective: To determine that the applicant:
1. Exhibits knowledge by explaining the aerodynamic factors and flight situations that may result in stalls - power off, including proper recovery procedures, and hazards of stalling during uncoordinated flight.

2. Selects an entry altitude that will allow a recovery to be completed no lower than 1,500 feet above the ground.
3. Establishes a normal approach to landing configuration and airspeed with the throttle closed or at a reduced power setting.
4. Establishes a straight glide or a gliding turn with a bank angle of 30 degrees, plus or minus 10 degrees, in coordinated flight.
5. Establishes and maintains a landing pitch attitude that will induce a stall.
6. Recognizes the indications of a stall and promptly recovers with a minimum loss of altitude by simultaneously decreasing the angle of attack, leveling the wings, and adjusting the power as necessary to regain normal flight attitude.
7. Avoids a secondary stall.
8. Retracts the wing flaps and establishes straight and level flight.

C. Task: maneuvering during slow flight

Objective: To determine that the applicant:
1. Exhibits knowledge by explaining the flight characteristics and controllability associated with maneuvering during slow flight.
2. Selects an entry altitude that will allow the maneuver to be performed at no lower that 1,500 feet above the ground.
3. Establishes and maintains slow flight during coordinated straight and turning flight in various configurations and bank angles.
4. Maintains the desired altitude within plus or minus 100 feet.
5. Maintains the specified heading during straight flight within plus or minus 10 degrees.
6. Maintains the specified bank angle within plus or minus 10 degrees during turning flight.
7. Maintains an airspeed of 10 knots above stall speed by plus or minus 5 knots.

PRIVATE PILOT CHECKRIDE STALL STANDARDS

VI. Area of operation: flight by reference to instruments

E. Task: unusual flight attitudes

Objective: To determine that the applicant:
1. Exhibits knowledge by explaining flight solely by reference to instruments as related to unusual flight attitudes.
2. Recognizes unusual flight attitudes promptly.
3. Properly interprets the instruments.
4. Recovers to a stabilized level flight attitude by prompt, smooth, coordinated control, applied in the proper sequence.
5. Avoids excessive load factor, airspeed and stall.
NOTE: Unusual attitudes, such as a start of a power-on spiral or an approach to a climbing stall, shall not exceed 45 degrees bank or 10 degrees pitch from level flight.

VII. Area of operation: flight at critically slow airspeeds

A. Task: stalls - power off

Objective: To determine that the applicant:

1. Exhibits knowledge by explaining the aerodynamic factors and flight situations that may result in full stalls power off, including proper recovery procedures, and hazards of stalling during uncoordinated flight.
2. Selects an entry altitude that will allow the recoveries to be completed no lower than 1,500 feet above ground.
3. Establishes the normal approach or landing configuration and airspeed with the throttle closed or at a reduced power setting.
4. Establishes a straight glide or a gliding turn with a bank angle of 30 degrees, plus or minus 10 degrees in coordinated flight.
5. Establishes and maintains a pitch attitude that will induce a stall.
6. Recognizes the indications of a full stall and promptly recovers by decreasing the angle of attack, leveling the wings, and adjusting the power, as necessary to regain normal flight attitude.
7. Retracts the wing flaps and landing gear (if retractable) and establishes straight and level flight or climb.
8. Avoids secondary stalls, excessive airspeed, excessive altitude loss, spins, and flight below 1,500 feet above ground level.

B. Task: full stalls - power on

Objective: To determine that the applicant:

1. Exhibits knowledge by explaining the aerodynamic factors and flight situations that may result in full stalls - power on, including proper recovery procedures, and hazards of stalling during uncoordinated flight.
2. Selects an entry altitude that will allow recoveries to be completed no lower than 1,500 feet above ground.
3. Establishes takeoff or normal climb configuration.
4. Establishes takeoff or climb airspeed before applying takeoff or climb power. (Reduced power may only be used to avoid excessive pitch-up during entry only).
5. Establishes and maintains a pitch attitude straight ahead or in a turn with a bank angle of 20 degrees, plus or minus 10 degrees, that will induce a full stall.
6. Applies proper control to maintain coordinated flight.
7. Recognizes the indications of a full stall and promptly recovers by decreasing the angle of attack, leveling the wings and adjusting power, as necessary, to regain normal flight attitude.
8. Retracts the wing flaps and landing gear (if retractable) and establishes straight and level flight or climb.
9. Avoids secondary stall, excessive airspeed, excessive altitude loss, spin, and flight below 1,500 feet AGL.

C. Task: imminent stalls - power on and power off

Objective: To determine that the applicant:

1. Exhibits knowledge by explaining the aerodynamic factors associated with imminent stalls (power on and power off), an awareness of speed loss in different configurations, and the procedure for resuming normal flight attitude.
2. Selects an entry altitude that will allow recoveries to be completed no lower than 1,500 feet above the ground.
3. Establishes either a takeoff or climb, or an approach configuration with the appropriate power setting.
4. Establishes a pitch attitude on a constant heading, plus or minus 10 degrees, or 20 degree bank turns, plus or minus 10 degrees, that will induce an imminent stall.
5. Applies proper control to maintain coordinated flight.
6. Recognizes and recovers from imminent stalls at the first indication of buffeting or decay of control effectiveness by reducing angle of attack and adjusting power, as necessary, to regain normal flight attitude.
7. Avoids full stalls, secondary stall, excessive altitude change, spin, and flight below 1,500 feet above the ground.

D. Task: maneuvering at critically slow airspeed

Objective: To determine that the applicant:

1. Exhibits knowledge by explaining the flight characteristics and controllability associated with maneuvering at critically slow airspeeds.
2. Selects an entry altitude that will allow the maneuver to be performed no lower than 1,500 feet above the ground.
3. Establishes and maintains a critically slow airspeed while-
   (a) in coordinated straight and level flight in various configurations and bank angles, and
   (b) in coordinated departure climbs and landing approach descents in various configurations.
4. Maintains the desired altitude within plus or minus 100 feet, when a constant altitude is specified, and level off from climbs and descents within plus or minus 100 feet.
5. Maintains the desired heading during straight flight within plus or minus 10 degrees.
6. Maintains the specified bank angle within plus or minus 10 degrees while in coordinated flight.
7. Maintains a critically slow airspeed within plus 5 knots and minus 0 knots.

INSTRUMENT RATING CHECKRIDE STANDARDS

No tasks directly involve stalls listed in the *Instrument Rating - Airplane Practical Test Standards*; however, recovery from unusual flight attitudes is included. This leaves the door open for "under-the-hood" stalls on the checkride. This maneuver also incorporates a simulated loss of the vacuum system by covering the attitude gyro.

III. Area of operation: flight by reference to instruments.

G. Task: recovery from unusual flight attitudes.

Objective: To determine that the applicant:

1. Exhibits adequate knowledge of the factors relating to attitude instrument flying during recovery from unusual flight attitudes (both nose-high and nose-low).

2. Uses proper instrument cross-check and interpretation, and applies the appropriate pitch, bank, and power corrections in the correct sequence to return the aircraft to a stabilized level flight attitude.

   NOTE: Any intervention by the examiner to prevent the aircraft from exceeding any operating limitation, or entering an unsafe flight condition, shall be disqualifying.

   NOTE: Task G will be performed without the use of the attitude indicator.

COMMERCIAL PILOT CHECKRIDE STALL STANDARDS

The *Commercial Pilot Practical Test Standards* only call for stall to reach the imminent stage. Unlike recreational pilot and private pilot standards, the commercial pilot applicant is not required to do full stalls.

V. Area of operation: flight at critically slow airspeeds

A. Task: imminent stalls

1. Objective: To determine that the applicant:

   a. Exhibits commercial pilot knowledge by explaining the aerodynamic factors associated with imminent stalls in various configurations, pitch attitudes and flight situations; ("flight situations" means takeoffs, departures with at least climb power, cruising flight, and landing approaches), the changes in stall speed in various configurations, power settings, weights, and bank angles; and the procedure for recovery.

   b. Selects an entry altitude that will allow recoveries to be completed no lower than 1,500 feet above the ground.

   c. Stabilizes the airplane during entry at the airspeed, configuration, and power setting appropriate to the flight situation from which the imminent stall is to be demonstrated.

   d. Maintains a specified heading within plus or minus 10 degrees, in straight flight; the specified angle of bank within plus or minus 10 degrees, in turning flight.

   e. Establishes a pitch attitude that will induce an imminent stall.

   f. Applies proper control to maintain coordinated flight.

   g. Recognizes and recovers promptly at the first indication of buffeting or decay of control effectiveness with or without power applications as directed.

   h. Recovers with minimum loss of altitude consistent with safety during power-on recoveries; recovers to the glide airspeed within plus or minus 10 knots, during power-off recoveries.

      i. Resumes the specified airspeed and retracts wing flaps and landing gear, as appropriate.

      j. Avoids full stalls, excessive pitch changes, spirals, spins, or flight below 1,500 feet above the ground.

  2. Action. The examiner will:

      a. Ask the applicant to explain the aerodynamic factors associated with imminent stalls in various configurations and flight situations; the changes in stall speed in various configurations, power settings, pitch attitudes, weights, and bank angles; and the procedure for resuming normal flight.

      b. Ask the applicant to perform imminent stalls in a specified flight situation, and determine that the applicant's performance meets the objective.

B. Task: maneuvering during slow flight

  1. Objective. To determine that the applicant:

      a. Exhibits knowledge by explaining the flight characteristics and controllability associated with maneuvering during slow flight.

      b. Selects an entry altitude that will allow the maneuver to be performed no lower than 1,500 feet above the ground.

      c. Establishes and maintains slow flight, specified gear position (as appropriate), various flap settings, and angles of bank, during straight-and-level flight and level turns.

      d. Maintains a specified altitude within plus or minus 50 feet.

      e. Maintains a specified heading during straight flight within plus or minus 10 degrees.

      f. Maintains a specified bank angle within plus or minus 5 degrees, during turning flight.

      g. Maintains an airspeed of 5 knots, within plus or minus 5 knots, above the stall speed.

  2. Action. The examiner will:

      a. Ask the applicant to explain the flight characteristics and controllability involved in slow flight.

      b. Ask the applicant to perform slow flight, specifying the configuration and flight maneuver, and determine that the applicant meets the objective.

FLIGHT INSTRUCTOR CHECKRIDE STALL/SPIN STANDARDS

NOTE: The intent of tasks A and B (proficiency) is to ensure that the flight instructor applicant is tested on proficiency for the purpose of teaching these tasks to students.

The intent of tasks C, D, and E (demonstration) is to ensure that the flight instructor applicant is knowledgeable of the maneuvers and can demonstrate them to students for both familiarization and stall/spin awareness purposes.

NOTE: The term "instructional knowledge" means the "what," "why," and "how" of a subject matter topic, procedure, or maneuver.

IX. Area of operation: stalls, spins, and maneuvering during slow flight.

A. Task: Power-on stalls (proficiency)

Objective: To determine that the applicant:

1. Exhibits instructional knowledge of the elements of power-on stalls, in climbing flight (straight or turning), with selected landing gear and flap configurations, by describing–

    (a.) aerodynamics of power-on stalls

    (b.) relationship of various factors such as landing gear and flap configuration, weight, center of gravity, load factor, and bank angle to stall speed.

    (c.) flight situations where unintentional power-on stalls may occur.

    (d.) recognition of the first indication of power-on stalls.

    (e.) performance of power-on stalls in climbing flight (straight and turning).

    (f.) entry technique and minimum entry altitude.

    (g.) coordinated flight controls.

    (h.) recovery technique and minimum recovery altitude.

2. Exhibits instructional knowledge of common errors related to power-on stalls, in climbing flight (straight and turning), with selected landing gear and flap configurations by describing–

    (a.) failure to establish the specified landing gear and flap configuration prior to entry.

    (b.) improper pitch, heading, and bank control during straight ahead stalls.

    (c.) improper pitch and bank control during turning stalls.

    (d.) rough or uncoordinated control techniques.

    (e.) failure to recognize the first indications of a stall.

    (f.) failure to achieve a stall.

    (g.) improper torque correction.

    (h.) poor stall recognition and delayed recovery.

    (i.) excessive altitude loss or excessive airspeed during recovery.

    (j.) secondary stall during recovery.

3. Demonstrates and simultaneously explains power on stalls, in climbing flight (straight or turning), with selected landing gear and flap configurations, from an instructional standpoint.

4. Analyzes and corrects simulated common errors related to power on stalls, in climbing flight (straight and turning), with selected landing gear and flap configurations.

B. Task: power-off stalls (proficiency)

Objective: To determine that the applicant:

1. Exhibits instructional knowledge of the elements of power-off stalls, in descending flight (straight and turning), with selected landing gear and flap configurations, by describing–

    (a.) aerodynamics of power-off stalls.

    (b.) relationship of various factors such as landing gear and flap configuration, weight, center of gravity, load factor, and bank angle to stall speed.

    (c.) flight situations where unintentional power-off stalls may occur.

    (d.) recognition of the first indications of power-off stalls.

    (e.) performance of power-off stalls in descending flight (straight and turning).

    (f.) entry technique and minimum entry altitude.

    (g.) coordination of flight controls.

    (h.) recovery technique and minimum recovery altitude.

2. Exhibits instructional knowledge of common errors related to power-off stalls, descending flight (straight and turning), with selected landing gear and flap configurations, by describing–

    (a.) failure to establish the specified landing gear and flap configuration prior to entry.

    (b.) improper pitch, heading, and bank control during straight ahead stalls.

    (c.) improper pitch and bank control during turning stalls.

    (d.) rough or uncoordinated control technique.

    (e.) failure to recognize the first indications of a stall.

    (f.) failure to achieve a stall.

    (g.) improper torque corrections.

    (h.) poor stall recognition and delayed recovery.

    (i.) excessive altitude loss or excessive airspeed during recovery.

    (j.) secondary stall during recovery.

3. Demonstrates and simultaneously explains power-off stalls, in descending flight (straight and turning) with selected landing gear and flap configurations, from an instructional standpoint.

4. Analyzes and corrects simulated common errors related to power-off stalls, in descending flight (straight and turning), with selected landing gear and flap configurations.

C. Task: crossed-control stalls (demonstration)

Objective: To determine that the applicant:

1. Exhibits instructional knowledge of the elements of crossed-control stalls, with the landing gear extended, by describing–

    (a.) aerodynamics of crossed-control stalls.

    (b.) effects of crossed controls in gliding or reduced airspeed descending turns.

    (c.) hazards of crossed controls in a base leg to final approach turn.

    (d.) entry technique and minimum entry altitude.

    (e.) recognition of crossed-control stalls.

    (f.) flight situations where unintentional crossed-control stalls may occur.

    (g.) recovery technique and minimum recovery altitude.

2. Exhibits instructional knowledge of common errors related to crossed-control stalls, with the landing gear extended, by describing–

    (a.) failure to establish selected configuration prior to entry.

(b.) failure to establish a cross-control turn and stall condition that will adequately demonstrate the hazards of a crossed-control stall.

(c.) improper or inadequate demonstration of the recognition of and recovery from a crossed-control stall.

(d.) failure to present simulated student instruction that adequately emphasizes the hazards of a crossed-control condition in a gliding or reduced airspeed condition.

3. Demonstrates and simultaneously explains a crossed-control stall, with the landing gear extended, from an instructional standpoint.

4. Analyzes and corrects simulated common errors related to crossed-control stall with the landing gear extended.

D. Task: elevator trim stalls (demonstration)

Objective: To determine that the applicant:

1. Exhibits instructional knowledge of the elements of elevator trim stalls, in selected landing gear and flap configurations, by describing–

(a.) aerodynamics of elevator trim stalls.

(b.) hazards of inadequate control pressures to compensate for thrust, torque and up elevator trim during go-arounds and other related maneuvers.

(c.) entry technique and minimum entry altitude.

(d.) recognition of elevator trim stalls.

(e.) importance of recovering from an elevator trim stall immediately upon recognition.

(f.) flight situations where elevator trim stalls occur.

(g.) recovery technique and minimum recovery altitude.

2. Exhibits instructional knowledge of common errors related to elevator trim stalls, in selected landing gear and flap configurations by describing–

(a.) failure to establish selected configuration prior to entry.

(b.) failure to establish the thrust, torque and up elevator trim conditions that will result in a realistic demonstration.

(c.) improper or inadequate demonstration of the recognition of and the recovery from an elevator trim stall.

(d.) failure to present simulated student instruction that adequately emphasizes the hazards of poor correction for torque and up elevator trim during go-around and other maneuvers.

3. Demonstrates and simultaneously explains elevator trim stalls, in selected landing gear and flap configurations, from an instructional standpoint.

4. Analyze and correct simulated common errors related to elevator trim stalls in selected landing gear and flap configurations

E. Task: secondary stalls (demonstration)

Objective: To determine that the applicant:

1. Exhibits instructional knowledge of the elements of secondary stalls in selected landing gear and flap configurations, by describing–

(a.) aerodynamics of secondary stalls.

    (b.) flight situations where secondary stalls may occur.

    (c.) hazards of secondary stalls during normal stall or spin recovery.

    (d.) entry technique and minimum entry altitude.

    (e.) recognition of a secondary stall.

    (f.) recovery technique and minimum recovery altitude.

2. Exhibits instructional knowledge of common errors related to secondary stalls, in selected landing gear and flap configurations, by describing–

    (a.) failure to establish selected configuration prior to entry.

    (b.) improper or inadequate demonstration of the recognition of and recovery from a secondary stall.

    (c.) failure to establish a condition that will cause a secondary stall to occur.

    (d.) failure to present simulated student instruction that adequately emphasizes the hazards of poor technique in recovering from a primary stall.

3. Demonstrates and simultaneously explains secondary stalls, in selected landing gear and flap configurations, from an instructional standpoint.

4. Analyzes and corrects simulated common errors related to secondary stalls in selected landing gear and flap configurations.

F. Task: spins

Objective: To determine that the applicant:

1. Exhibits instructional knowledge of the elements of spins by describing–

    (a.) aerodynamics of a spin.

    (b.) airplanes approved for the spin maneuvers based on airworthiness category and type certificate.

    (c.) relationships of various factors such as configuration, weight, center of gravity, and control coordination to spins.

    (d.) flight situations where unintentional spins may occur.

    (e.) how to recognize and recover from imminent unintentional spins.

    (f.) entry technique and minimum entry altitude for intentional spins.

    (g.) control technique to maintain a stabilized spin.

    (h.) orientation during a spin.

    (i.) recovery technique and minimum recovery altitude for intentional spins.

    (j.) anxiety factors associated with spin instruction.

2. Exhibits instructional knowledge of common errors related to spins by describing–

    (a.) failure to establish proper configuration prior to spin entry.

    (b.) failure to achieve and maintain a full stall during spin entry.

    (c.) failure to close the throttle when a spin entry is achieved.

    (d.) failure to recognize the indications of an imminent, unintentional spin.

    (e.) improper use of flight controls during spin entry, rotation, or recovery.

    (f.) disorientation in a spin.

    (g.) failure to distinguish between high speed spiral and spin.

    (h.) excessive speed or accelerated stall during recovery.

    (i.) failure to recover with minimum altitude loss.

(j.) hazards of attempting to spin an airplane not approved for spins.

3. Demonstrates and simultaneously explains a spin (one turn) from an instructional standpoint.

4. Analyzes and corrects simulated common errors related to spins.

NOTE: At the discretion of the examiner, a logbook record attesting applicant instructional competency in spin entries, spins, and spin recoveries may be accepted in lieu of this Task. Logbook record shall be certified by the flight instructor who conducted the spin instruction (spin endorsement recommended in AC 61-65C for logbook record):

I certify that I have given Mr./Ms._____ flight training in spin entry, spins, and spin recovery techniques and he/she has demonstrated instructional competency in those maneuvers.

G. Task: maneuvering during slow flight

Objective: To determine that the applicant:

1. Exhibits instructional knowledge of the elements of maneuvering during slow flight by describing–
   (a.) relationship of configuration, weight, center of gravity, maneuvering loads, angle of bank, and power to flight characteristics and controllability.
   (b.) relationship of the maneuver to critical flight situations, such as go-arounds.
   (c.) performance of the maneuver in various landing gear and flap configurations during straight and level flight and level turns.
   (d.) specified airspeed for the maneuver.
   (e.) coordination of flight controls.
   (f.) trim technique.
   (g.) reestablishment of cruise flight.

2. Exhibits instructional knowledge of common errors related to maneuvering during slow flight by describing–
   (a.) failure to establish a specified configuration.
   (b.) improper entry technique.
   (c.) failure to establish and maintain the specified airspeed.
   (d.) excessive variations of altitude, heading and bank when constant altitude, heading, and bank are specified.
   (e.) rough or uncoordinated control technique.
   (f.) faulty trim technique.
   (g.) unintentional stall.
   (h.) inappropriate removal of hand from throttle.

3. Demonstrates and simultaneously explains maneuvering during slow flight from an instructional standpoint.

4. Analyzes and corrects simulated common errors related to maneuvering during slow flight.

MULTIENGINE AIRPLANE CHECKRIDE STALL STANDARDS
VII. Area of operation: flight at critically slow airspeeds

NOTE: Stalls will not be performed with one engine at reduced power or inoperative and the other engine(s) developing effective power.

A. Task: stalls

1. Objective: To determine that the applicant:
   a. Exhibits knowledge by explaining the aerodynamic factors associated with stalls and recoveries.
   b. Selects an entry altitude that allows a recovery to be completed no less than 3,000 feet above the ground.
   c. Stabilizes the aircraft at Vyse in level flight with gear and flap configuration as specified by the examiner.
   d. Establishes straight-and-level flight or level 20 degree turns within plus or minus 5 degrees, as specified by the examiner.
   e. Adjusts pitch and power as necessary to induce a stall while maintaining altitude within plus or minus 50 feet.
   f. Recognizes a stall and recovers at the first indication through proper power and control applications. Artificial means of determining a stall, such as stall warning horns or stick shakers, are acceptable only in those cases where such action is recommended or required by the aircraft manufacturer. The intent of this task is to evaluate a stall, NOT an imminent stall.
      (1) Straight ahead standards:
         (a.) Maintains heading within plus or minus 10 degrees, and altitude plus or minus 50 feet during the entry.
         (b.) Maintains heading within plus or minus 10 degrees and altitude plus or minus 100 feet during the recovery.
      (2.) Turning standards:
         (a.) Maintains 20 degrees of bank within plus or minus 5 degrees and altitude plus or minus 50 feet during entry.
         (b.) Levels the wings and maintains heading within plus or minus 10 degrees, and altitude within plus or minus 100 feet during recovery.
   g. Avoids excessive pitch changes or secondary stall during the recovery.
   h. Returns to airspeed and configuration as specified by the examiner.
2. Action. The examiner will:
   a. Ask the applicant to explain aerodynamic factors associated with stalls under various aircraft configurations, and determine that the applicant meets the objective.
   b. Ask the applicant to perform stalls under specified aircraft configurations(at least one stall must be evaluated in the landing configuration), and determine that the applicant's performance meets the objective.

B. Task: maneuvering during slow flight
  1. Objective: To determine that the applicant:
     a. Exhibits knowledge by explaining the flight characteristics and controllability associated with maneuvering during slow flight.
     b. Select an entry altitude that will allow the maneuver to be performed no lower than 3,000 feet above the ground.
     c. Establishes and maintains slow flight, specified gear position, various flap settings, and angles of bank, during straight-and-level flight and level turns.
     d. Maintains the specified altitude within plus or minus 100 feet.
     e. Maintains the specified heading during straight flight within plus or minus 10 degrees.
     f. Maintains the specified bank angle within plus or minus 5 degrees during turning flight.
     g. Maintains airspeed of 5 knots, within plus or minus 5 knots, above stall speed or Vmc, whichever is greater.
  2. Action. The examiner will:
     a. Ask the applicant to explain the flight characteristics and controllability involved in slow flight, and determine that the applicant's knowledge meets the objective.
     b. Ask the applicant to perform slow flight, specifying the configuration and flight maneuver, and determine that the applicant's performance meets the objective.

VIII. Area of operations: emergency operations

C. Task: engine inoperative loss of directional control demonstration.
NOTE: Entering this maneuver by increasing pitch attitude to a high point with both engines operating and then reducing power on the critical engine should be avoided because the airplane may become uncontrollable.
  1. Objective: To determine that the applicant:
     a. Exhibits knowledge by explaining the causes of loss of directional control at airspeeds less than V_{MC}, the factors affecting V_{MC}, and the safe recovery procedures.
     b. Selects an entry altitude that will allow recoveries to be completed no less than 3,000 feet above the ground
     c. Establishes the airplane configuration with:
        (1.) propeller set to high rpm
        (2.) landing gear retracted
        (3.) flaps set in takeoff position
        (4.) cowl flaps set in takeoff position
        (5.) airspeed at V_{YSE}
     (6.) trim set for takeoff
     (7.) power on the critical engine reduced to idle (avoid abrupt power reduction)

    d. Establishes a single-engine climb attitude (inoperative engine propeller wind-milling) with climb power applied to the operating engine.

    e. Establishes a bank toward the operating engine, as necessary for best performance.

    f. Reduces the airspeed slowly with the elevators while applying rudder to maintain directional control until all available rudder is applied.

    g. Recognizes the indications of loss of directional control.

    h. Recovers promptly by simultaneously reducing the power on the operating engine and reducing the angle of attack as necessary to regain directional control and airspeed.

    i. Maintains directional control within plus or minus 20 degrees, during the entry and recovery.

    j. Accelerates to V_{YSE}, plus or minus 5 knots during the recovery.

2. Action. The examiner will:

    a. Ask the applicant to explain the cause of loss of directional control, the factors affecting V_{MC}, and safe recovery procedures, and determine that the applicant's knowledge meets the objective.

    b. Ask the applicant to demonstrate engine inoperative loss of directional control, and determine that the applicant's performance meets the objective.

26
Practice, understand, recognize, and respect

THIS HAS NOT BEEN AN EXAMINATION OF HOT AIR BALLOONS, BUT ABOUT airplanes. Unlike hot air balloons, airplanes must continuously move forward or they will stall. Unfortunately, pilots get killed every year because they let the airplane that they are flying get too slow, then panic or inexperience prevents them from preventing disaster.

To be a safe pilot, you must practice stalls and airspeed maneuvers.

To be a safe pilot, you must understand that deadly stalls do not happen in the practice area, but when you least expect them.

To be a safe pilot, you must recognize and respect the stall/spin threats that are present on every flight.

The debate over spin training has not been resolved. Certainly we need to do whatever we can to prevent a situation where a pilot inadvertently enters a spin and fear steals his ability to recover. A pilot frozen at the controls is no pilot at all.

I am in favor of spin training for all pilots, but I know it is a Pandora's box.

I am against "recreational" spinning.

Spinning should be done only with a qualified instructor as part of an organized training syllabus.

Pilots must accept spin training with maturity. But when the forbidden fruit is given to the general flying public, there will be abuses. A private pilot flying to the practice area to execute spins solely to impress his friends, scares me to death. Of course, nothing stops them from doing that today, but most pilots, even ones without good judgment, stay away from spins unless they have received proper instruction and know proper recovery techniques.

Will spin training kill more people than it is supposed to save? We cannot answer that question.

If you do choose to spin until it becomes required, spin with responsibility. Be selective when it comes to spin instructors and spin airplanes.

Anytime you spin, it should be to honestly improve your ability to safely fly the airplane. Spinning is not just for kicks.

Appendices

Appendix A
Flight test distractions

FAA Advisory Circular 61-92 covers the use of distractions during pilot certification flight tests.

1. **PURPOSE.** This advisory circular announces the Federal Aviation Administration's policy of incorporating into all flight tests the use of certain distractions during the performance of flight test maneuvers.

2. **BACKGROUND.**

a. According to the General Aviation Pilot Stall Awareness Study (Report No. FAA-RD-77-26), stall/spin related accidents accounted for about twenty-five percent of the total general aviation fatal accidents. National Transportation Safety Board statistics reveal that most stall/spin accidents occurred when the pilot's attention was diverted from the primary task of flying the aircraft. Sixty percent of stall/spin accidents occurred during takeoff or landing; and twenty percent were preceded by engine failure (a distraction). Other distractions included preoccupation inside or outside the cockpit while changing power, configuration or trim; maneuvering to avoid other traffic; or clearing hazardous obstacles during takeoff and climb.

b. The intentional practice of stalls and spins seldom resulted in an accident. The real danger was inadvertent stalls induced by distractions during routine flight situations.

3. **DISCUSSION.** In view of the data revealed by the Stall Awareness Study, the Federal Aviation Administration has established the use of certain distractions in conjunction with pilot certification flight tests. Distractions may be included in the evaluation of performance to determine that applicants possess the skills required to cope with distractions while maintaining the degree of aircraft control required for safe flight.

4. **EXAMPLES OF DISTRACTIONS FOR A GIVEN MANEUVER.** During an applicant's performance of "S" Turns Across A Road, the Federal Aviation Administration inspector or

other authorized pilot examiner may observe and note performance while providing distractions such as requesting the applicant to:

    a. Simulate radio communications.

    b. Read outside air temperature gauge.

    c. Remove object from the glove compartment.

    d. Identify terrain features or objects on the ground.

    e. Climb 200 feet and maintain altitude, then descend 200 feet and maintain altitude.

    f. Reverse course after a series of "S" turns.

    g. Identify fields suitable for forced landings.

    5. **SUMMARY.** At the time of their next revision, all flight test guides will be changed to include distractions appropriate to selected flight maneuvers listed under pilot operations. During the interim, Federal Aviation Administration inspectors and designated pilot examiners may incorporate the use of realistic distractions during the performance of flight test maneuvers.

Appendix B
Awareness training

Subject: **STALL AND SPIN AWARENESS TRAINING**   Date: **5/17/91**   AC No: **61-67B**
Initiated by: **AFS-840**   Change:

1. PURPOSE. This advisory circular (AC) explains the stall and spin awareness training required under Part 61 of the Federal Aviation Regulations (FAR) and offers guidance to flight instructors who provide that training. In addition, this AC informs pilots of the airworthiness standards for the type certification of small airplanes prescribed in FAR Section 23.221 concerning spin maneuvers and it emphasizes the importance of observing restrictions that prohibit the intentional spinning of certain airplanes.

2. CANCELLATION. AC 61-67A dated October 8, 1982, and AC 61-92 dated January 25, 1980, are canceled.

3. RELATED READING MATERIAL
   a. *Report No. FAA-RD-77-26, General Aviation Pilot Stall Awareness Training Study.* This document may be purchased from the National Technical Information Service (NTIS), U.S. Department of Commerce, 5285 Port Royal Road, Springfield, Virginia 22161. Telephone orders: (703) 487-4650. NTIS identification number ADA041310.
   b. The following documents may be purchased from the Superintendent of Documents, U.S. Government Printing Office, Washington, D.C., 20402.
      (1) AC 61-21, Flight Training Handbook, current edition.
      (2) AC 91-23, Pilot's Weight and Balance Handbook, current edition.
      (3) FAA-S-8081-1, Private Pilot - Practical Test Standards, current edition.

(4) FAA-S-8081-2, Commercial Pilot-Practical Test Standards, current edition

(5) FAA-S-8081-6, Flight Instructor - Airplane Practical Test Standards, current edition.

4. BACKGROUND. In January 1980, the Federal Aviation Administration (FAA) issued AC 61-92, "Use of Distractions During Pilot Certification Flight Tests," announcing its policy of incorporating the use of certain distractions during the performance of flight test maneuvers. This policy came about as a result of Report No. FAA-RD-77-26 which revealed that stall/spin related accidents accounted for approximately, one-quarter of all fatal general aviation accidents. National Transportation Safety Board statistics indicate that most stall/spin accidents result when a pilot is distracted momentarily from the primary task of flying the aircraft.

5. CHANGES. Changes to FAR Part 61, completed in 1991, included increased spin awareness training for applicants for recreational, private, and commercial pilot certificates. The training is intended to emphasize recognition of situations that could lead to an inadvertent stall and/or spin by using realistic distractions such as those suggested in Report No. FAA-RD-77-26 and incorporated into the performance of flight test maneuvers. Although the training is intended to emphasize stall and spin awareness and recovery techniques for all pilots, only flight instructor-airplane and flight instructor-glider candidates are required to demonstrate instructional proficiency in spin entry, spins, and spin recovery techniques as a requirement for certification. Where applicable, AC 61-67B supersedes AC 61-21A.

6. COMMENTS INVITED. Comments regarding this publication should be directed to:
Federal Aviation Administration
Field Programs Division, AFS-500
Advisory Circular Staff
P.O. Box 20034, Gateway Building
Dulles International Airport
Washington, DC 20041-2034
Every comment will not necessarily generate a direct acknowledgement to the commenter. Comments received will be considered in the development of upcoming revisions to AC's or other related technical material.

CONTENTS

CHAPTER 1. GROUND TRAINING - STALL AND SPIN AWARENESS
    1. DEFINITIONS
    2. DISTRACTIONS
    3. STALL RECOGNITION
    4. TYPES OF STALLS
    5. STALL RECOVERY
    6. SECONDARY STALLS
    7. SPINS
    8. WEIGHT AND BALANCE
    9. PRIMARY CAUSE
   10. TYPES OF SPINS
   11. SPIN RECOVERY

CHAPTER 2. FLIGHT TRAINING - STALLS
   12. STALL TRAINING

CHAPTER 3. FLIGHT TRAINING - SPINS
   13. SPIN TRAINING

CHAPTER 4. AIRWORTHINESS STANDARDS
   14. OPERATING LIMITATIONS
   15. PLACARDS
   16. PILOT AWARENESS

CHAPTER 1. GROUND TRAINING - STALL AND SPIN AWARENESS

1. DEFINITIONS. A stall is a loss of lift and increase in drag that occurs when an aircraft is flown at an angle of attack greater than the angle for maximum lift. If recovery from a stall is not effected in a timely and appropriate manner by reducing the angle of attack, a secondary stall and/or a spin may result. All spins are preceded by a stall on at least part of the wing. The angle of the relative wind is determined primarily by the aircraft's airspeed. Other factors are considered, such as aircraft weight, center of gravity, configuration, and the amount of acceleration used in a turn. The speed at which the critical angle of the relative wind is exceeded is the stall speed. Stall speeds are listed in the Airplane Flight Manual (AFM) or the Pilot Operating Handbook (POH) and pertain to certain conditions or aircraft configurations, e.g., landing configuration. Other specific operational speed are calculated based upon the aircraft's stall speed in the landing configuration. Airspeed values specified in the AFM or POH may vary under different circumstances. Factors such as weight, center of gravity, altitude, temperature, turbulence, and the presence of snow, ice, or frost on the wings will affect an aircraft's stall speed. To thoroughly understand the stall/spin phenomenon, some basic factors affecting aircraft aerodynamics and flight should be reviewed with particular emphasis on their relation to stall speeds. (This advisory circular is principally concerned with and discusses airplanes. However, much of the information also is applicable to gliders.) The following terms are defined as they relate to stalls/spins.
   a. Angle of Attack. Angle of attack is the angle at which the wing meets the relative wind. The angle of attack must be small enough to allow attached airflow over and under the airfoil to produce lift. A change in angle of attack will affect the amount of lift that is produced. An excessive angle of attack will eventually disrupt the flow of air over the airfoil. If the angle of attack is not reduced, a section of the airfoil will reach its critical angle of attack, lose lift, and stall. Exceeding the critical angle of attack for a particular airfoil section will always result in a stall.
   b. Airspeed. Airspeed is controlled primarily by the elevator or longitudinal control position for a given configuration and power. If an airplane's speed is too slow, the angle of attack required for level flight will be so large that the air can no longer follow the upper curvature of the wing. The result is a separation of airflow from the wing, loss of lift, a large increase in drag, and eventually a stall if the angle of attack is not reduced. The stall is the result of excessive angle of attack - not airspeed. **A stall can occur at any airspeed. In any altitude, and at any power setting.**
   c. Configuration. Flaps, landing gear, and other configuring devices can affect an airplane's stall speed. Extension of flaps and/or landing gear in flight will usually increase drag. Flap extension will generally increase the lifting ability of the wings, thus reducing the airplane's stall speed. The effect of flaps on an airplane's stall speed can be seen by markings on the airplane's airspeed indicator, where the lower airspeed limit of the white arc (power-off stall speed with gear and flaps in the landing configuration) is less than the lower airspeed limit of the green arc (power-off stall speed in the clean configuration).
   d. V_{SO}. V_{SO} means the stall speed or the minimum steady flight speed in the landing configuration.
   e. V_{S1}. V_{S1} means the stall speed or the minimum steady flight speed obtained in a specific configuration.

f. V_A. V_A is the design maneuvering speed which is the speed at which an airplane can be stalled without exceeding its structural limits.

g. Load Factor. Load factor is the ratio of the lifting force produced by the wings to the actual weight of the airplane and its contents. Load factors are usually expressed in terms of "G." The aircraft's stall speed increases in proportion to the square root of the load factor. For example, an airplane that has a normal unaccelerated stall speed of 45 knots can be stalled at 90 knots when subjected to a load factor of 4 G's. The possibility of inadvertently stalling the airplane by increasing the load factor (by putting the airplane in a steep turn or spiral, for example) is therefore much greater than in normal cruise flight. A stall entered from straight and level flight or from an unaccelerated straight climb will not produce additional load factors. In a constant rate turn, increased load factors will cause an airplane's stall speed to increase as the angle of bank increases. Excessively steep banks should be avoided because the airplane will stall at a much higher speed or, if the aircraft exceeds maneuvering speed, structural damage to the aircraft may result before it stalls. If the nose falls during a steep turn, the pilot might attempt to raise it to the level flight attitude without shallowing the bank. This situation tightens the turn and can lead to a diving spiral. A feeling of weightlessness will result if a stall recovery is performed by abruptly pushing the elevator control forward, which will reduce the up load on the wings. Recoveries from stalls and spins involve a tradeoff between loss of altitude (and an increase in airspeed) and an increase in load factor in the pullup. However, recovery from the dive following spin recovery generally causes higher airspeeds and consequently higher load factors than stall recoveries due to the much lower position of the nose. Significant load factor increases are sometimes induced during pullup after recovery from a stall or spin. It should be noted that structural damage can result from the high load factors imposed by intentional stalls practiced above the airplane's design maneuvering speed.

h. Center of Gravity (CG). The CG location has an indirect effect on the effective lift and angle of attack of the wing, the amount and direction of force on the tail, and the degree of stabilizer deflection needed to supply the proper tail force for equilibrium. The CG position, therefore, has a significant effect on stability and stall/spin recovery. As the CG is moved aft, the amount of elevator deflection will be reduced. An increased angle of attack will be achieved with less elevator control force. This could make the entry into inadvertent stalls easier, and during the subsequent recovery, it would be easier to generate higher load factors, due to the reduced forces. In an airplane with an extremely aft CG, very light back elevator control forces may lead to inadvertent stall entries and if a spin is entered, the balance of forces on the airplane may result in a flat spin. Recovery from a flat spin is often impossible. A forward CG location will often cause the stalling angle of attack to be reached at a higher airspeed. Increased back elevator control force is generally required with a forward CG location.

i. Weight. Although the distribution of weight has the most direct effect on stability, increased gross weight can also have an effect on an aircraft's flight characteristics, regardless of the CG position. As the weight of the airplane is increased, the stall speed increases. The increased weight requires a higher angle of attack to produce additional lift to support the weight.

j. Altitude and Temperature. Altitude has little or no effect on an airplane's indicated stall speed. Thinner air at higher altitudes will result in decreased aircraft performance and a higher true airspeed for a given indicated airspeed. Higher than standard temperatures will also contribute to increased true airspeed. However, the higher true airspeed has no effect on indicated approach or stall speeds. The manufacturer's recommended indicated airspeeds should therefore be maintained during the landing approach, regardless of the elevation or the density altitude at the airport of landing.

k. Snow, Ice, or Frost on the Wings. Even a small accumulation of snow, ice, or frost on an aircraft's surface can cause an increase in that aircraft's stall speed. Such accumulation changes the shape of the wing, disrupting the smooth flow of air over the surface and, consequently, increasing drag and decreasing lift. Flight should not be attempted when snow, ice, or frost has accumulated on the aircraft surfaces.

l. Turbulence. Turbulence can cause an aircraft to stall at a significantly higher airspeed than in stable conditions. A vertical gust or windshear can cause a sudden change in the relative wind, and result in an abrupt increase in angle of attack. Although a gust may not be maintained long enough for a stall to develop, the aircraft may stall while the pilot is attempting to control the flight path, particularly during an approach in gusty conditions. When flying in moderate to severe turbulence or strong crosswinds, a higher than normal approach speed should be maintained. In cruise flight in moderate or severe turbulence, an airspeed well above the indicated stall speed and below maneuvering speed should be used.

2. DISTRACTIONS. Improper airspeed management resulting in stalls are most likely to occur when the pilot is distracted by one or more other tasks, such as locating a checklist or attempting a restart after an engine failure; flying a traffic pattern on a windy day; reading a chart or making fuel and/or distance calculations; or attempting to retrieve items from the floor, back seat, or glove compartment. Pilots at all skill levels should be aware of the increased risk of entering into an inadvertent stall or spin while performing tasks that are secondary to controlling the aircraft.

3. STALL RECOGNITION. There are several ways to recognize that a stall is impending before it actually occurs. When one or more of these indicators is noted, initiation of a recovery should be instinctive (unless a full stall is being practiced intentionally from an altitude that allows recovery above 1,500 feet above ground level (AGL) for single-engine airplanes and 3,000 feet AGL for multiengine airplanes). One indication of a stall is a mushy feeling in the flight controls and less control effect as the aircraft's speed is reduced. This reduction in control effectiveness is attributed in part to reduced airflow over the flight control surfaces. In fixed-pitch propeller airplanes, a loss of revolutions per minute (RPM) may be evident when approaching a stall in power-on conditions. For both airplanes and gliders, a reduction in the sound of air flowing along the fuselage is usually evident. Just before the stall occurs, buffeting, uncontrollable pitching or vibrations may begin. Many aircraft are equipped with stall warning devices that will alert the pilot when the airflow over the wing(s) approaches a point that will not allow lift to be sustained. Finally, kinesthesia (the sensing of changes in direction or speed of motion), when properly learned and developed, will warn the pilot of a decrease in speed or the beginning of a "mushing" of the aircraft. These preliminary indications serve as a warning to the pilot to increase airspeed by adding power, and/or lowering the nose, and/or decreasing the angle of bank.

4. TYPES OF STALLS. Stalls can be practiced both with and without power. Stalls should be practiced to familiarize the student with the aircraft's particular stall characteristics without putting the aircraft into a potentially dangerous condition. In multiengine airplanes, single-engine stalls must be avoided. A description of some different types of stalls follows:

a. Power-off stalls (also known as approach-to-landing stalls) are practiced to simulate normal approach-to-landing conditions and configuration. Many stall/spin accidents have occurred in these power-off situations, such as crossed control turns from base leg to final approach (resulting in a skidding or slipping turn); attempting to recover from a high sink rate on final approach by using only an increased pitch attitude; and improper airspeed control on final approach or in other segments of the traffic pattern.

b. Power-on stalls (also known as departure stalls) are practiced to simulate takeoff and climb-out conditions and configuration. Many stall/spin accidents have occurred during these phases of flight, particularly during go-arounds. A causal factor in such accidents has been the pilot's failure to maintain positive control due to a nose-high trim setting or premature flap retraction. Failure to maintain positive control during short field takeoffs has also been an accident causal factor.

c. Accelerated stalls can occur at higher-than-normal airspeeds due to abrupt and/or excessive control applications. These stalls may occur in steep turns, pullups, or other abrupt changes in flight path. Accelerated stalls usually are more severe than unaccelerated stalls and are often unexpected because they occur at higher-than-normal airspeeds.

5. STALL RECOVERY. The key factor in recovering from a stall is regaining positive control of the aircraft by reducing the angle of attack. At the first indication of a stall, the aircraft angle of attack must be decreased to allow the wings to regain lift. Every aircraft in upright flight may require a different amount of forward pressure to regain lift. It should be noted that too much forward pressure can hinder recovery by imposing a negative load on the wing. The next step in recovering from a stall is to smoothly apply maximum allowable power (if applicable) to increase the airspeed and to minimize the loss of altitude. Certain high performance airplanes may require only an increase in thrust and relaxation of the back pressure on the yoke to effect recovery. As airspeed increases and the recovery is completed, power should be adjusted lo return the airplane to the desired flight condition. Straight and level flight should be established with full coordinated use of the controls. The airspeed indicator or tachometer, if installed, should never be allowed to reach their high-speed red lines at anytime during a practice stall.

7. SPINS. A spin in a small airplane or glider is a controlled or uncontrolled maneuver in which the glider or airplane descends in a helical path while flying at an angle of attack greater than the angle of maximum lift. Spins result from aggravated stalls in either a slip or a skid. If a stall does not occur, a spin cannot occur. In a stall, one wing will often drop before the other and the nose will yaw in the direction of the low wing.

8. WEIGHT AND BALANCE. Minor weight or balance changes can affect an aircraft's spin characteristics. For example, the addition of a suitcase in the aft baggage compartment will affect the weight and balance of the aircraft. An aircraft that may be difficult to spin intentionally in the utility category (restricted aft CG and reduced weight) could have less resistance to spin entry in the normal category (loss restricted aft CG and increased weight) due to its ability to generate a higher angle of attack and increased load factor. Furthermore, an aircraft that is approved for spins in the utility category, but loaded in the normal category, may not recover from a spin that is allowed to progress beyond one turn.

9. PRIMARY CAUSE. The primary cause of an inadvertent spin is exceeding the critical angle of attack for a given stall speed while executing a turn with excessive or insufficient rudder and, to a lesser extent, aileron. In an uncoordinated maneuver, the pilot/static instruments, especially the altimeter and airspeed indicator, are unreliable due to the uneven distribution of air pressure on the fuselage. The pilot may not be aware that a critical angle of attack has been exceeded until the stall warning device activates. If a stall recovery is not promptly initiated, the airplane is more likely to enter an inadvertent spin. The spin that occurs from cross controlling an aircraft usually results in rotation in the direction of the rudder being applied, regardless of which wing tip is raised. In a skidding turn, where both aileron and rudder are applied in the same direction, rotation will be in the direction the controls are applied. However, in a slipping turn, where opposite aileron is held against the rudder, the resultant spin will usually occur in the direction opposite the aileron that is being applied.

10. TYPES OF SPINS.
a. An incipient spin is that portion of a spin from the time the airplane stalls and rotation starts, until the spin becomes fully developed. Incipient spins that are not allowed to develop into a steady state spin are commonly used as an introduction to spin training and recovery techniques.

b. A fully developed spin occurs when the aircraft angular rotation rates, airspeed, and vertical speed are stabilized from turn-to-turn in a flight path that is close to vertical.

c. A flat spin is characterized by a near level pitch and roll altitude with the spin axis near the CG of the airplane. Recovery from a flat spin may be extremely difficult and, in some cases, impossible.

11. SPIN RECOVERY. Before flying any aircraft, in which spins are to be conducted, the pilot should be familiar with the operating characteristics and standard operating procedures, including spin recovery techniques, specified in the approved AFM or POH. The first step in recovering from an upright spin is to close the throttle completely to eliminate power and minimize the loss of altitude. If the particular aircraft spin recovery techniques are not known, the next step is to neutralize the ailerons, determine the direction of the turn, and apply full opposite rudder. When the rotation slows, briskly move the elevator control forward to approximately the neutral position. Some aircraft require merely a relaxation of back pressure; others require full forward elevator control pressure. Forward movement of the elevator control will decrease the angle of attack. Once the stall is broken, the spinning will stop. Neutralize the rudder when the spinning stops to avoid entering a spin in the opposite direction. When the rudder is neutralized, gradually apply enough aft elevator pressure to return to level flight. Too much or abrupt aft elevator pressure and/or application of rudder and ailerons during the recovery can result in a secondary stall and possibly another spin. If the spin is being performed in an airplane, the engine will sometimes stop developing power due to centrifugal force acting on the fuel in the airplane's tanks causing fuel interruption. It is, therefore, recommended to assume that power is not available when practicing spin recovery. As a rough estimate, an altitude loss of approximately 500 feet per each 3-second turn can be expected in most small aircraft in which spins are authorized. Greater losses can be expected at higher density altitudes.

CHAPTER 2. FLIGHT TRAINING - STALLS

12. STALL TRAINING. Flight instructor-airplane and flight instructor-glider applicants must be able to give stall training. The flight instructor should emphasize that techniques and procedures for each aircraft may differ and that pilots should be aware of the flight characteristics of each aircraft flown. Single-engine stalls should not be demonstrated or practiced in multiengine airplanes. Engine-out minimum control speed demonstrations in multiengine airplanes should not be attempted when the density altitude and temperature are such that the engine-out minimum control speed is close to the stall speed, since loss of directional or lateral control could result. The flight training required by FAR Part 61 does not entail the actual practicing of spins for other than flight instructor-airplane and flight instructor-glider applicants, but emphasizes stall and spin avoidance. The most effective training method contained in Report No. FAA-RD-T7-26 is the simulation of scenarios that can lead to inadvertent stalls by creating distractions while the student is practicing certain maneuvers. Stall demonstrations and practice, including maneuvering during slow flight and other maneuvers with distractions that can lead to inadvertent stalls, should be conducted at a sufficient altitude to enable recovery above 1,500 feet AGL in single-engine airplanes and 3,000 feet AGL in multiengine airplanes. The following training elements are based on Report No. FAA-RD-77-26:

a. Stall Avoidance Practice at Slow Airspeeds.

(1) Assign a heading and an altitude. Have the student reduce power and slow to an airspeed just above the stall speed, using trim as necessary.

(2) Have the student maintain heading and altitude with the stall warning device activated.

(3) Demonstrate the effect of elevator trim (use neutral and full nose-up settings) and rudder trim, if available.

(4) Note the left turning tendency and rudder effectiveness for lateral/directional control.

(5) Emphasize how right rudder pressure is necessary to center the ball indicator and maintain heading.

(6) Release the rudder and advise the student to observe the left yaw.

(7) Adverse yaw demonstration. While at a low airspeed, have the student enter left and right turns without using rudder pedals.

(8) Have the student practice turns, climbs, and descents at low airspeeds.

(9) Demonstrate the proper flap extension and retraction procedures while in level flight to avoid a stall at low airspeeds. Note the change in stall speeds with flaps extended and retracted.

(10) Realistic distractions at low airspeeds. Give the student a task to perform while flying at a low airspeed. Instruct the student to divide his/her attention between the task and flying the aircraft to maintain control and avoid a stall. The following distractions can be used:

(i) Drop a pencil. Ask the student to pick it up. Ask the student to determine a heading to an airport using a chart.

(ii) Ask the student to reset the clock to Universal Coordinated Time.

(iii) Ask the student to get something from the back seat.

(iv) Ask the student to read the outside air temperature.

(v) Ask the student to call the Flight Service Station (FSS) for weather Information.

(vi) Ask the student to compute true airspeed with a flight computer.

(vii) Ask the student to identify terrain or objects on the ground.

(viii) Ask the student to identify a field suitable for a forced landing.

(ix) Have the student climb 200 feet and maintain altitude, then descend 200 feet and maintain altitude.

(x) Have the student reverse course after a series of S-turns.

(11) Flight at low airspeeds with the airspeed indicator covered. Use various flap settings and distractions.

b. Departure Stall.

(1) At a safe altitude, have the student attempt coordinated power-on (departure) stalls straight ahead and in turns. Emphasize how these stalls could occur during takeoff.

(2) Ask the student to demonstrate a power-on (departure) stall and distract him/her just before the stall occurs. Explain any effects the distraction may have had on the stall or recovery.

c. Engine Failure in a Climb Followed by a 180-Degree Gliding Turn. This demonstration will show the student how much altitude the airplane loses following a power failure after takeoff and during a 180-degree turn back to the runway and why returning to the airport after losing an engine is not a recommended procedure. This can be performed using either a medium or steep bank in the 180-degree turn, but emphasis should be given to stall avoidance.

(1) Set up best rate of climb (V_Y).

(2) Reduce power smoothly to idle as the airplane passes through a cardinal altitude.

(3) Lower the nose to maintain the best glide speed and make a 180-degree turn at the best glide speed.

(4) Point out the altitude loss and emphasize how rapidly airspeed decreases following a power failure in a climb attitude?

d. Cross Controlled Stalls in Gliding Turns. Perform stalls in gliding turns to simulate turns from base to final. Perform the stalls from a properly coordinated turn, a slipping turn, and a skidding turn. Explain the difference between slipping and skidding turns. Explain the ball indicator position in each turn and the aircraft behavior in each of the stalls.

e. Power-off (Approach-to-Landing) Stalls.

(1) Have the student perform a full-flap, gear extended, power-off stall with the correct recovery and cleanup procedures. Note the loss of altitude.

(2) Have the student repeat this procedure and distract the student during the stall and recovery and note the effect of the distraction. Show how errors in flap retraction procedure can cause a secondary stall.

f. Stalls during Go-Arounds.

(1) Have the student perform a full-flap, gear extended, power-off stall, then recover and attempt to climb with flaps extended. If a higher than normal climb pitch attitude is held, a secondary stall will occur. (In some airplanes, a stall will occur if a normal climb pitch attitude is held.)

(2) Have the student perform a full-flap, gear extended, power-off stall, then recover and retract the flaps rapidly as a higher than normal climb pitch altitude is held. A secondary stall or settling with a loss of altitude may result.

g. Elevator Trim-Stall.

(1) Have the student place the airplane in a landing approach configuration, in a trimmed descent.

(2) After the descent is established, initiate a go-around by adding full power, holding only light elevator and light rudder pressure.

(3) Allow the nose to pitch up and torque to swerve the airplane left. At the first indication of a stall, recover to a normal climbing pitch attitude.

(4) Emphasize the importance of correct attitude control, application of control pressures, and proper trim during go-arounds.

CHAPTER 3. FLIGHT TRAINING - SPINS

13. SPIN TRAINING. Spin training is required for flight instructor-airplane and flight instructor-glider applicants only. Upon completion of the training, the applicant's logbook or training record should be endorsed by the flight instructor who provided the training. A sample endorsement of spin training for flight instructor applicants is available in AC 61-65, *Certification: Pilots and Flight Instructors*, current edition.

a. Spin training must be accomplished in an aircraft that is approved for spins. Before practicing intentional spins, the AFM or POH should be consulted for the proper entry and recovery techniques.

b. The training should begin by practicing both power-on and power-off stalls to familiarize the applicant with the aircraft's stall characteristics. Spin avoidance, incipient spins, and actual spin entry, spin, and spin recovery techniques should be practiced from an altitude above 3,500 feet AGL.

c. Spin avoidance training should consist of stalls and maneuvering during slow flight using realistic distractions such as those listed in Chapter 2. Performance is considered unsatisfactory if it becomes necessary for the instructor to take control of the aircraft to avoid a fully developed spin.

d. Incipient spins should be practiced to train the instructor applicant to recover from a student's poorly performed stall or unusual attitude that could lead to a spin.

(1) Configure the aircraft for a power-on or power-off stall, and continue to apply back elevator pressure. As the stall occurs, apply right or left rudder and allow the nose to yaw toward the stalled wing. Release the spin inducing controls and recover as the spin begins by applying opposite rudder and forward elevator pressure. The instructor should discuss control application in the recovery.

e. Spin entry, spin, and spin recovery should be demonstrated by the instructor and repeated, in both directions, by the applicant.

(1) Apply the entry procedure for a power-off stall. As the airplane approaches a stall, smoothly apply full rudder in the direction of desired spin rotation and continue to apply back elevator to the limit of travel. The ailerons should be neutral.

(2) Allow the spin to develop, and be fully recovered no later than one full turn. Observe the airspeed indicator during the spin and subsequent recovery to ensure that it does not reach the red line (V_{NE}).

(3) Follow the recovery procedures recommended by the manufacturer in the AFM or POH. In most aircraft, spin recovery techniques consist of retarding power (if in a powered aircraft), applying opposite rudder to slow the rotation, neutralizing the ailerons, applying positive forward-elevator movement to break the stall, neutralizing the rudder as the spinning stops, and returning to level flight.

CHAPTER 4. AIRWORTHINESS STANDARDS

14. OPERATING LIMITATIONS. Operating limitations are imposed for the safety of pilots and their passengers. Operations contrary to these restrictions are a serious compromise of safety. It is, therefore most important that all pilots, flight and ground instructors, and pilot examiners apply the following information on spinning to pilot training and flight operations.

a. Normal Category. Single-engine normal category airplanes are placarded against intentional spins. However, to provide a margin of safety when recovery from a stall is delayed, these airplanes are tested during certification and must be able to recover from a one-turn spin or a 3-second spin, whichever takes longer, in not more than one additional turn with the controls used in the manner normally used for recovery. In addition:

(1) For both the flaps-retracted and flaps-extended conditions, the applicable airspeed limit and positive limit maneuvering load factor may not be exceeded. For the flaps-extended condition, the flaps may be retracted during recovery;

(2) There may be no excessive back pressure during the spin recovery; and

(3) It must be impossible to obtain uncontrollable spins with any use of the controls.

Note: Since airplanes certificated in the normal category have not been tested for more than a one-turn or 3-second spin, their performance characteristics beyond these limits are unknown. This is the reason they are placarded against intentional spins.

b. Acrobatic Category. An acrobatic category airplane must meet the following requirements:

(1) The airplane must recover from any point in a spin, in not more than one and one-half additional turns after normal recovery application of the controls. Prior to normal recovery application of the controls, the spin test must proceed for six turns or 3 seconds, whichever takes longer, with flaps retracted, and one turn or 3 seconds, whichever takes longer, with flaps extended. However, beyond 3 seconds, the spin may be discontinued when spiral characteristics appear with flaps retracted.

(2) For both the flaps-retracted and flaps-extended conditions, the applicable airspeed limit and the positive limit maneuvering load factor may not be exceeded. For the flaps-extended condition, the flaps may be retracted during recovery, if a placard is installed prohibiting intentional spins with flaps extended.

(3) It must be impossible to obtain uncontrollable spins with any use of the controls.

Note: Since airplanes certificated in the acrobatic category have not been tested for more than six turns or 3-second spin, their performance characteristics beyond these limits are unknown.

c. Utility Category. A utility category airplane must meet the requirements for either the normal or acrobatic category.

15. PLACARDS. Under FAR Section 23.1567, all airplanes type certificated under FAR Part 23 must have a flight maneuver placard containing the following information:

a. For normal category airplanes, there must be a placard in front of and in clear view of the pilot stating: "No acrobatic maneuvers, including spins, approved."

b. Additionally, for those utility category airplanes, with a certification basis after March 1978 and that do not meet the spin requirements for acrobatic category airplanes, there must be an additional placard in clear view of the pilot stating: "Spins Prohibited."

c. For acrobatic category airplanes, there must be a placard in clear view of the pilot listing the approved acrobatic maneuvers and the recommended entry airspeed for each. If inverted flight maneuvers are not approved, the placard must include a notation to this affect.

16. PILOT AWARENESS. The pilot of an airplane placarded against intentional spins should assume that the airplane may become uncontrollable in a spin. In addition, stall warning devices should not be deactivated for pilot certification flight tests in airplanes for which they are required equipment.

Appendix C

FAR Part 23 stall and spin airworthiness standards

These are selected airworthiness standards for normal, utility, acrobatic, and commuter category airplanes (effective February 1, 1965; current through change 28; revised September 29, 1990).

§23.49 Stalling speed.

(a) V_{SO} is the stalling speed, if obtainable, or the minimum steady speed, in knots (CAS), at which the airplane is controllable, with the—

(1) Applicable power or thrust condition set forth in paragraph (e) of this section;

(2) Propellers in the takeoff position;

(3) Landing gear extended;

(4) Wing flaps in the landing position;

(5) Cowl flaps closed;

(6) Center of gravity in the most unfavorable position within the allowable landing range; and

(7) Weight used when V_{SO} is being used as a factor to determine compliance with a required performance standard.

(b) V_{SO} at maximum weight may not exceed 61 knots for—

(1) Single-engine airplanes; and

(2) Multiengine airplanes of 6,000 pounds or less maximum weight that cannot meet the minimum rate of climb specified in §23.67(b) with the critical engine inoperative.

(c) V_{S1} is the calibrated stalling speed, if obtainable, or the minimum steady speed, in knots, at which the airplane is controllable with the—

(1) Applicable power or thrust condition set forth in paragraph (e) of this section;

(2) Propellers in the takeoff position;

(3) Airplane in the condition existing in the test in which V_{S1} is being used; and

(4) Weight used when V_{S1} is being used as a factor to determine compliance with a required performance standard.

(d) V_{SO} and V_{S1} must be determined by flight tests, using the procedure specified in §23.201.

(e) The following power or thrust conditions must be used to meet the requirements of this section:

(1) For reciprocating engine-powered airplanes, engines idling, throttles closed or at not more than the power necessary for zero thrust at a speed not more than 110 percent of the stalling speed.

(2) For turbine engine-powered airplanes, the propulsive thrust may not be greater than zero at the stalling speed, or, if the resultant thrust has no appreciable effect on the stalling speed, with engines idling and throttles closed.

Flight characteristics
§23.141 General.

The airplane must meet the requirements of §§23.143 through 23.253 at the normally expected operating altitudes without exceptional piloting skill, alertness, or strength.

Controllability and maneuverability
§23.143 General.

(a) The airplane must be safely controllable and maneuverable during—

(1) Takeoff;

(2) Climb;

(3) Level flight;

(4) Dive; and

(5) Landing (power on and power off) with the wing flaps extended and retracted.

(b) It must be possible to make a smooth transition from one flight condition to another (including turns and slips) without danger of exceeding the limit load factor, under any probable operating condition, (including, for multiengine airplanes, those conditions normally encountered in the sudden failure of any engine).

(c) If marginal conditions exist with regard to required pilot strength, the "strength of pilots" limits must be shown by quantitative tests. In no case may the limits exceed those prescribed in TABLE C-1.

§23.145 Longitudinal control.

(a) It must be possible, at speeds below the trim speed, to pitch the nose downward so that the rate of increase in airspeed allows prompt acceleration to the trim speed with—

(1) Maximum continuous power on each engine and the airplane trimmed at V_X,

(2) Power off and the airplane trimmed at a speed determined in accordance with §23.161 (c) (3), or (4), as appropriate, or at the minimum trim speed, whichever is higher; and

(3) Wing flaps and landing gear (i) retracted, and (ii) extended.

Table C-1

Values in pounds of force as applied to the control wheel or rudder pedals	Pitch	Roll	Yaw
(a) For temporary application:			
Stick	60	30	. . . .
Wheel (applied to rim).	75	60	. . . .
Rudder pedal	. . .	. . .	150
(b) For prolonged application	10	5	20

(b) With the landing gear extended, no change in trim or exertion of more control force than can be readily applied with one hand for a short period of time may be required for the following maneuvers:

    (1) With power off, flaps retracted, and the airplane trimmed at $1.4V_{S1}$ or the minimum trim speed, whichever is higher, extend the flaps as rapidly as possible and allow the airspeed to transition from $1.4V_{S1}$ to $1.4V_{S0}$, or, if appropriate, from the minimum trim speed to a speed equal to V_{S0} increased by the same percentage that the minimum trim speed at the initial condition was greater than V_{S1}.

    (2) With power off, flaps extended, and the airplane trimmed at $1.4V_{S0}$ or the minimum trim speed, whichever is higher, retract the flaps as rapidly as possible and allow the airspeed to transition from $1.4V_{S0}$ to $1.4V_{S1}$ or, if appropriate, from the minimum trim speed to a speed equal to $1.4V_{S1}$ increased by the same percentage that the minimum trim speed at the initial condition was greater than V_{S0}.

    (3) Repeat subparagraph (2) of this paragraph except with maximum continuous power.

    (4) With power off, flaps retracted, and the airplane trimmed at a speed determined in accordance with §23.161 (c) (3), or (4), as appropriate, or at the minimum trim speed, whichever is higher, apply takeoff power rapidly while maintaining the same airspeed.

    (5) Repeat subparagraph (4) of this paragraph, except with the flaps extended.

    (6) With power off, flaps extended, and the airplane trimmed at a speed determined in accordance with §23.161 (c) (3), or (4), as appropriate, or at the minimum trim speed, whichever is higher, obtain and maintain airspeeds between $1.1\ V_{S1}$ and either $1.7\ V_{S1}$ or V_F, whichever is lower.

(c) It must be possible to maintain approximately level flight when flap retraction from any position is made during steady horizontal flight at $1.1\ V_{S1}$ with simultaneous application of not more than maximum continuous power.

(d) It must be possible, with a pilot control force of not more than 10 pounds, to maintain a speed of not more than the speed determined in accordance with §23.161 (c) (4), during a poweroff glide with landing gear and wing flaps extended.

(e) By using normal flight and power controls, except as otherwise noted in paragraphs (e)(1) and (e)(2), it must be possible in the following airplanes to establish a zero rate of descent at an attitude suitable for a controlled landing without exceeding the operational and structural limitations of the airplane:

    (1) For single engine and multiengine airplanes, without the use of the primary longitudinal control system.

    (2) For multiengine airplanes-

    (I) Without the use of the primary directional control; and

    (II) If a single failure of any one connecting or transmitting link would affect both the longitudinal and directional primary control system, without the primary longitudinal and directional control system.

§23.147 Directional and lateral control.

(a) For each multiengine airplane, it must be possible to make turns with 15° of bank both towards and away from an inoperative engine, from a steady climb at 1.4 V_{S1} or V_Y with—

    (1) One engine inoperative and its propeller in the minimum drag position;

    (2) The remaining engines at not more than maximum continuous power;

    (3) The rearmost allowable center of gravity;

    (4) The landing gear (i) retracted, and (ii) extended;

    (5) The flaps in the most favorable climb position; and

    (6) Maximum weight.

(b) For each multiengine airplane, it must be possible, while holding the wings level within 5°, to make sudden changes in heading safely in both directions. This must be shown at 1.4 V_{S1} or V_Y with heading changes up to 15° (except that the heading change at which the rudder force corresponds to the limits specified in 23.143 need not be exceeded), with the—

    (1) Critical engine inoperative and its propeller in the minimum drag position;

    (2) Remaining engines at maximum continuous power;

    (3) Landing gear (i) retracted, and (ii) extended;

    (4) Flaps in the most favorable climb position; and

    (5) Center of gravity at its rearmost allowable position.

[§23.149 Minimum control speed.

[(a) V_{MC} is the calibrated airspeed, at which, when the critical engine is suddenly made inoperative, it is possible to recover control of the airplane with that engine still inoperative, and maintain straight flight either with zero yaw or, at the option of the applicant, with an angle of bank not more than five degrees. The method used to simulate critical engine failure must represent the most critical mode of powerplant failure with respect to controllability expected in service.

[(b) For reciprocating engine-powered airplanes, V_{MC} may not exceed 1.2 V_{S1} (where V_{S1} is determined at the maximum takeoff weight) with—

    [(1) Takeoff or maximum available power on the engines;

    [(2) The most unfavorable center of gravity;

    [(3) The airplane trimmed for takeoff;

    [(4) The maximum sea level takeoff weight (or any lesser weight necessary to show V_{MC});

    [(5) Flaps in the takeoff position;

    [(6) Landing gear retracted;

    [(7) Cowl flaps in the normal takeoff position;

    [(8) The propeller of the inoperative engine

        [(i) Windmilling;

        [(ii) In the most probable position for the specific design of the propeller control; or

        [(iii) Feathered, if the airplane has an automatic feathering device; and

[**(9)** The airplane airborne and the ground effect negligible.

[**(c)** For turbine engine-powered airplanes, V_{MC} may not exceed $1.2V_{S1}$ (where V_{S1} is determined at the maximum takeoff weight) with—

    [**(1)** Maximum available takeoff power or thrust on the engines;

    [**(2)** The most unfavorable center of gravity;

    [**(3)** The airplane trimmed for takeoff;

    [**(4)** The maximum sea level takeoff weight (or any lesser weight necessary to show V_{MC});

    [**(5)** The airplane in the most critical takeoff configuration, except with the landing gear retracted; and

    [**(6)** The airplane airborne and the ground effect negligible.

[**(d)** At V_{MC}, the rudder pedal force required to maintain control may not exceed 150 pounds, and it may not be necessary to reduce power or thrust of the operative engines. During recovery, the airplane may not assume any dangerous attitude and it must be possible to prevent a heading change of more than 20 degrees.] Ch. 8 (Amdt. 23-21, eff. 3/1/78)(Corrected)

§23.151 Acrobatic maneuvers.

Each acrobatic and utility category airplane must be able to perform safely the acrobatic maneuvers for which certification is requested. Safe entry speeds for these maneuvers must be determined.

Stalls
§23.201 Wings level stall.

    (a) For an airplane with independently controlled roll and directional controls, it must be possible to produce and to correct roll by unreversed use of the rolling control and to produce and to correct yaw by unreversed use of the directional control, up to the time the airplane pitches.

    (b) For an airplane with interconnected lateral and directional controls (2 controls) and for an airplane with only one of these controls, it must be possible to produce and correct roll by unreversed use of the rolling control without producing excessive yaw, up to the time the airplane pitches.

    (c) The wing level stall characteristics of the airplane must be demonstrated in flight as follows: The airplane speed must be reduced with the elevator control until the speed is slightly above the stalling speed, then the elevator control must be pulled back so that the rate of speed reduction will not exceed one knot per second until a stall is produced, as shown by an uncontrollable downward pitching motion of the airplane, or until the control reaches the top. Normal use of the elevator control for recovery is allowed after the pitching motion has unmistakably developed.

    (d) Except where made inapplicable by the special features of a particular type of airplane, the following apply to the measurement of loss of altitude during a stall:

        (1) The loss of altitude encountered in the stall (power on or power off) is the change in altitude (as observed on the sensitive altimeter testing installation) between the altitude at which the airplane pitches and the altitude at which horizontal flight is regained.

        (2) If power or thrust is required during stall recovery the power or thrust used must be that which would be used under the normal operating procedures selected by the applicant for this maneuver. However, the power used to regain level flight may not be applied until flying control is regained.

(e) During the recovery part of the maneuver, it must be possible to prevent more than 15 degrees of roll or yaw by the normal use of controls.

(f) Compliance with the requirements of this section must be shown under the following conditions:

(1) Wing Flaps: Full up, full down, and intermediate, if appropriate.

(2) Landing Gear: Retracted and extended.

(3) Cowl Flaps: Appropriate to configuration.

(4) Power: Power or thrust off, and 75 percent maximum continuous power or thrust.

(5) Trim: 1.5 V_{S1} or at the minimum trim speed, whichever is higher.

(6) Propeller: Full increase rpm position for the power off condition.

§23.203 Turning flight and accelerated stalls.

Turning flight and accelerated stalls must be demonstrated in tests as follows:

(a) Establish and maintain a coordinated turn in a 30 degree bank. Reduce speed by steadily and progressively tightening the turn with the elevator until the airplane is stalled or until the elevator has reached its stop. The rate of speed reduction must be constant, and—

(1) For a turning flight stall, may not exceed one knot per second; and

(2) For an accelerated stall, be 3 to 5 knots per second with steadily increasing normal acceleration.

(b) When the stall has fully developed or the elevator has reached its stop, it must be possible to regain level flight without—

(1) Excessive loss of altitude;

(2) Undue pitchup;

(3) Uncontrollable tendency to spin;

(4) Exceeding 60 degree of roll in either direction from the established 30 degree bank; and

(5) For accelerated entry stalls, without exceeding the maximum permissible speed or the allowable limit load factor.

(c) Compliance with the requirements of this section must be shown with—

(1) Wing Flaps: Retracted and fully extended for turning flight and accelerated entry stalls, and intermediate, if appropriate, for accelerated entry stalls;

(2) Landing Gear: Retracted and extended;

(3) Cowl Flaps: Appropriate to configuration;

(4) Power: 75 percent maximum continuous power; and

(5) Trim: 1.5 V_{S1} or minimum trim speed, whichever is higher.

§23.205 Critical engine inoperative stalls.

(a) A multiengine airplane may not display any undue spinning tendency and must be safely recoverable without applying power to the inoperative engine when stalled. The operating engines may be throttled back during the recovery from stall.

(b) Compliance with paragraph (a) of this section must be shown with—

(1) Wing flaps: Retracted.

(2) Landing gear: Retracted.

(3) Cowl flaps: Appropriate to level flight critical engine inoperative.

(4) Power: Critical engine inoperative and the remaining engine(s) at 75 percent maximum continuous power or thrust or the power or thrust at which the use of

maximum control travel just holds the wings laterally level in the approach to stall, whichever is lesser.

(5) Propeller: Normal inoperative position for the inoperative engine.

(6) Trim: Level flight, critical engine inoperative, except that for an airplane of 6,000 pounds or less maximum weight that has a stalling speed of 61 knots or less and cannot maintain level flight with the critical engine inoperative, the airplane must be trimmed for straight flight, critical engine inoperative, at a speed not greater than $1.5\ V_{S1}$.

§23.207 Stall warning.

(a) There must be a clear and distinctive stall warning, with the flaps and landing gear in any normal position, in straight and turning flight.

(b) The stall warning may be furnished either through the inherent aerodynamic qualities of the airplane or by a device that will give clearly distinguishable indications under expected conditions of flight. However, a visual stall warning device that requires the attention of the crew within the cockpit is not acceptable by itself.

(c) The stall warning must begin at a speed exceeding the stalling speed by a margin of not less than 5 knots, but not more than the greater of 10 knots or 15 percent of the stalling speed, and must continue until the stall occurs.

Spinning
§23.221 Spinning.

(a) *Normal category.* A single-engine, normal category airplane must be able to recover from a one-turn spin or a 3-second spin, whichever takes longer, in not more than one additional turn, with the controls used in the manner normally used for recovery. In addition—

  (1) For both the flaps-retracted and flaps-extended conditions, the applicable airspeed limit and positive limit maneuvering load factor may not be exceeded;

  (2) There may be no excessive back pressure during the spin or recovery; and

  (3) It must be impossible to obtain uncontrollable spins with any use of the controls. For the flaps-extended condition, the flaps may be retracted during recovery.

(b) *Utility category.* A utility category airplane must meet the requirements of paragraph (a) of this section or the requirements of paragraph (c) of this section.

(c) *Acrobatic category.* An acrobatic category airplane must meet the following requirements:

  (1) The airplane must recover from any point in a spin, in not more than one and one-half additional turns after normal recovery application of the controls. Prior to normal recovery application of the controls, the spin test must proceed for six turns or 3 seconds, whichever takes longer, with flaps retracted, and one turn or 3 seconds, whichever takes longer, with flaps extended. However, beyond 3 seconds, the spin may be discontinued when spiral characteristics appear with flaps retracted.

  (2) For both the flaps-retracted and flaps-extended conditions, the applicable airspeed limit and positive limit maneuvering load factor may not be exceeded. For the flaps extended condition, the flaps may be retracted during recovery, if a placard is installed prohibiting intentional spins with flaps extended.

  (3) It must be impossible to obtain uncontrollable spins with any use of the controls.

(d) *Airplanes "characteristically incapable of spinning."* If it is desired to designate an airplane as "characteristically incapable of spinning," this characteristic must be shown with—

(1) A weight five percent more than the highest weight for which approval is requested;

(2) A center of gravity at least three percent aft of the rearmost position for which approval is requested;

(3) An available elevator up-travel 4° in excess of that to which the elevator travel is limited for approval; and

(4) An available rudder travel 7°, in both directions, in excess of that to which the rudder travel is to be limited for approval.

Control systems
§23.671 General.

(a) Each control must operate easily, smoothly, and positively enough to allow proper performance of its functions.

(b) Controls must be arranged and identified to provide for convenience in operation and to prevent the possibility of confusion and subsequent inadvertent operation.

§23.673 Primary flight controls.

(a) Primary flight controls are those used by the pilot for the immediate control of pitch, roll, and yaw.

(b) The design of two-control airplanes must minimize the likelihood of complete loss of lateral or directional control in the event of failure of any connecting or transmitting element in the control system.

§23.675 Stops.

(a) Each control system must have stops that positively limit the range of motion of each movable aerodynamic surface controlled by the system.

(b) Each stop must be located so that wear, slackness, or takeup adjustments will not adversely affect the control characteristics of the airplane because of a change in the range of surface travel.

(c) Each stop must be able to withstand any loads corresponding to the design conditions for the control system.

§23.677 Trim systems.

(a) Proper precautions must be taken to prevent inadvertent, improper, or abrupt trim tab operation. There must be means near the trim control to indicate to the pilot the direction of trim control movement relative to airplane motion. In addition, there must be means to indicate to the pilot the position of the trim device with respect to the range of adjustment. This means it must be visible to the pilot and must be located and designed to prevent confusion.

(b) Trimming devices must be designed so that, when any one connecting or transmitting element in the primary flight control system fails, adequate control for safe flight and landing available with—

(1) For single-engine airplanes, the longitudinal trimming devices; or

(2) For multiengine airplanes, the longitudinal and directional trimming devices.

(c) Tab controls must be irreversible unless the tab is properly balanced and has no unsafe flutter characteristics. Irreversible tab systems must have adequate rigidity and reliability in the portion of the system from the tab to the attachment of the irreversible unit to the airplane structure.

[(d) In addition, for commuter category airplanes, a demonstration must show that the airplane is safely controllable and that a pilot can perform all the maneuvers and operations necessary to effect a safe landing following any probable electric trim tab runaway which might be reasonably expected in service allowing for appropriate time delay after pilot recognition of the runaway. This demonstration must be conducted at the critical airplane weights and center of gravity positions.] Ch. 22 (Amdt. 2334, eff. 2/17/87)

§23.679 Control system locks.

If there is a device to lock the control system on the ground or water there must be means to—
(a) Give unmistakable warning to the pilot when the lock is engaged; and
(b) Prevent the lock from engaging in flight.

§23.681 Limit load static tests.

(a) Compliance with the limit load requirements of this Part must be shown by tests in which—
   (1) The direction of the test loads produces the most severe loading in the control system; and
   (2) Each fitting, pulley, and bracket used in attaching the system to the main structure is included.
(b) Compliance must be shown (by analyses or individual load tests) with the special factor requirements for control system joints subject to angular motion.

§23.683 Operation tests.

(a) It must be shown by operation tests that, when the controls are operated from the pilot compartment with the system loaded as prescribed in paragraph (b) of this section, the system is free from—
   (1) Jamming;
   (2) Excessive friction; and
   (3) Excessive deflection.
(b) The prescribed test loads are—
   (1) For the entire system, loads corresponding to the limit airloads on the appropriate surface, or the limit pilot forces in §23.397(b), whichever are less; and
   (2) For secondary controls, loads not less than those corresponding to the maximum pilot effort established under §23.405.

§23.685 Control system details.

(a) Each detail of each control system must be designed and installed to prevent jamming, chafing, and interference from cargo, passengers, loose objects, or the freezing of moisture.
(b) There must be means in the cockpit to prevent the entry of foreign objects into places where they would jam the system.
(c) There must be means to prevent the slapping of cables or tubes against other parts.
(d) Each element of the flight control system must have design features, or must be distinctively and permanently marked, to minimize the possibility of incorrect assembly that could result in malfunctioning of the control system.

APPENDIX C

§23.687 Spring devices.

The reliability of any spring device used in the control system must be established by tests simulating service conditions unless failure of the spring will not cause flutter or unsafe flight characteristics.

§23.689 Cable systems.

(a) Each cable, cable fitting, turnbuckle, splice, and pulley used must meet approved specifications. In addition—

    (1) No cable smaller than ⅛ inch diameter may be used in primary control systems;

    (2) Each cable system must be designed so that there will be no hazardous change in cable tension throughout the range of travel under operating conditions and temperature variations; and

    (3) There must be means for visual inspection at each fairlead, pulley, terminal, and turnbuckle.

(b) Each kind and size of pulley must correspond to the cable with which it is used. Each pulley must have closely fitted guards to prevent the cables from being misplaced or fouled, even when slack. Each pulley must lie in the plane passing through the cable so that the cable does not rub against the pulley flange.

(c) Fairleads must be installed so that they do not cause a change in cable direction of more than 3°.

(d) Clevis pins subject to load or motion and retained only by cotter pins may not be used in the control system.

(e) Turnbuckles must be attached to parts having angular motion in a manner that will positively prevent binding throughout the range of travel.

(f) Tab control cables are not part of the primary control system and may be less than ⅛ inch diameter in airplanes that are safely controllable with the tabs in the most adverse positions.

§23.693 Joints.

Control system joints (in push-pull systems) that are subject to angular motion, except those in ball and roller bearing systems, must have a special factor of safety of not less than 3.33 with respect to the ultimate bearing strength of the softest material used as a bearing. This factor may be reduced to 2.0 for joints in cable control systems. For ball or roller bearings, the approved ratings may not be exceeded.

§23.697 Wing flap controls.

(a) Each wing flap control must be designed so that, when the flap has been placed in any position upon which compliance with the performance requirements of this Part is based, the flap will not move from that position unless the control is adjusted or is moved by the automatic operation of a flap load limiting device.

(b) The rate of movement of the flaps in response to the operation of the pilot's control or automatic device must give satisfactory flight and performance characteristics under steady or changing conditions of airspeed, engine power, and attitude.

§23.699 Wing flap position indicator.

There must be a wing flap position indicator for—

(a) Flap installations with only the retracted and fully extended position, unless—

    (1) A direct operating mechanism provides a sense of "feel" and position (such as when a mechanical linkage is employed); or

(2) The flap position is readily determined without seriously detracting from other piloting duties under any flight condition, day or night; and

(b) Flap installation with intermediate flap positions if—

(1) Any flap position other than retracted or fully extended is used to show compliance with the performance requirements of this part; and

(2) The flap installation does not meet the requirements of paragraph (a) (1) of this section.

§23.701 Flap interconnection.

(a) The motion of flaps on opposite sides of the plane of symmetry must be synchronized by a mechanical interconnection unless the airplane has safe flight characteristics with the flaps retracted on one side and extended on the other.

(b) If an interconnection is used in multiengine airplanes, it must be designed to account for the unsymmetrical loads resulting from flight with the engines on one side of the plane of symmetry inoperative and the remaining engines at takeoff power. For single-engine airplanes, and multiengine airplanes with no slipstream effects on the flaps, it may be assumed that 100 percent of the critical air load acts on one side and 70 percent on the other.

§23.1545 Airspeed indicator.

(a) Each airspeed indicator must be marked as specified in paragraph (b) of this section, with the marks located at the corresponding indicated airspeeds.

(b) The following markings must be made:

(1) For the never-exceed speed V_{NE}, a radial red line.

(2) For the caution range, a yellow arc extending from the red line specified in subparagraph (1) of this paragraph to the upper limit of the green arc specified in subparagraph (3) of this paragraph.

(3) For the normal operating range, a green arc with the lower limit at V_{S1}, with maximum weight and with landing gear and wing flaps retracted, and the upper limit at the maximum structural cruising speed V_{NO} established under §23.1505(b).

(4) For the flap operating range, a white arc with the lower limit at V_{SO} at the maximum weight and the upper limit at the flaps-extended speed V_{FE} established under §23.1511.

(5) For the one-engine-inoperative best rate of climb speed, V_y, a blue sector extending from the V_y speed at sea level to the V_y speed at—

  (i) An altitude of 5,000 feet, if the one-engine-inoperative best rate of climb at that altitude is less than 100 feet per minute, or

  (ii) The highest 1,000-foot altitude (at or above 5,000 feet) at which the one-engine-inoperative best rate of climb is 100 feet per minute or more. Each side of the sector must be labeled to show the altitude for the corresponding V_y.

(6) For the minimum control speed (one-engine-inoperative) V_{mc}, a red radial line.

(c) If V_{NE} or V_{NO} vary with altitude, there must be means to indicate to the pilot the appropriate limitations throughout the operating altitude range.

(d) Subparagraphs (1) through (3) of paragraph (b) and paragraph (c) of this section do not apply to aircraft for which a maximum operating speed V_{MO} / M_{MO} is established under §23.1505(c). For those aircraft there must either be a maximum allowable airspeed indication showing the variation of V_{MO} / M_{MO} with altitude or compressibility limitations (as appropriate), or a radial red line marking for V_{MO} / M_{MO} must be made at lowest value of V_{MO} / M_{MO} established for any altitude up to the maximum operating altitude for the airplane.

§23.1547 Magnetic direction indicator.

(a) A placard meeting the requirements of this section must be installed on or near the magnetic direction indicator.

(b) The placard must show the calibration of the instrument in level flight with the engines operating.

(c) The placard must state whether the calibration was made with radio receivers on or off.

(d) Each calibration reading must be in terms of magnetic headings in not more than 30° increments.

(e) If a magnetic nonstabilized direction indicator can have a deviation of more than 10 degrees caused by the operation of electrical equipment, the placard must state which electrical loads, or combination of loads, would cause a deviation of more than 10 degrees when turned on.

§23.1563 Airspeed placards.

There must be an airspeed placard in clear view of the pilot and as close as practicable to the airspeed indicator: This placard must list—

(a) The design maneuvering speed V_A; and

(b) The maximum landing gear operating speed V_{LO}.

§23.1567 Flight maneuver placard.

(a) For normal category airplanes, there must be a placard in front of and in clear view of the pilot stating: "No acrobatic maneuvers, including spins, approved."

(b) For utility category airplanes, there must be—

    (1) A placard in clear view of the pilot stating: "Acrobatic maneuvers are limited to the following _____ (list approved maneuvers and the recommended entry speed for each); and

    (2) For those airplanes that do not meet the spin requirements for acrobatic category airplanes, an additional placard in clear view of the pilot stating: "Spins Prohibited."

(c) For acrobatic category airplanes, there must be a placard in clear view of the pilot listing the approved acrobatic maneuvers and the recommended entry airspeed for each. If inverted flight maneuvers are not approved, the placard must bear a notation to this effect.

Appendix D
Factors affecting stall speed

(The FAA's *VFR Pilot Exam-O-Gram Number 58* examines the factors that affect stall speed.) A recent report indicates that approximately 80 percent of all accidents are pilot caused. The major cause of **fatal** accidents is listed as "failed to maintain airspeed (or flying speed) resulting in a stall." Although many of these stalls may have occurred under the stress and duress of other problems such as **disorientation** during limited visibility or at night, **improper division of attention**, etc., a review of statistical analyses of written examinations indicates a lack of knowledge and understanding of the various factors that can cause or contribute to a stall. This Exam-O-Gram discusses some of the more important, ever-present factors of which the pilot must have an understanding so that he will instinctively avoid or compensate for situations, conditions, and attitudes which may lead to a stall—even under the stress and duress of additional problems he may encounter in flight.

WHAT CAUSES AN AIRPLANE TO STALL? All stalls are caused by exceeding the critical angle of attack. Knowing this particular fact does not necessarily help the pilot. What is more important to the pilot is to know what factors are likely to contribute to or cause this angle of attack to be exceeded.

IS IT NECESSARY FOR THE AIRPLANE TO HAVE A RELATIVELY LOW AIRSPEED IN ORDER FOR IT TO STALL? No! An airplane can be stalled **at any airspeed**. All that is necessary is to exceed the critical angle of attack. This can be done at any airspeed if the pilot applies abrupt or excessive back pressure on the elevator control. A stall that occurs at a relatively high speed is referred to as an accelerated or high speed stall.

IS IT NECESSARY FOR THE AIRPLANE TO HAVE A RELATIVELY HIGH PITCH ATTITUDE IN ORDER FOR IT TO STALL? No! An airplane can be stalled **in any attitude**. Repeating again the statement made above—all that is necessary is to exceed the critical angle of attack. This can occur in any attitude by application of abrupt or excessive back pressure on the elevator control.

DOES WEIGHT AFFECT THE STALLING SPEED? Yes! As the weight of the airplane is increased, the stall speed increases. Due to the greater weight, a higher angle of attack must be maintained to produce the additional lift to support the additional weight in flight. Therefore, the critical angle of attack will be reached at a higher airspeed when loaded to maximum gross weight than when flying solo with no baggage.

DOES THE CENTER-OF-GRAVITY LOCATION (WEIGHT DISTRIBUTION) AFFECT STALL SPEED? Yes! The farther forward the center of gravity, the higher the stalling speed. The farther aft the center of gravity, the lower the stalling speed.

DOES THIS MEAN THAT THE WEIGHT SHOULD BE DISTRIBUTED IN THE AIRPLANE SO THAT THE CG IS AS FAR TO THE REAR AS POSSIBLE? No! This may present problems with stability that will far outweigh any advantages obtained by the decrease in stall speed.

DO FLAPS AFFECT STALLING SPEED? Yes! The use of flaps reduces stalling speed. The Stall Speed Chart (FIG. D-1) excerpted from an airplane flight manual illustrates this fact. This also can be readily verified by checking the color coding of any airspeed indicator. The lower airspeed limit of the white arc (power-off stalling speed with gear and flaps in the landing configuration) is less than the lower airspeed limit of the green arc (power-off stalling speed in the clean configuration). This fact is important to the pilot in that when making no-flap landings, a higher indicated airspeed should be maintained than when landing with flaps. The manufacturers' recommendations should be adhered to as to approach speeds with various configurations.

STALL SPEED, POWER OFF

Gross Weight 3000 lbs.

CONFIGURATION	ANGLE OF BANK			
	0°	20°	40°	60°
Gear & flaps up	65	67	74	92
Gear down, flaps 20°	61	63	70	86
Gear down, flaps 40°	60	62	69	85

Speeds are mph, TIAS

Fig. D-1

DOES AN ACCUMULATION OF FROST, SNOW, OR ICE ON THE WINGS AFFECT STALLING SPEED? Yes! Even a light accumulation of frost, snow, or ice on the wings can cause a significant increase in stalling speed. It can increase it so much that the airplane is unable to take off. The accumulation disrupts the smooth flow of air over the wing thus decreasing the lift it produces.

To make up for the lost lift, a higher angle of attack must be used or a higher speed must be attained on the takeoff roll. The runway may not be long enough to attain the necessary speed and even though the airplane may become airborne, it could be so close to the stall speed that it would not be possible to maintain flight once the airplane climbs above the comparatively shallow zone where ground effect prevails. DO NOT TAKE OFF UNTIL ALL FROST, SNOW, OR ICE HAS MELTED OR BEEN REMOVED FROM THE AIRPLANE.

DOES AN INCREASE IN ALTITUDE AFFECT THE INDICATED AIRSPEED AT WHICH AN AIRPLANE STALLS? An increase in altitude has no effect on the **indicated** airspeed at which an airplane stalls at altitudes normally used by general aviation aircraft. That is, for all practical purposes, the indicated stalling speed remains the same regardless of altitude in this range. This fact is important to the pilot in that the same indicated airspeed should be maintained during the landing approach regardless of the elevation or the density altitude at the airport of landing. (Follow the manufacturer's recommendations in this regard.) If higher than normal approach airspeed is used, a longer landing distance will be required.

DOES AN INCREASE IN ALTITUDE AFFECT THE TRUE AIRSPEED AT WHICH AN AIRPLANE STALLS? Since true airspeed normally increases as altitude increases (for a given indicated airspeed), then true airspeed at which an airplane stalls generally increases with an increase in altitude. Under non-standard conditions (temperature warmer than standard) there is an additional increase in true airspeed above the indicated airspeed.

OF WHAT SIGNIFICANCE IS THIS TO THE PILOT? It is significant in that when landing at higher elevations or under higher density altitudes, he is operating at higher true airspeeds (and therefore higher ground speeds) throughout the approach, touchdown, and landing roll. This results in a greater distance to clear obstacles during the approach, a longer ground roll, and consequently, the need for a longer runway. If, in addition, the pilot is operating under the misconception that a higher than normal indicated airspeed should be used under these conditions, the situation is further compounded due to the additional increase in groundspeed.

DOES TURBULENCE AFFECT STALLING SPEED? Yes! Turbulence can cause a large increase in stalling speed. Encountering an upward vertical gust causes an abrupt change in relative wind. This results in an equally abrupt, increase in angle of attack which could result in a stall. This fact is important to the pilot in that when making an approach under turbulent conditions, a higher than normal approach speed should be maintained. Also, in moderate or greater turbulence, an airplane should not be flown above maneuvering speed. At the same time, it should not be flown too far below maneuvering speed since a sudden severe vertical gust may cause an inadvertent stall due to the higher angle of attack at which it will already be flying.

DOES ANGLE OF BANK AFFECT STALLING SPEED? Yes! As the angle of bank increases in a constant altitude turn, the stalling speed increases. This is easily seen from the STALL SPEED CHARTS (FIGS. D-1 and D-2) which show the increase in stall speed as the angle of bank increases— FIG. D-2 in terms of percent, FIG. D-1 the actual values for one airplane. At a 600 bank stalling speed is 40 percent greater than in straight-and-level flight (25–27 mph for the specific example). At angles of bank above 600, stall speed increases very rapidly, and at approximately 75° it is doubled with respect to straight-and-level stall speed (FIG. D-2).

DOES LOAD FACTOR AFFECT STALLING SPEED? Yes! As the load factor increases, stalling speed increases. When the load factor is high, stalling speed is high. A comparison of the two

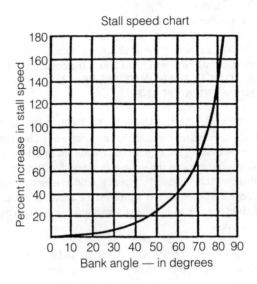

Stall speed chart

Fig. D-2

charts (FIGS. D-2 and D-3) should easily show this relationship. Load factor is the ratio of the load supported by the wings to the actual weight of the airplane and its contents. At a load factor of 2, the wings support twice the weight of the airplane; at a load factor of 4, they support four times the weight of the airplane. Normal category airplanes with a maximum gross weight of less than 4,000 pounds are required to have a minimum limit load factor of 3.8. (The limit load factor is that load factor an airplane can sustain without taking a permanent set in the structure.) Note from the load factor chart (FIG. D-3) that this minimum limit load factor is attained in a constant altitude turn at a bank of approximately 75°. Also note from the stall speed chart (FIG. D-2) that at this angle of bank, the stall speed is twice as great as in straight-and-level flight. There are two reasons then why excessively steep banks should be avoided—an airplane will stall at a much higher airspeed and the limit load factor can be exceeded. The danger can be compounded when the nose gets down in a steep turn if the pilot attempts to raise it to the level flight attitude without shallowing the bank since the load factor may be increased even more. This is the situation as it generally exists when, due to disorientation, the pilot enters a diving spiral (often referred to as the "graveyard spiral") and attempts to recover with elevator pressure alone.

WHAT FACTORS CAUSE AN INCREASE IN LOAD FACTOR? Any maneuvering of the airplane that produces an increase in centrifugal force will cause an increase in load factor. Turning the airplane or pulling out of a dive are examples of maneuvering that will increase the centrifugal force and thus produce an increase in load factor. When you have a combination of turning and pulling out of a dive, such as recovering from a diving spiral, you are, in effect, placing yourself in double jeopardy. This is why you must avoid high-speed diving spirals or if you accidentally get into one—be careful how you recover. Turbulence can also produce large load factors. This is why an airplane should be slowed to maneuvering speed or below when encountering moderate or greater turbulence.

CAN THE PILOT RECOGNIZE WHEN THERE IS AN INCREASE IN LOAD FACTOR? Yes! He can recognize it by the feeling of increased body weight or the feeling that he is being forced down into the seat—the greater the load factor the greater this feeling of increased weight or of be-

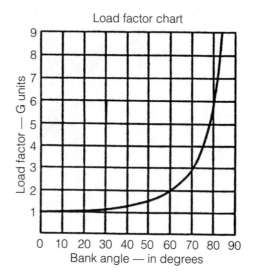

Fig. D-3

ing forced down in the seat. It is the same feeling one has when riding the roller coaster at the bottom of a dip or going around a banked curve. This feeling of increased body weight is important to the pilot because it should, if it becomes excessive, have the immediate effect of a red flag being waved in his face to warn him that the airplane will now stall at a higher airspeed or that the limit load factor can be exceeded, resulting in structural failure.

DOES SPEED AFFECT LOAD FACTOR? Speed does not, in itself, affect load factor. However, it has a pronounced effect on how much of an increase in load factor can be produced by strong vertical gusts, or by the pilot through abrupt or excessive application of back pressure on the elevator control. This is why airspeed should be reduced to maneuvering speed or below if moderate or greater turbulence is encountered. At maneuvering speed or below, the airplane is stressed to handle any vertical gust that normally will be encountered. Also, below this speed, the pilot can make abrupt full deflection of the elevator control and not exceed the maximum load factor for which the airplane is stressed. However, it should be noted that the reason this is possible is because **the airplane will stall**, thus relieving the load factor. At airspeeds above maneuvering speed, abrupt full deflection of the elevator control or strong vertical gusts can cause the limit load factor to be exceeded. As airspeed continues to increase above maneuvering speed, the limit load factor can be exceeded with less and less turbulence or abrupt use or deflection of the controls.

WHAT IS THE RELATIONSHIP BETWEEN A HIGH SPEED (ACCELERATED) STALL AND LOAD FACTOR? The higher the airspeed when an airplane is stalled, the greater the load factor. When an airplane stalls at a slow airspeed, the load factor will be very little more than one. When stalled at an airspeed twice as great as the normal stall speed, the limit load factor for normal category airplanes probably will be exceeded. This fact can be determined from the stall speed (FIG. D-2) and load factor (FIG. D-3) charts. See also the discussion of "Does Load Factor Affect Stalling Speed?"

Appendix E
Stall and spin lesson plans

POWER-ON STALLS

WHAT? A power-on stall is a stall that can be done while in a straight climb, and climbing turns with 15 deg to 20 deg banks, to simulate an accidental stall occurring during takeoffs and departure climbs. A power-on occurs when the stalling angle of attack is exceeded with power-on, normally at takeoff or climb power. This will cause the stall to have a very high angle of attack.

HOW? After establishing takeoff or departure configuration, the airplane should be slowed to the normal lift-off speed while clearing the area for other air traffic. When the desired speed is attained, the power should be set at takeoff power for the takeoff stall or the recommended climb power for the departure stall while establishing a climb attitude. After the climb attitude is established, the nose is then brought smoothly upward to an attitude obviously impossible for the airplane to maintain and is held at that attitude until the stall occurs. If an imminent stall is desired then recover at the first sign of a stall (stall warning horn). Recovery from the stall should be accomplished by immediately reducing the angle of attack by positively releasing back elevator pressure and smoothly advancing the throttle to maximum allowable power. The nose should be lowered as necessary to regain flying speed. Then the airplane should be returned to the normal straight-and-level flight attitude. When in normal level flight, the throttle should be returned to cruise power setting.

WHY? To develop the pilots skill to recognize instantly when the stall has occurred and take prompt action to prevent a prolonged stalled condition. These types of stalls can be encountered during take-off and climbs from airports when attention has been directed to another object like looking for traffic or ATC communications.

LESSON Power-On Stalls   STUDENT   DATE

OBJECTIVE	* TO DEVELOP THE STUDENT'S SKILL IN DETECTION AND RECOVERING FROM IMMINENT AND FULL STALLS WITH POWER ON AND WITH LITTLE OR NO ALTITUDE LOST.

ELEMENTS
* USE OF A SAFE ALTITUDE
* CONTROL OF AIRPLANE ATTITUDE, ALTITUDE, AND HEADING.
* CONTROL OF AIRSPEED

SCHEDULE
* PREFLIGHT DISCUSSION   :15
* INSTRUCTOR DEMONSTRATIONS :15
* STUDENT-PRACTICE   :35
* POSTFLIGHT CRITIQUE   :15

EQUIPMENT
* MODEL AIRPLANE TO DEMONSTRATE ATTITUDES
* AIRPLANE COCKPIT FOR PROCEDURES DEMO (GROUND)
* IFR HOOD FOR MANEUVERS REVIEWED.

INSTRUCTOR'S
ACTION
* PREFLIGHT–DISCUSS LESSON OBJECTIVE. REVIEW MANEUVER FOR AC 61-21. DEMONSTRATE ATTITUDE WITH MODEL AIRPLANE.
* INFLIGHT–DEMONSTRATE ELEMENTS. DEMONSTRATE POWER-ON STALLS, FULL AND IMMINENT. COACH STUDENT PRACTICE.
* POSTFLIGHT–CRITIQUE STUDENT PERFORMANCE, REVIEW OBJECTIVE, MAKE STUDY ASSIGNMENT.

STUDENT'S
ACTION
* PREFLIGHT–DISCUSS LESSON OBJECTIVE
* INFLIGHT–REVIEW MCA, STRAIGHT-LEVEL FLT, TURNS, CLIMBS, DESCENTS. PREFORM EACH NEW MANEUVER AS DIRECTED.
* POSTFLIGHT–ASK PERTINENT QUESTIONS

COMPLETION
STANDARDS
* STUDENT SHOULD DEMONSTRATE COMPETENCY IN MAINTAINING ORIENTATION
* SELECTING ALTITUDE WHERE RECOVERY CAN BE MADE ABOVE 1500' AGL
* ESTABLISHES TAKEOFF OR NORMAL CLIMB CONFIGURATION
* ESTABLISHES TAKEOFF OR CLIMB SPEED BEFORE ADDING FULL POWER
* MAINTAINS PITCH ATTITUDE AND BANK IF IN TURN 20 DEG, ± 10 DEG
* RECOGNIZES THE STALL AND RECOVERS BY DECREASING THE ANGLE OF ATTACK, LEVELING THE WINGS, AND ADJUSTING THE POWER TO REGAIN NORMAL FLIGHT ATTITUDE, RETRACTS WING FLAPS AND LANDING GEAR (IF RG)
* AVOID SECONDARY STALL
* EXCESSIVE AIRSPEED

> * EXCESSIVE ALTITUDE LOSS
> * SPINS

COMMON
ERRORS   * UNCOORDINATED FLIGHT
           * ADDING POWER TOO SOON
           * RELAXED PITCH ATTITUDE
           * EXCESSIVE AIRSPEED
           * EXCESSIVE ALTITUDE LOSS
           * FORGETS TO RETRACT FLAPS TO RECOMMENDED SETTING
           * FAILS TO REDUCE POWER AND LOWER NOSE BELOW THE HORIZON

POWER-OFF STALLS (FULL)

WHAT? A practice maneuver that demonstrated, in simulation of actual landing conditions, an accidental full stall.

WHY? To teach the student to avoid stalls and to recover from such a stall were one to occur, with little or no altitude lost. Also to show proper control usage for flight near stalling speed that is essential for take-offs and landings.

HOW?   a) Clearing turn
          b) Extend landing gear (if so equipped)
          c) Apply carburetor heat
          d) Retard throttle to idle
          e) Hold attitude while decelerating to approach airspeed
          f) Establish approach attitude to maintain approach airspeed
          g) Extend wing flaps, adjust pitch attitude to maintain approach airspeed
          h) Raise nose to pitch attitude that will induce a full stall (recognized by buffeting)
          i) Recover by reducing angle of attack, releasing back elevator pressure, applying full power, retracting flaps to 20 deg.
          j) When positive rate-of-climb is established retract flaps in increments to 0 deg.
          k) Return to normal cruise flight

LESSON POWER-OFF STALL (FULL)   STUDENT   DATE

OBJECTIVE   * TO DEVELOP THE STUDENT'S SKILL IN DETECTION AND RECOVERING FROM FULL STALLS WITH POWER OFF AND WITH LITTLE OR NO ALTITUDE LOST ON THE RECOVERY.

ELEMENTS   * USE OF SAFE ALTITUDE
             * CONTROL COORDINATION
             * CONTROL RESPONSIVENESS AT SLOW AIRSPEEDS
             * CONTROL OF AIRPLANE ATTITUDE, ALTITUDE, AND HEADING
             * STALL CHARACTERISTICS
             * STALL RECOVERY

SCHEDULE   * PREFLIGHT DISCUSSION   :10
             * INSTRUCTOR DEMONSTRATIONS   :10

*	STUDENT PRACTICE	:20
*	POSTFLIGHT CRITIQUE	:10

EQUIPMENT
* MODEL-AIRPLANE FOR ATTITUDE DEMONSTRATION
* CHALKBOARD TO LIST PROCEDURES

INSTRUCTOR'S
ACTION
* PREFLIGHT: DISCUSS LESSON OBJECTIVE, LIST PROCEDURES ON CHALKBOARD, DEMONSTRATE ATTITUDES WITH MODEL AIRPLANE
* INFLIGHT: DEMONSTRATE ELEMENTS, DEMONSTRATE POWER-OFF STALL (FULL), COACH STUDENT PRACTICE
* POSTFLIGHT: CRITIQUE STUDENT PERFORMANCE, REVIEW OBJECTIVE, MAKE STUDY ASSIGNMENT

STUDENT'S
ACTION
* PREFLIGHT: DISCUSS LESSON OBJECTIVE, RESOLVE QUESTIONS
* INFLIGHT: PERFORM MANEUVER AS DIRECTED
* POSTFLIGHT: ASK PERTINENT QUESTIONS

COMPLETION
STANDARDS
* STUDENT SHOULD DEMONSTRATE COMPETENCY IN: SELECTING AN ENTRY ALTITUDE THAT WILL ALLOW THE RECOVERIES TO BE COMPLETED NO LOWER THAN 1500 FT. AGL, ESTABLISHING THE NORMAL APPROACH OR LANDING CONFIGURATION AND AIRSPEED WITH THE THROTTLE CLOSED OR AT A REDUCED POWER SETTING, ESTABLISHING A STRAIGHT GLIDE OR GLIDING TURN WITH A BANK ANGLE OF 30 DEG., ± 10 DEG., IN COORDINATED FLIGHT, ESTABLISHING AND MAINTAINING A LANDING PITCH ATTITUDE THAT WILL INDUCE A FULL STALL, RECOGNIZING THE INDICATIONS OF A FULL STALL AND PROMPTLY RECOVERING BY DECREASING ANGLE OF ATTACK, LEVELING WINGS, AND ADJUSTING THE POWER, AS NECESSARY TO REGAIN NORMAL FLIGHT ATTITUDE, RETRACTING THE FLAPS AND LANDING GEAR (IF SO EQUIPPED), AND ESTABLISHING STRAIGHT AND LEVEL FLIGHT OR CLIMB, AVOIDING SECONDARY STALLS, EXCESSIVE AIRSPEED, EXCESSIVE ALTITUDE LESS, SPINS, AND FLIGHT BELOW 1500 FT. AGL.

COMMON:
ERRORS
* FAILURE TO ESTABLISH THE SPECIFIED LANDING GEAR AND FLAP CONFIGURATION PRIOR TO ENTRY.
* IMPROPER PITCH, HEADING, AND BANK CONTROL DURING STRAIGHT AHEAD STALLS.
* IMPROPER PITCH AND BANK CONTROL DURING TURNING STALLS.
* ROUGH OR UNCOORDINATED CONTROL TECHNIQUE
* FAILURE TO RECOGNIZE THE FIRST INDICATIONS OF A STALL.
* FAILURE TO ACHIEVE A FULL STALL.

* IMPROPER TORQUE CORRECTION.
* POOR STALL RECOGNITION AND DELAYED RECOVERY.
* EXCESSIVE ALTITUDE LOSS OR EXCESSIVE AIRSPEED DURING THE RECOVERY.
* SECONDARY STALL DURING RECOVERY.

POWER-OFF STALLS (IMMINENT)

WHAT? A practice maneuver that demonstrated, in simulation of actual landing conditions, a partial or imminent stall and allows for recognition of stall warning and recovery before a full stall occurs.

WHY? For practice in retaining or regaining full control of the airplane immediately upon recognizing that it is almost in a full stall or that a full stall is likely to occur if timely preventative action is not taken.

HOW?
a) Clearing turn
b) Extend landing gear (if so equipped)
c) Apply carburetor heat
d) Retard throttle to idle
e) Hold attitude while decelerating to approach airspeed
f) Establish approach attitude to maintain approach airspeed
g) Extend wing flaps, adjust pitch attitude to maintain approach airspeed
h) Raise nose to pitch attitude that will induce a stall
i) At first sign of an ensuing stall (full up elevator, high sink rate, uncontrollable, nose-down pitching) begin a recovery by reducing the angle of attack, releasing back elevator pressure, applying full power, retracting flaps to 20 deg.
j) When positive rate-of-climb is established retract flaps in increments to 0 deg.
k) Return to normal cruise flight

LESSON POWER-OFF STALL (IMMINENT):   STUDENT   DATE

OBJECTIVE   * TO DEVELOP THE STUDENT'S SKILL IN DETECTION AND RECOVERY FROM AN IMMINENT STALL WITH POWER OFF AND WITH LITTLE OR NO ALTITUDE LOST ON THE RECOVERY.

ELEMENTS
* USE OF SAFE ALTITUDE
* CONTROL COORDINATION:
* CONTROL RESPONSIVENESS AT SLOW AIRSPEEDS
* CONTROL OF AIRPLANE ATTITUDE, ALTITUDE, AND HEADING
* STALL CHARACTERISTICS (IMMINENT)
* IMMINENT STALL RECOVERY

SCHEDULE
* PREFLIGHT DISCUSSION   :10
* INSTRUCTOR DEMONSTRATIONS :10
* STUDENT PRACTICE   :20
* POSTFLIGHT CRITIQUE   :10

EQUIPMENT
* MODEL AIRPLANE FOR ATTITUDE DEMONSTRATION
* CHALKBOARD TO LIST PROCEDURES

INSTRUCTOR'S
ACTION

* PREFLIGHT: DISCUSS LESSON OBJECTIVE, LIST PROCEDURES ON CHALKBOARD, DEMONSTRATE ATTITUDES WITH MODEL AIRPLANE
* INFLIGHT: DEMONSTRATE ELEMENTS, DEMONSTRATE POWER-OFF STALL (IMMINENT), COACH STUDENT PRACTICE
* POSTFLIGHT: CRITIQUE STUDENT PERFORMANCE, REVIEW OBJECTIVE, MAKE STUDY ASSIGNMENT

STUDENT'S
ACTION

* PREFLIGHT: DISCUSS LESSON OBJECTIVE, RESOLVE ACTION QUESTIONS
* INFLIGHT: PERFORM MANEUVER AS DIRECTED
* POSTFLIGHT: ASK PERTINENT QUESTIONS

COMPLETION
STANDARDS

* STUDENT SHOULD DEMONSTRATE COMPETENCY IN: SELECTING AN ENTRY ALTITUDE THAT WILL ALLOW THE RECOVERIES TO BE COMPLETED NO LOWER THAN 1500 FT. AGL, ESTABLISHING THE NORMAL APPROACH OR LANDING CONFIGURATION AND AIRSPEED WITH THE THROTTLE CLOSED OR AT A REDUCED POWER SETTING, ESTABLISHING A PITCH ATTITUDE AT A CONSTANT HEADING, ± 10 DEG., OR 20 DEG. BANKED TURNS, ± 10 DEG. THAT WILL INDUCE AN IMMINENT STALL, APPLYING PROPER CONTROL TO MAINTAIN COORDINATED FLIGHT, RECOGNIZING AND RECOVERING FROM IMMINENT STALLS AT THE FIRST INDICATION OF BUFFETING OR DECAY OF CONTROL EFFECTIVENESS BY REDUCING ANGLE OF ATTACK AND ADJUSTING POWER, AS NECESSARY, TO REGAIN NORMAL FLIGHT ATTITUDE. AVOIDING–FULL STALL, SECONDARY STALL, EXCESSIVE AIRSPEED EXCESSIVE ALTITUDE CHANGE, SPIN, AND FLIGHT BELOW 1500 FT. AGL.

COMMON
ERRORS:

* FAILURE TO ESTABLISH THE SPECIFIED LANDING ERRORS GEAR AND FLAP CONFIGURATION PRIOR TO ENTRY.
* IMPROPER PITCH, HEADING, AND BANK CONTROL DURING STRAIGHT AHEAD STALLS.
* IMPROPER PITCH AND BANK CONTROL DURING TURNING STALLS.
* ROUGH OR UNCOORDINATED CONTROL TECHNIQUE
* FAILURE TO RECOGNIZE THE FIRST INDICATIONS OF AN IMMINENT STALL.
* IMPROPER TORQUE CORRECTION.
* POOR STALL RECOGNITION AND DELAYED RECOVERY.
* EXCESSIVE ALTITUDE LOSS OR EXCESSIVE AIRSPEED DURING THE RECOVERY.

CROSSED-CONTROL STALL

WHAT? A demonstration maneuver that shows the result when a stall occurs with the controls "crossed"–that is, aileron pressure applied in one direction and rudder pressure in the opposite direction.

WHY? To show the effect of improper control technique and to emphasize the importance of using coordinated control pressures whenever making turns.

HOW?
    a) Clearing turn while retarding throttle
    b) Extend landing gear (if so equipped)
    c) Close throttle–maintain altitude until airplane approaches normal glide speed
    d) Retrim airplane while establishing attitude and airspeed
    e) When glide is stabilized, roll airplane into a medium-banked turn to simulate a final approach turn which would overshoot the centerline of the runway.
    f) Apply rudder pressure–increased back-elevator pressure is needed to keep the nose from lowering
    g) Increase these control pressures until the airplane stalls
    h) Recover by releasing the control pressures and increasing power as necessary to recover.

LESSON CROSSED-CONTROL STALL   STUDENT   DATE

OBJECTIVE
    * TO SHOW THE EFFECT OF IMPROPER CONTROL TECHNIQUE AND TO EMPHASIZE THE IMPORTANCE OF USING COORDINATED CONTROL PRESSURES WHENEVER MAKING TURNS.

ELEMENTS
    * AERODYNAMICS OF CROSSED-CONTROL STALLS
    * EFFECTS OF CROSSED-CONTROLS IN GLIDING OR REDUCED AIRSPEED DESCENDING TURNS
    * HAZARDS OF CROSSED CONTROLS IN A BASE LEG TO FINAL APPROACH TURN
    * ENTRY TECHNIQUE AND MINIMUM ENTRY ALTITUDE
    * RECOGNITION OF CROSSED-CONTROL STALLS
    * FLIGHT SITUATIONS WHERE UNINTENTIONAL CROSSED-CONTROL STALLS MAY OCCUR
    * RECOVERY TECHNIQUE AND MINIMUM RECOVERY ALTITUDE

SCHEDULE
    * PREFLIGHT DISCUSSION   :10
    * INSTRUCTOR DEMONSTRATIONS   :10

EQUIPMENT
    * MODEL AIRPLANE FOR ATTITUDE DEMONSTRATION

INSTRUCTOR'S ACTION
    * PREFLIGHT: DISCUSS LESSON OBJECTIVE, DEMONSTRATE ATTITUDES WITH MODEL AIRPLANE
    * INFLIGHT: DEMONSTRATE ELEMENTS, DEMONSTRATE CROSSED-CONTROL STALLS.
    * POSTFLIGHT: REVIEW OBJECTIVE, MAKE STUDY ASSIGNMENT

STUDENT'S
ACTION
* PREFLIGHT: DISCUSS LESSON OBJECTIVE, RESOLVE QUESTIONS
* INFLIGHT: OBSERVE INSTRUCTOR DEMONSTRATION
* POSTFLIGHT: ASK PERTINENT QUESTIONS

COMPLETION
STANDARDS
* STUDENT SHOULD DEMONSTRATE KNOWLEDGE OF: AERODY-
NAMICS OF CROSSED-CONTROL STALLS, EFFECTS OF CROSSED-
CONTROLS IN GLIDING OR REDUCED AIRSPEED DESCENDING
TURNS, HAZARDS OF CROSSED CONTROLS IN A BASE LEG TO FI-
NAL APPROACH TURN, ENTRY TECHNIQUE AND MINIMUM EN-
TRY ALTITUDE, RECOGNITION OF CROSSED-CONTROL STALLS,
FLIGHT SITUATIONS WHERE UNINTENTIONAL CROSSED-CON-
TROL STALLS MAY OCCUR, RECOVERY TECHNIQUE AND MINI-
MUM RECOVERY ALTITUDE.

COMMON
ERRORS:
* FAILURE TO ESTABLISH SELECTED CONFIGURATION PRIOR TO
ENTRY
* FAILURE TO ESTABLISH A CROSSED-CONTROL TURN AND STALL
CONDITION THAT WILL ADEQUATELY DEMONSTRATE THE HAZ-
ARDS OF A CROSSED-CONTROL STALL.
* IMPROPER OR INADEQUATE DEMONSTRATION OF THE RECOGNI-
TION OF ANY RECOVERY FROM A CROSSED-CONTROL STALL.
* FAILURE TO PRESENT SIMULATED STUDENT INSTRUCTION
THAT ADEQUATELY EMPHASIZES THE HAZARDS OF A CROSSED-
CONTROL CONDITION IN A GLIDING OR REDUCED AIRSPEED
CONDITION.

ELEVATOR TRIM STALL

WHAT? Elevator trim stall is a stall resulting from the application of full power for a go-around
when the airplane is trimmed for slow airspeed and positive control of the airplane is not maintained.

WHY? To show the importance of making smooth power applications, overcoming strong trim
forces and maintaining positive control of the airplane to hold safe flight attitudes and using proper
and timely trim techniques.

HOW?
1. Clear the area of traffic And select the proper altitude for performing the maneuver
2. Reduce power and extend the landing gear (if retractable)
3. Lower flaps 1/2 to full and reduce power to idle
4. Maintain altitude and bleed off airspeed to establish a normal glide
5. Trim the airplane for a landing approach (nose-up trim)
6. Add full power to simulate a go-around procedure
7. When stall is imminent, apply forward pressure to return to the normal climbing attitude (a full stall must not occur)
8. Adjust trim to relieve control pressures
9. Complete the normal go-around and level-off procedures

LESSON Elevator Trim Stalls   STUDENT   DATE

OBJECTIVE
* TO DEVELOP THE STUDENT'S SKILL IN DEMONSTRATING THE IMPORTANCE OF SMOOTH POWER APPLICATIONS AND THE USE OF PROPER AND TIMELY TRIM TECHNIQUES IN OVERCOMING STRONG TRIM FORCES AND MAINTAINING POSITIVE CONTROL OF THE AIRPLANE.

ELEMENTS
* CONTROL OF AIRSPEED
* LANDING APPROACH CONFIGURATION
* DEMONSTRATION OF STALL
* RECOVERY

SCHEDULE
* PREFLIGHT DISCUSSION   :10
* INSTRUCTOR DEMONSTRATIONS   :10
* STUDENT PRACTICE   :20
* POSTFLIGHT CRITIQUE   :10

EQUIPMENT
* FLIGHT TRAINING HANDBOOK
* WRITING MATERIAL

INSTRUCTOR'S ACTION
* PREFLIGHT–DISCUSS LESSON OBJECTIVE AND ELEMENTS
* INFLIGHT–DEMONSTRATE ELEMENTS. COACH STUDENT PRACTICE.
* POSTFLIGHT–CRITIQUE STUDENT PERFORMANCE, MAKE STUDY ASSIGNMENT

STUDENT'S ACTION
* PREFLIGHT–DISCUSS LESSON OBJECTIVE
* INFLIGHT–PERFORM MANEUVER AS DIRECTED
* POSTFLIGHT–ASK PERTINENT QUESTIONS

COMPLETION STANDARDS
* STUDENT SHOULD DEMONSTRATE COMPETENCY IN RECOGNIZING THE IMMINENT STALL (A FULL STALL SHOULD NOT OCCUR) AND IN TAKING PROMPT, CORRECT ACTION FOR RECOVERY BY MAINTAINING AIRSPEED WITHIN 10 KNOTS, AND ALTITUDE WITHIN 100 FEET

COMMON ERRORS

SECONDARY STALL

WHAT? A secondary stall is a stall because of recovering too soon from a stall before the airplane has regained sufficient flying speed.

WHY? Pilots practice secondary stalls so they know what may happen if they recover too soon if they were at a low altitude.

How? 1. Pilot does a normal stall.
      2. After the airplane stalls the pilot pulls back on the yoke quickly by then stalling the airplane again.

LESSON SECONDARY STALLS   STUDENT   DATE

OBJECTIVE   * TO DEVELOP THE STUDENT'S KNOWLEDGE OF WHAT MAY HAPPEN IF THEY TRY TO RECOVER FROM A STALL BEFORE THE AIRPLANE HAS REGAINED SUFFICIENT FLYING AIRSPEED

ELEMENTS   * CONTROL OF AIRSPEED
                   * COORDINATION
                   * CONTROL OF ATTITUDE, ALTITUDE

SCHEDULE   * PREFLIGHT INSTRUCTION   :15
                   * DEMONSTRATION   :10
                   * STUDENT PRACTICE   :10
                   * POST-FLIGHT CRITIQUE   :10

EQUIPMENT   * MODEL
                   * FLIGHT TRAINING HANDBOOK (149)

INSTRUCTOR'S
ACTIONS   * PREFLIGHT–DISCUSS LESSON OBJECTIVE–EXPLAIN CORRECT STALL RECOVERY TECHNIQUE
                   * DEMONSTRATE CORRECT STALL RECOVERY TECHNIQUE
                   * POST-FLIGHT–CRITIQUE STUDENT PERFORMANCE–MAKE STUDY ASSIGNMENT

STUDENT'S
ACTION   * PREFLIGHT–DISCUSS OBJECTIVE AND STALL RECOVERY TECHNIQUE
                   * IN-FLIGHT–FOLLOW THROUGH WITH CONTROLS IN DEMONSTRATION–PRACTICE STALL RECOVERY
                   * POST-FLIGHT–DISCUSS CRITIQUE

COMPLETION
STANDARDS   * EXHIBITS KNOWLEDGE OF ELEMENTS OF SECONDARY STALLS
                   * DEMONSTRATES AND SIMULTANEOUSLY EXPLAINS SECONDARY STALLS
                   * MAKES SMOOTH AND COORDINATED CONTROL APPLICATIONS
                   * ANALYZES AND CORRECTS SIMULATED COMMON ERRORS RELATED TO SECONDARY STALLS IN SELECTED LANDING GEAR AND FLAP CONFIGURATIONS

COMMON
ERRORS   * DOES NOT HAVE DIRECTIONAL CONTROL OF THE AIRPLANE
             * DOES NOT EXPLAIN SECONDARY STALLS
             * DOES NOT CONTROL AIRSPEED

SPINS

WHAT? A spin may be described as an aggravated stall that results in what is termed *autorotation* wherein the airplane follows a corkscrew path in a downward direction. The wings are producing some lift and the airplane is forced downward by gravity, wallowing and yawing in a spiral path. To have a spin you must have two things present, stall and yaw.

HOW? First be sure that the airplane to be spinned is authorized by the manufacturer and the FAA regulations. To begin a spin, the airplane must stall. During the stall lower one wing slightly in the direction of the desired spin. As the airplane begins to stall the nose of the airplane will want to yaw toward the low wing. Normally in stall practice you would use opposite rudder to keep the nose from yawing. To spin the airplane you will need to let the nose yaw in the direction of the low wing, then the airplane will begin to slip in the direction of the low wing; as it does, the air meeting the side of the fuselage, the vertical fin, and other vertical surfaces, tends to weathervane the airplane into the relative wind. This accounts for the continuing yaw which is present in a spin. At the same time, rolling is also occurring about the longitudinal axis of the airplane. This is caused by the lowered wing having an increasingly greater angle of attack, due to the upward motion of the relative wind against its surfaces. This wing, then, is well beyond stalling angle of attack, and accordingly suffers an extreme loss of lift. The rising wing, since the relative wind is striking it at a smaller angle, has a smaller angle of attack than the opposite wing. Thus, the rising wing has more lift than the lowering wing, so that the airplane begins to rotate about its longitudinal axis. This rotation, combined with the effects of centrifugal force and the different amount of drag on the two wings, then becomes a spin and the airplane descends vertically, rolling and yawing until recovery is effected.

To recover from a spin, the pilot should first be sure that the power is at idle, then apply full opposite rudder; then after the rotation slows, apply brisk, positive straight forward movement of the elevator control (forward of the neutral position). The control should be held firmly in this position. The forceful movement of the elevator will decrease the excessive angle of attack and hence will break the stall. When the stall is broken the spinning will stop. This straight forward position should be maintained and as the spin rotation stops, the rudder should be neutralized. If the rudder is not neutralized at the proper time, the succeeding increased airspeed acting upon the fully deflected rudder will cause an excessive and unfavorable yawing effect. This places strain on the airplane, and may cause a secondary spin in the opposite direction.Slow and overly-cautious control movements during spin recovery must be avoided. In certain cases it has been found that such movements result in the airplane continuing to spin indefinitely, even with the application of full opposite controls. Brisk and positive operation, on the other hand, results in a more positive recovery. After the spin rotation stops and the rudder has been neutralized; the pilot should begin applying back elevator pressure to raise the nose to level flight. Caution must be used so as not to apply excessive back pressure after the rotation stops. Sometimes a pilot does this because of being too anxious to stop the descent. To do so will cause a secondary stall and may result in another spin, more violent than the first.

WHY? To help a pilot recognize when a spin condition exists and take prompt action to prevent a fully developed spin. In flight instructor training it is used to demonstrate that the instructor can recognize and recover from spin situations that might be encountered in poorly executed maneuvers during student training flights.

LESSON Spins   STUDENT   DATE

OBJECTIVE
* TO DEVELOP THE STUDENT'S SKILL IN RECOGNIZING WHEN A SPIN CONDITION EXISTS AND TO TAKE PROMPT ACTION TO PREVENT A FULLY DEVELOPED SPIN.

ELEMENTS
* AIRPLANE CONFIGURATION
* COLLISION AVOIDANCE
* CONTROL OF POWER
* STALL AND YAW
* LOW WING
* RUDDER AND ELEVATORS
* MINIMUM SAFE ALTITUDE
* RELATED SAFETY FACTORS

SCHEDULE
* PREFLIGHT DISCUSSION :15
* INSTRUCTOR DEMONSTRATIONS :15
* STUDENT PRACTICE :35
* POSTFLIGHT CRITIQUE :15

EQUIPMENT
* MODEL AIRPLANE TO DEMONSTRATE ATTITUDES
* AIRPLANE COCKPIT FOR PROCEDURES DEMO (GROUND)
* IFR HOOD FOR MANEUVERS REVIEWED.

INSTRUCTOR'S ACTION
* PREFLIGHT–DISCUSS LESSON OBJECTIVE. REVIEW MANEUVER FROM AC 61-21. DEMONSTRATE SPINS WITH MODEL AIRPLANE. DISCUSS THE RELATED SAFETY FACTORS.
* INFLIGHT–DEMONSTRATE ELEMENTS. DEMONSTRATE SPINS. COACH STUDENT PRACTICE.
* POSTFLIGHT–CRITIQUE STUDENT PERFORMANCE, REVIEW OBJECTIVE, MAKE STUDY ASSIGNMENT.

STUDENT'S ACTION
* PREFLIGHT–DISCUSS LESSON OBJECTIVE
* INFLIGHT–REVIEW MANEUVERS, PREFORM SPINS AS DIRECTED.
* POSTFLIGHT–ASK PERTINENT QUESTIONS

COMPLETION STANDARDS
* STUDENT SHOULD DEMONSTRATE COMPETENCY AND INSTRUCTIONAL KNOWLEDGE OF THE ELEMENTS OF SPINS BEING DESCRIBED
* AERODYNAMICS OF SPINS
* AIRPLANES APPROVED FOR SPIN MANEUVER BASED ON AIRWORTHINESS CATEGORY AND TYPE CERTIFICATE

* RELATIONSHIP OF VARIOUS FACTORS SUCH AS CONFIGURATION, WEIGHT, CENTER OF GRAVITY, AND CONTROL COORDINATION TO SPINS.
* FLIGHT SITUATIONS WHERE UNINTENTIONAL SPINS MAY OCCUR
* HOW TO RECOGNIZE AND RECOVER FROM IMMINENT UNINTENTIONAL SPINS
* ENTRY TECHNIQUE AND MINIMUM ENTRY ALTITUDE FOR INTENTIONAL SPINS
* CONTROL TECHNIQUE TO MAINTAIN A STABILIZED SPIN
* ORIENTATION DURING A SPIN
* RECOVERY TECHNIQUE AND MINIMUM RECOVERY ALTITUDE FOR INTENTIONAL SPINS
* ANXIETY FACTORS ASSOCIATED WITH SPIN INSTRUCTION

COMMON
ERRORS

* FAILURE TO ESTABLISH PROPER CONFIGURATION PRIOR TO SPIN ENTRY
* FAILURE TO ACHIEVE AND MAINTAIN A FULL STALL DURING SPIN ENTRY
* FAILURE TO CLOSE THROTTLE WHEN A SPIN ENTRY IS ACHIEVED
* FAILURE TO RECOGNIZE THE INDICATIONS OF AN IMMINENT, UNINTENTIONAL SPIN
* IMPROPER USE OF FLIGHT CONTROLS DURING SPIN ENTRY, ROTATION, OR RECOVERY
* DISORIENTATION DURING A SPIN
* FAILURE TO DISTINGUISH BETWEEN A HIGH SPEED SPIRAL AND A SPIN
* EXCESSIVE SPEED OR ACCELERATED STALL DURING RECOVERY
* FAILURE TO RECOVER WITH MINIMUM LOSS OF ALTITUDE
* HAZARDS OF ATTEMPTING TO SPIN AN AIRPLANE NOT APPROVED FOR SPINS

MINIMUM CONTROLLABLE AIRSPEED
(SLOW FLIGHT)

WHAT? Minimum Controllable Airspeed is the slowest airspeed at which straight and level controlled flight can be maintained. This airspeed is normally within +5 knots of stall speed of the airplane. This is a speed at which any further increase of angle of attack, load factor, or loss of power will cause an immediate stall. Gross weight, CG location, and Density Altitude all play an important part in this speed.

HOW? Reduce power and maintain altitude by increasing pitch attitude. When the airspeed is within normal flap range, add desired flaps, only 10 deg at a time. If full flaps are used, maintain airspeed at the bottom of the white arc +5 knots. If less than full flaps are used, maintain airspeed at the bottom of green arc +5 knots. When this airspeed is attained, maintain altitude with power, and airspeed with pitch attitude.

WHY? Minimum Controllable Airspeed is taught to develop the pilot's sense of feel and ability to use the controls correctly while inside the region of reverse command. This gives the pilot practice at controlling the airplane in critically slow airspeeds such as those used during takeoff and landing. Also this gives the pilot practice at recognizing imminent stalls and avoiding them.

LESSON Slow Flight   STUDENT   DATE

OBJECTIVE
* TO DEVELOP THE STUDENT'S SKILL, SENSE OF FEEL AND ABILITY TO USE CORRECT CONTROL IN THE REGION OF REVERSE COMMAND WHILE MAINTAINING A CONSTANT ALTITUDE AND AIRSPEED.

ELEMENTS
* USE OF A SAFE ALTITUDE
* USE OF CORRECT CONFIGURATION
* CONTROL OF AIRSPEED
* REGION OF REVERSE COMMAND
* CONTROL OF AIRPLANE ATTITUDE, ALTITUDE, AND HEADING.
* COLLISION AVOIDANCE

SCHEDULE
* PREFLIGHT DISCUSSION   :15
* INSTRUCTOR DEMONSTRATIONS   :15
* STUDENT PRACTICE   :35
* POSTFLIGHT CRITIQUE   :15

EQUIPMENT
* MODEL AIRPLANE TO DEMONSTRATE ATTITUDES
* AIRPLANE COCKPIT FOR PROCEDURES DEMO (GROUND)

INSTRUCTOR'S ACTION
* PREFLIGHT–DISCUSS LESSON OBJECTIVE. EXPLAIN: THE REGION OF REVERSE COMMAND, AIRPLANE CHARACTERISTICS AT MCA, ENTRY AND RECOVERY PROCEDURES.
* INFLIGHT–DEMONSTRATE MCA WITHIN COMPLETION STANDARDS. COACH STUDENT PRACTICE.
* POSTFLIGHT–CRITIQUE STUDENT PERFORMANCE, REVIEW OBJECTIVE, MAKE STUDY ASSIGNMENT.

STUDENT'S ACTION
* PREFLIGHT–DISCUSS LESSON OBJECTIVE
* INFLIGHT–REVIEW STRAIGHT-LEVEL FLT, TURNS, CLIMBS, DESCENTS. PREFORM EACH MANEUVER AS DIRECTED.
* POSTFLIGHT–ASK PERTINENT QUESTIONS

COMPLETION STANDARDS
* STUDENT SHOULD DEMONSTRATE COMPETENCY IN MAINTAINING ORIENTATION
* AIRSPEED +5, – 0 KNOTS
* ALTITUDE ± 100 FEET
* LEVEL OFF FROM CLIMBS AND DESCENTS ± 100 FEET
* MAINTAINS HEADING ± 10° DURING STRAIGHT FLIGHT
* MAINTAINS BANK ANGLE ± 10°
* IN COORDINATED FLIGHT

Index

Other Bestsellers of Related Interest

THE ILLUSTRATED GUIDE TO AERODYNAMICS—2nd Edition—H.C. "Skip" Smith

Avoiding technical jargon and scientific explanations, this guide demonstrates how aerodynamic principles effect every aircraft in terms of lift, thrust, drag, in-air performance, stability, and control. It includes new material on airfoil development and design, accelerated climb performance, takeoff velocities, load and velocity-load factors, hypersonic flight, area rules, laminar flow airfoils, planform shapes, computer-aided design, and high-performance lightplanes. 352 pages, 269 illustrations. Book No. 3786, $18.95 paperback only

BE A BETTER PILOT: Making the Right Decisions —Paul A. Craig

Why do good pilots sometimes make bad decisions? This book takes an in-depth look at the ways pilots make important preflight and in-flight decisions. It dispels the myths surrounding the pilot personality, provides straightforward solutions to poor decision-making, and determines traits that pilots appear to share—traits that affect the way they approach situations. 240 pages, 76 illustrations. Book No. 3675, $15.95 paperback, $24.95 hardcover

ABCs of SAFE FLYING—3rd Edition —David Frazier

Take a step-by-step look at operational safety. This book presents a wealth of flight safety information in a fun-to-read format. The author's anecdotal episodes, as well as NTSB accident reports, lend both humor and sobering reality to the text. Detailed photographs, maps, and illustrations ensure you understand key concepts and techniques. 192 pages, illustrated. Book No. 3757, $17.95 paperback, $22.95 hardcover

AVOIDING COMMON PILOT ERRORS: An Air Traffic Controller's View—John Stewart

This essential reference—written from the controller's perspective—interprets the mistakes pilots often make when operating in controlled airspace. It cites situations frequently encountered by controllers that show how improper training, lack of preflight preparation, poor communication skills, and confusing regulations can lead to pilot mistakes. 240 pages, 32 illustrations. Book No. 2434, $17.95 paperback only

GENERAL AVIATION LAW—Jerry A. Eichenberger

Although the regulatory burden that is part of flying sometimes seems overwhelming, it need not take the pleasure out of your flight time. This survey of aviation regulations gives you a solid understanding of FAA procedures and functions, airman ratings and maintenance certificates, the implications of aircraft ownership, and more. It allows you to recognize legal problems before they result in FAA investigations and potentially serious consequences. 240 pages. Book No. 3431, $16.95 paperback only

STANDARD AIRCRAFT HANDBOOK—5th Edition —Edited by Larry Reithmaier, originally compiled and edited by Stuart Leavell and Stanley Bungay

Now updated to cover the latest in aircraft parts, equipment, and construction techniques, this classic reference provides classical information on FAA-approved metal airplane hardware. Techniques are presented in step-by-step fashion and explained in shop terms without unnecessary theory and background. All data on materials and procedures is derived from current reports by the nation's largest aircraft manufacturers. 240 pages, 213 illustrations. Book No. 3634, $11.95 paperback only

UNDERSTANDING AERONAUTICAL CHARTS—
Terry T. Lankford

Filled with practical applications for beginning and veteran pilots, this book will show you how to plan your flights quickly, easily, and accurately. It covers all the charts you'll need for flight planning, including those for VFR, IFR, SID, STAR, Loran, and helicopter flights. As you examine the criteria, purpose, and limitations of each chart, you'll learn the author's proven system for interpreting and using charts. 320 pages, 183 illustrations. Book No. 3844, $17.95 paperback only

THE PILOT'S GUIDE TO WEATHER REPORTS, FORECASTS & FLIGHT PLANNING
—Terry T. Lankford

Don't get caught in weather you're not prepared to handle. Learn how to use today's weather information services with this comprehensive guide. It shows you how to access weather services efficiently, translate briefings correctly, and apply reports and forecasts to specific preflight and in-flight situations to expand your margin of safety. 397 pages, 123 illustrations. Book No. 3582, $19.95 paperback only

GOOD TAKEOFFS AND GOOD LANDINGS
—2nd Edition—Joe Christy,
revised and updated by Ken George

Perform safe, precise takeoffs and landings. This complete guide includes material on obstructions to visibility, wind shear avoidance, unlighted night landings, and density altitude. You'll also find a recap of recent takeoff and landing mishaps and how to avoid them, expanded coverage of FARs, and information on the new recreational license. 208 pages, 76 illustrations. Book No. 3611, $15.95 paperback only

CROSS-COUNTRY FLYING—3rd Edition
R. Randall Padfield;
Prior editions by Paul Garrison and Norval Kennedy

Establish and maintain sound flying habits with this classic cockpit reference. It includes revised information on Mode-C requirements, direct user access terminal usage (DUAT), LORAN-C navigation, hand-held transceivers, affordable moving maps, and over-water flying techniques. Plus, you'll find expanded coverage of survival equipment, TCAs, fuel management and conservation, mountain flying techniques, and off-airport landings. 328 pages, 148 illustrations. Book No. 3640, $19.95 paperback only

The classic you've been searching for . . .
STICK AND RUDDER:
An Explanation of the Art of Flying
—Wolfgang Langewiesche

Students, certificated pilots, and instructors alike have praised this book as "the most useful guide to flying ever written." The book explains the important phases of the art of flying, in a way the learner can use. It shows precisely what the pilot does when he flies, just how he does it, and why. 400 pages, 88 illustrations. Book No. 3820, $19.95 hardcover only

Look for These and Other TAB Books at Your Local Bookstore

To Order Call Toll Free 1-800-822-8158
(24-hour telephone service available.)

or write to TAB Books, Blue Ridge Summit, PA 17294-0840.

Title	Product No.	Quantity	Price

☐ Check or money order made payable to TAB Books

Charge my ☐ VISA ☐ MasterCard ☐ American Express

Acct. No. _____ Exp. _____

Signature: _____

Name: _____

Address: _____

City: _____

State: _____ Zip: _____

Subtotal $ _____

Postage and Handling
($3.00 in U.S., $5.00 outside U.S.) $ _____

Add applicable state and local
sales tax $ _____

TOTAL $ _____

TAB Books catalog free with purchase; otherwise send $1.00 in check or money order and receive $1.00 credit on your next purchase.

Orders outside U.S. must pay with international money in U.S. dollars drawn on a U.S. bank.

TAB Guarantee: If for any reason you are not satisfied with the book(s) you order, simply return it (them) within 15 days and receive a full refund.

BC